"It is shameful but true. Chr[...] their most astounding privile[...] and talking to God, communicating with the one who created and redeems us, who loves us with a love even stronger than death. This thought-provoking book is precisely what we need to put our prayer lives on track. It points us to the one who initiates this marvelous divine communication and invites us to answer him in fear, love, honesty, and ceaseless, awestruck, self-giving speech."

Douglas A. Sweeney, Dean and Professor of Divinity, Beeson Divinity School, Samford University

"The chief virtue of this book is that it is not about prayer; it is about God. Of course the title gives that away: prayer is a response to who God is and what he has said and done. As the author wisely says, prayer is a way of perceiving what really is. Many of us believe that, but it often does not inform the way we pray. This wonderful book will help you move in the right direction. I highly recommend it."

William Edgar, Professor Emeritus of Apologetics, Westminster Theological Seminary

"If Dan Brendsel is right—and I believe he is—that a primary pastoral task in the life of the church is teaching God's people to pray, then the church today needs to read this book! The message of *Answering Speech* is the profound biblical truth that our life with God is a life of prayer—dialogue with a gracious God who has initiated conversation and covenanted with us. In essence, prayer is living in response to the Trinitarian God. By rooting prayer in canon, church, and creed, and by showing the glorious marriage between the prayer life and the Christian life, Brendsel pastors the individual Christian and the corporate church into deeper communion with Christ. I could not recommend this book more highly!"

Edward W. Klink III, Senior Pastor, Hope Evangelical Free Church, Roscoe, Illinois; author, *The Local Church* and *John*

"Prayer is theology in miniature, the essence of the creature's interpersonal relation with the Creator: human answering speech to the divine address. Prayer is also the beating heart of the Christian life, a participation through the gift of the Spirit in the Son's response to the Father: "Not my will, but yours, be done" (Luke 22:42). Jesus's disciples asked him to teach them to pray, and as Brendsel rightly notes in this important book, teaching God's people to pray is one of the pastor's chief tasks. *Answering Speech* is an excellent resource for doing just that. Brendsel helpfully engages both theological and practical matters and, in the process, helps us see all of life as eminently theological, an ongoing dialogue in different registers—confession, intercession, adoration—with our covenantal, triune God."

Kevin J. Vanhoozer, Research Professor of Systematic Theology, Trinity Evangelical Divinity School

"This book lights up our place in the life of prayer—in relation to God, who speaks first. Dan Brendsel has given us a thought-provoking, Scripture-saturated, and deeply encouraging discussion of prayer as our answer to God's initiating word, fully spoken to us in Christ."

Kathleen Nielson, author; speaker

"This is a book I've been waiting for. It approaches prayer in a way that accents and celebrates the initiative of God: he speaks first; then we respond in prayer, answering his word. Dan Brendsel is a careful pastor-scholar who brings together both biblical insights and treasures from the great tradition. Just look at the bibliography. Most of us need to go deeper with prayer—which can seem so simple, even natural, and yet is a bottomless wonder, past finding out. To speak with the living God! There is far more to prayer than we presume—riches here set before us by a learned jeweler."

David Mathis, Senior Teacher and Executive Editor, desiringGod.org; Pastor, Cities Church, Saint Paul, Minnesota; author, *Habits of Grace*

Answering Speech

Answering Speech

The Life of Prayer as Response to God

Daniel J. Brendsel

WHEATON, ILLINOIS

Library of Congress Control Number: 2022046429

Crossway is a publishing ministry of Good News Publishers.

NP			32	31	30	29	28	27	26	25	24	23
15	14	13	12	11	10	9	8	7	6	5	4	3	2	1

To the members of
First Presbyterian Church,
Hinckley, Minnesota

May the God of endurance and encouragement grant
you to live in such harmony with one another, in accord
with Christ Jesus, that together you may with one voice
glorify the God and Father of our Lord Jesus Christ.

ROMANS 15:5–6

Contents

Acknowledgments

THIS BOOK BEGAN AS ESSAYS for discussion at our weekly church staff meetings when I served as an associate pastor at Grace Church of DuPage in Warrenville, Illinois. As we considered together the life of prayer, the questions raised and the comments made were invaluable for sharpening my thoughts and articulation. Along the way, others at Grace had the chance to read the manuscript I was noodling on (e.g., our women's ministry small groups), from whom I received further helpful feedback. "Answering speech" itself is inseparable from the life of Christ's church. Much the same could be said about the book *Answering Speech* and the life shared with my brothers and sisters at Grace Church.

In the summer of 2021, I prepared a new draft and an incipient book proposal for review at a symposium of the St. John Fellowship of the Center for Pastor Theologians. Through the years the CPT has been a major boon to my maturation and invigoration as a pastor-theologian, and I am grateful for their scholarship and camaraderie at an important stage in this work.

Lindsey Knott kindly gave of her time and wisdom to read the whole manuscript and to write out detailed comments and encouragements, improving this book in dozens of ways. It is a rare privilege to have such an able and insightful dialogue partner, and it is a great joy to have such a friend.

Thanks are owed to Don Jones, Doug O'Donnell, and Justin Taylor at Crossway for showing initial interest in the project, and for their continued enthusiasm for it. The good people at Crossway more generally have been a delight to work with. In particular, Thom Notaro has proved consistently reliable in his edits, patient and creative in dealing with my many writing quirks, and tremendously gifted in improving the overall expression and realizing my intentions.

My wonderment for my wife Jen continues to grow, as well as for the God who supplies her strength to serve many with untiring gladness. Jen is, of course, naturally tired at the end of long and taxing days. Yet, even then she's eager to read the latest installment of whatever project I'm working on; to speak wisdom, life, and clarity into the writing; and to encourage an oft-insecure soul by reminding him of our sufficiency in Christ. As if that were not enough, every evening I also get the refreshment and mirth of a story, a game, or a not-infrequent dance party with John, Anna, Elinor, and Evangeline. Where would *Answering Speech* be—indeed, where would *I* be—without such a slew of undeserved mercies?

During the writing of this book, the Lord called me to serve as pastor of First Presbyterian Church of Hinckley, Minnesota. There, with great joy and gratitude, I was able to walk through the chapters of *Answering Speech* in conjunction with our Sunday evening prayer services. It was a wonderful, fitting way to finalize the manuscript. It is to the members of First Presbyterian that

I dedicate this work. May the years to come find us fervently praying together in answer to the God who addresses us in Christ, being formed by the Spirit ever more into Christ's image, and glorifying our God and Father with one voice.

Soli Deo gloria.

*Teach me to seek You, and reveal yourself to me as I seek,
because I can neither seek You if You do not teach me how,
nor find You unless You reveal Yourself. Let me seek You in
desiring You; let me desire You in seeking You; let me find You
in loving You; let me love You in finding You. . . . I do not try,
Lord, to attain Your lofty heights, because my understanding
is in no way equal to it. But I do desire to understand
Your truth a little, that truth that my heart believes and
loves. For I do not seek to understand so that I may believe;
but I believe so that I may understand. For I believe this
also, that "unless I believe, I shall not understand."*

ANSELM OF CANTERBURY
Proslogion

Introduction

Prayer as "Answering Speech"

THOUGH, SADLY, HE IS NOT WELL KNOWN in many Christian circles today, Anselm of Canterbury (1033–1109) remains one of the giants in the Western theological and philosophical tradition. Anselm seems to have coined the highly influential shorthand definition of theology as "faith seeking understanding." His satisfaction theory of the atonement was an important forerunner for later Reformed formulations of the penal substitutionary accomplishment of Christ's cross. And numerous contemporary apologists, in seeking to offer theistic proofs to skeptics, draw from the well of Anselm's writings. In this last respect, Anselm's *Monologion* is an outstanding example. In this work, Anselm offers some eighty chapters of arguments (though he referred to it as a "short tract"!) for the existence and the necessary nature and attributes of God. Dense and thought-provoking, the *Monologion* is a marvel of philosophical and theological meditation.

From Monologue to Dialogue

But its sequel is what interests us here. For but a year after writing *Monologion*, Anselm again took up the pen to write *Proslogion*.

In the *Proslogion*, Anselm can still be seen to be arguing for the existence of God, but his manner is very different from the year prior. What differed, or in what way did Anselm think his reasoning needed to improve? For one thing, he wanted to offer a simpler, more streamlined (only twenty-six-chapter) argument. But another crucial difference comes through a mundane point of grammar. Consider how the first chapter of the *Monologion* begins:

Of all things that exist, there is one nature that is supreme. It alone is self-sufficient in eternal happiness, yet through its all-powerful goodness it creates and gives to all other things their very existence and their goodness. Now, take someone who either has never heard of, or does not believe in, and so does not know this.[1]

And on it goes in this mode.

Compare this with how the *Proslogion* opens. Anselm rouses his soul to "fly for a moment from your affairs" and turn "to God and rest for a little in Him." He gives an invitation: "Speak now, my whole heart, speak now *to God*." Then he commences his renewed theological labor: "Come then, Lord my God, teach my heart where and how to seek You, where and how to find You."[2] And on the *Proslogion* goes in this mode.

What is the difference between the modes of the *Monologion* and the *Proslogion*? In grammatical terms, the former is written in the third person, while the latter is written in the second person. The first is written *about* God; the second is written *to* God. The

---

1 In *Anselm of Canterbury: The Major Works*, ed. Brian Davies and G. R. Evans (Oxford: Oxford University Press, 1998), 11.

2 Davies and Evans, *Anselm of Canterbury*, 84–85, emphasis added.

Monologion is a personal meditation, a soliloquy of the would-be theologian alone with his own thoughts (*mono* = alone; *logion* = word); the *Proslogion* is a word of address (*pros* = to; *logion* = word), the true theologian's truthful discourse with the God who speaks to his creatures. The *Monologion* is philosophical study; the *Proslogion* is prayer. In the space between these two writings, as Eugene Peterson puts it, Anselm "realized that however many right things he had said about God, he had said them all in the wrong language."[3] He was compelled to "translate" philosophizing into the true theology of prayer, for all true knowledge of God begins in prayer.

If Anselm was on target, then crucial for growing in truthful understanding of and relationship with God is the life of prayer. One (if not *the*) main pastoral task in the life of the church is teaching God's people to pray. One (if not *the*) main personal responsibility for every Christian is to learn to pray.

Our Part in the Dialogue

Thankfully, the Christian tradition is filled with resources offering instruction and inspiration for the life of prayer: expositions of biblical prayers (e.g., the Psalms), systematic treatments of the nature of prayer, meditations on the "power of prayer," and devotional collections of advice and encouragement for the ups and downs of praying continually. Some of these facets will also appear in the reflections below, but I want firmly to anchor all of what follows in the *dialogical* sensibility exhibited by Anselm. For our understanding of and engagement in prayer (our theory and our practice) will mature to the extent that we continually

3 Eugene H. Peterson, *The Contemplative Pastor: Returning to the Art of Spiritual Direction* (Dallas: Word, 1989), 100.

press into the fact that prayer is our part in a covenantal dialogue with God.

True prayer is communicative and relational. Prayer is not a strategy or mechanism to get things done. It is not a magical incantation to control the outcome of events. It is not thinking the right thoughts. It is part of a dialogue. Any growth in the life of prayer is necessarily a maturing in relationship with the one whom we would address in prayer, and a maturation in our dialogical skill and sensibility.

The word of our covenant Lord in Psalm 50 is instructive:

> Hear, O my people, and I will speak;
>> O Israel, I will testify against you.
>> I am God, your God. . . .
> Offer to God a sacrifice of thanksgiving,
>> and perform your vows to the Most High,
> and call upon me in the day of trouble;
>> I will deliver you, and you shall glorify me. (vv. 7, 14–15)

Here God first speaks (v. 7). He speaks to "my people," his covenant people (note God's self-identification with the covenant title "your God"). What does he say to his people, to us? It is an invitation to respond to him with a sacrifice not of thanks*feeling* but of thanks*giving*—that is, words given in thanks. These are to be joined with our words of commitment to God ("vows") and their attendant practices, as well as our words of petition to God for his help in the day of trouble (vv. 14–15a). God addresses us in his covenantal word, calling us to respond to his gracious word of address with fitting words of our own. What happens when we respond in this way? God responds in love to our response to him

(v. 15b). To what end? That we might respond yet again back to him with words of praise (v. 15c). Psalm 50 is God's invitation to enter into a practice, a rhythm, a life of dialogical prayer.

Charles Spurgeon once called Psalm 50 "Robinson Crusoe's text," because this was the text that proved instrumental in the conversion of Daniel Defoe's famous protagonist. What Robinson Crusoe was converted to by way of Psalm 50 was a life in which, as Spurgeon put it, "God and the praying man take shares."[4] Our life with God is a linguistic back and forth, an ever-continuing dialogue. That is, it is a life of prayer. My aim in this book is to sketch in, from various angles, the realities and rhythms of the ever-continuing dialogue that God graciously invites us to participate in, so that we might indeed participate in it and do so more fittingly and faithfully and fervently and fruitfully.

"Answering Speech"

But we can be more specific about the starting point and the connecting thread for the following explorations of prayer. It is not simply that prayer is our part in dialogue with God generally considered. More specifically, prayer is properly our word of response to the God who *initiates* the conversation. Notice again in Psalm 50 that God graciously initiates the relational dialogue by means of his word. He calls his people to attention and speaks first: "Hear, O my people, and I will speak" (Ps. 50:7). Without this initiating word, none of the ensuing words of thanksgiving and vow and petition and praise would be forthcoming or make sense. That is to say, there would be no *prayer* were it not for the initiating speech act of God.

---

4 Charles H. Spurgeon, "Robinson Crusoe's Text," sermon preached at the Metropolitan Tabernacle, Newington, August 30, 1885, https://archive.spurgeon.org/sermons/1876.php.

This is, in fact, the nature of all our life and all reality—it all flows from divine benevolence and initiating action. God is the one who always gets things going, as it were. From beginning to middle to end—from God's "Let there be light" (Gen. 1:3), to his shining in our hearts to give us the light of the knowledge of his glory in the face of Christ (2 Cor. 4:6), to his "Behold, I am making all things new" (Rev. 21:5)—everything that *is* is ever and only response to God's prior word and creative/saving activity. This includes prayer.

Prayer is not trying to twist God's arm to do something we have first conceived of. Prayer is not pleading with a God who is not already there to somehow show up. Prayer is not enticing a silent God to finally speak. Prayer is not mere sincerity and authenticity voiced to God, an outpouring to him of whatever we feel by instinct. Rather, prayer is always and properly our *response* to God's initiating word and work. Or, as Eugene Peterson has put it, prayer is fundamentally and always "answering speech."[5] As a result, "What is essential in prayer is not that we learn to express ourselves, but that we learn to answer God."[6]

I have found Peterson's formulation, his definitional gloss on "prayer," to be of immense help in my own deepened understanding of and engagement in the life of prayer. And this is the launching point and the main connecting thread in the coming pages. We will consider what it means for prayer to be "answering speech" in twelve chapters, divided into four parts.

Part 1 focuses on the *God* whose initiating word "gets prayer going." What could it mean to pray to this God who sovereignly ordains all things that come to pass, or why would we ever do it? What about those times when it seems like this God who invites

5   Peterson, *The Contemplative Pastor*, 16.
6   Eugene H. Peterson, *Answering God: The Psalms as Tools for Prayer* (San Francisco: Harper & Row, 1989), 6.

us to pray doesn't listen to our answering speech? What's the point, and what is God up to in this life of prayer anyway?

Part 2 offers guidance on how Scripture interfaces with the life of prayer. If prayer is speech that answers to God's initiating word, we should attend to that word earnestly. In so doing we will find our prayers shaped according to it and, indeed, enfolded in it.

Part 3 is much more philosophically (epistemologically) oriented than the other parts. In praying, we are necessarily engaging language, yet it is something like learning a whole new language. What does this "new language," the language of prayer, say about the reality that we would speak about and name? What does it say about who we are as God's people, citizens of his kingdom, among the nations of the world? And how and where might we learn this language?

For as theoretically oriented as part 3 is, it leads naturally into the final, most practical part. In part 4, I address regular rhythms in the life of prayer: weekly corporate rhythms, daily individual rhythms, and the rhythm and shape of typical prayers (or, at least, one model of prayer that has a long lineage in church history).

A crucial aspect of the shape of all prayer, of all answering speech, is that it is Trinitarian in form: to the Father, in the name of the Son, through the power of the Spirit. After considering that matter at the end of part 4, we will conclude with a focus on the middle member—praying in the name of Jesus. In the end, all our answering speech is a participation in the Son, who has answered the Father perfectly for our everlasting good and joy.

Orison and Everything

It is no accident that most major catechisms devote an entire section to instruction through the Lord's Prayer, so fundamental for

Christian life is learning how to pray. The present work may be understood to flow within this catechetical stream, seeking to provide so many different angles on the substance, form, and practicality of the Lord's Prayer as the Christian's model prayer.

Admittedly, many of the following chapters make no reference to the Lord's Prayer (though several do). The wording and movement of the Lord's Prayer does not dictate the subject matter and movement of the four major parts addressing God, Scripture, language, and rhythms. The ensuing pages frequently veer into regions like theology proper, epistemology, and ecclesiology—far afield, it would seem, from the practicalities of the prayerful life about which our Lord taught us. Yet I believe Tertullian was on target in his second-century tract *De oratione* when he suggested that the Lord's Prayer "is as comprehensive in its thought as it is succinct in language," for it encompasses "almost the whole of the Lord's teaching . . . so that really in the prayer there is contained an epitome of the whole Gospel."[7] When the Lord set himself to teach on prayer, he was, at the same time, beginning to teach on everything.

In this light, it may be reductionistic to *only* address God, Scripture, language, and rhythms—including forays into a theology of creation and providence, bibliology and hermeneutics, anthropology, epistemology, ecclesiology, and temporal rhythms—in relation to the life of prayer. To be sure, we must start somewhere and focus our attention on some few things. But it is important to highlight, before digging in, that a course in answering speech is no restriction of our attention to some limited heading under practical theology. Instead, a studied

---

7 Tertullian, *Concerning Prayer*, in *Tertullian's Treatises: Concerning Prayer, Concerning Baptism*, trans. Alexander Souter (London: SPCK, 1919), 20–21 (§1); see, further, 27–28 (§9).

consideration of the ins and outs of our Godward words is prolegomena for a well-ordered understanding of the cosmos, and
more. We come to know and name, and respond and relate to,
everything aright through the words of prayer in Jesus's name.
How could it be otherwise when everything came into being
through him who is the living Word?[8]

———

With a view to prompting more prayerful engagement throughout this book, and as a form of discipleship in the life of prayer
among God's historic praying people, a prayer from some past
figure or prayer tradition appears as a coda to every chapter.
Here, I conclude the introduction in the same way I began, by
quoting Anselm.

> *Almighty God, merciful Father, and my good Lord,*
>   *have mercy on me, a sinner.*
> *Grant me forgiveness of my sins. . . .*
> *May I shun utterly in word and in deed,*
>   *whatever you forbid,*
>   *and do and keep whatever you command.*
> *Let me believe and hope, love and live,*
>   *according to your purpose and your will.*
> *Give me heart-piercing goodness and humility;*
>   *discerning abstinence and mortification of the flesh.*

8 The present project has several points of overlap with, and many lines of influence from,
Michael S. Horton's covenantal (word-centered) theological prolegomenon. See Horton,
Covenant and Eschatology: The Divine Drama (Louisville: Westminster John Knox, 2002);
Horton, *The Christian Faith: A Systematic Theology for Pilgrims on the Way* (Grand Rapids,
MI: Zondervan, 2011), 35–222.

Help me to love you and pray to you,
praise you and meditate upon you. . . .
Deliver me from all evil
and lead me to eternal life
through the Lord.

PRAYER OF ANSELM (CA. 1070–1080)[9]

---

9 In *The Prayers and Meditations of St. Anselm with the Proslogion*, trans. and ed. Benedicta Ward (New York: Penguin, 1973), 91–92.

PART 1

GOD

But, someone will say, does God not know, even without being reminded, both in what respect we are troubled and what is expedient for us, so that it may seem in a sense superfluous that he should be stirred up by our prayers—as if he were drowsily blinking or even sleeping until he is aroused by our voice?

JOHN CALVIN
Institutes of the Christian Religion

You, O LORD of hosts, the God of Israel, have made this revelation to your servant, saying, "I will build you a house." Therefore your servant has found courage to pray this prayer to you.

2 SAMUEL 7:27

1

Answering the Sovereign God

PRAYER IS OUR PART IN DIALOGUE with our covenantal Lord. In the new exodus work of Christ, God has become our Father and our God (John 20:17), so we can address him in prayer as such (Matt. 6:9). But who is the Father and God that we address as ours in prayer? He is the Father *of Christ* first and by begetting, and he is *our* Father derivatively and by exodus-wrought adoption "in Jesus's name."[1] He is the God of Abraham, Isaac, and Jacob, who in Christ extends to all nations the covenantal blessing of being "my people" and of him being "your God." And he is the almighty Maker of earth and sea, the King who is sovereign over and in everything, the all-knowing and all-wise Lord of history, who does whatever he pleases.

It is here that we run into a roadblock when trying to comprehend prayer as dialogue with our covenantal Lord. What kind of *dialogue*

---

1   I connect the ability to address God in prayer as our *Father* with the *exodus* work of Christ because of the way Scripture typically uses the term *Father* with reference to God. In those (few!) Old Testament Scriptures where God is identified or addressed as Father, often it is with his work of the exodus from Egypt in view (e.g., Deut. 32:6; Isa. 63:15–16; I was first alerted to this pattern by Todd A. Wilson, "Wilderness Apostasy and Paul's Portrayal of the Crisis in Galatians," *NTS* 50, no. 4 [2004]: 554; see also, more generally, Joachim Jeremias, *The Prayers of Jesus*, trans. J. Bowden, C. Burchard, and J. Reumann [Philadelphia: Fortress, 1978], 11–15).

is possible with a God who sovereignly ordains all that comes to pass? As John Calvin asked long ago, what's the point of lifting up the thoughts and desires of our hearts to a God who already apparently knows them? If God has already made up his mind about what he's going to do, does it really matter whether we offer our input in prayer? To put it in its simplest form: why pray if God is sovereign?

The question is often raised. And several helpful answers are available, some of which inform coming chapters. Here, as Jesus often does in the Gospels, I want to answer the question with a question: How can we pray with anything like the boldness and persevering fervency on display among biblical pray-ers *unless* we are persuaded that God is sovereign over all things as Lord of history? To fill this out, let us consider a few examples of prayer from Scripture, beginning with something of a "ground clearing" example, before addressing two further examples that help us construct a sturdy house of prayer.

Hezekiah's Prayer in Isaiah 37

One of the major concerns of the first half of the book of Isaiah is the threat of Assyrian invasion in the eighth century BC.[2] Isaiah exhorts the southern kingdom of Judah to trust in the Lord for deliverance from Assyrian aggression, and not to trust in political alliances with other nations. In particular, throughout Isaiah 28–31, Judah and the house of David seem especially tempted to ally with the powerful Egypt for protection against the Assyrian threat. But

---

2   Here and in the section "Jesus's Prayer in John 17," below (p. 19), I am adapting and
    expanding material I wrote in a position paper for Grace Church of DuPage several years
    ago. The original paper, "The Doctrines of Grace at Grace Church of DuPage," can be found
    at https://www.gracedupage.org/beliefs/position-papers/doctrines-of-grace.

the Lord through the prophet makes remarkable promises to Israel, such as this one from Isaiah 31:8–9:

> "The Assyrian shall fall by a sword, not of man;
>   and a sword, not of man, shall devour him;
> and he shall flee from the sword,
>   and his young men shall be put to forced labor.
> His rock shall pass away in terror,
>   and his officers desert the standard in panic,"
> declares the LORD, whose fire is in Zion,
>   and whose furnace is in Jerusalem.

Be that as it may, in Isaiah 36–37, Sennacherib king of Assyria comes a-knockin'. His armies besiege Jerusalem. He mocks the living God and demands surrender. Trapped like a bird in a cage,[3] Judah seems hopeless. But it only *seems* this way. The good news for Israel is this: there is a righteous branch on the throne of David who will lead Israel into peace. King Hezekiah takes charge, but he does so in a remarkable way, in the right way. He prays to the divine King for deliverance.

> Hezekiah went up to the house of the LORD. . . . And Hezekiah prayed to the LORD: "O LORD of hosts, God of Israel, enthroned above the cherubim, you are the God, you alone, of all the kingdoms of the earth; you have made heaven and earth. Incline your ear, O LORD, and hear; open your eyes, O LORD, and see; and hear all the words of Sennacherib, which he has sent to mock the living God. Truly, O LORD, the kings

---

3 This was Sennacherib's own description of besieged Jerusalem; see James B. Pritchard, ed., *Ancient Near Eastern Texts Relating to the Old Testament*, 3rd ed. (Princeton, NJ: Princeton University Press, 1969), 288. Sennacherib conveniently left out mention of a final conquering of Jerusalem.

of Assyria have laid waste all the nations and their lands, and have cast their gods into the fire. For they were no gods, but the work of men's hands, wood and stone. Therefore they were destroyed. So now, O Lord our God, save us from his hand, that all the kingdoms of the earth may know that you alone are the Lord." (Isa. 37:14–20)

God responds immediately with a clear assurance:

Because you have prayed to me concerning Sennacherib king of Assyria, this is the word that the Lord has spoken concerning him:

"... I will put my hook in your [Sennacherib's] nose
 and my bit in your mouth,
and I will turn you back on the way
 by which you came." (Isa. 37:21–22, 29)

And God walks the talk. As Isaiah 37 goes on to relate, the angel of the Lord strikes down 185,000 Assyrians overnight, leaving Sennacherib and his armies (or what is left of them) with no choice but to retreat to their country.

For our purposes, the key question is this: What was responsible for the deliverance of Jerusalem? Was it Hezekiah's prayer? God seems to say so. He assures Hezekiah that he will thwart Assyria "*because* you have prayed to me" (Isa. 37:21). But didn't God earlier make promises to Judah that he would deliver from Assyrian oppression, for example in Isaiah 31:8–9? Shouldn't we say, instead, that Jerusalem's deliverance was owing to God's sovereign promise and purpose? After all, God himself in his response to Hezekiah's prayer says of Assyria's destruction,

"I determined it long ago" (Isa. 37:26). So which is responsible—Hezekiah's prayer or God's sovereign plan and promise? It is, of course, a faulty question posing a false alternative. We do not need to choose between God's promise and our prayers, between God's rule and our requests, between God's sovereignty and our supplications. The latter are, in God's mystery, wisdom, and goodness, the *means* through which the former works. The sovereign God of the cosmos, whose plan of redemption is perfect and cannot be thwarted, purposes to accomplish his work in the world through the faithful prayers of his people.

Prayer and the "Responsibility Pie Chart"

Far too easily we fall into the trap of pitting God's sovereign plan against the effectiveness of prayer. The question "Why pray if God is sovereign in everything?" carries in its very terms and structure a skewed outlook. It presents effective prayer as something undermined by God's sovereignty. If God is sovereign, then prayer doesn't really *do* anything. Or if prayer is effective, then God must *not* be sovereign or must somehow *limit* his sovereign power. We imagine that God's sovereignty and our responsibility are comparable items of the same order, related to each other as two divisions of a "responsibility pie chart," with their percentages being in inverse relationship to each other: the bigger the slice we give to God, the less reason will we have to pray.

Part of the problem with this is a breakdown in a healthy doctrine of creation. At the heart of the doctrine of creation is the conviction that the Creator is *fundamentally and absolutely other* than the creature. To imagine God's sovereignty and the necessity of prayer as species of the same genus, and therefore as vying for space in the "responsibility pie chart," is to contradict the doctrine of creation. It's to begin with false knowledge about who the Creator is and who we are. It is not adequate to say that God is a lot bigger than us and has a lot more power than us and thus typically bears more responsibility for events than us. Rather, he is wholly other than us. His responsibility and our responsibility are not two different slices of the same pie; rather, God is the *Maker* of the pie. The Creator *establishes* our responsibility as his creatures.[4] In the same manner, the Creator's sovereignty does not moot effective prayer but establishes it.

God really does engage our words addressed to him in prayer. He listens to them. He acts on them. But he does so in the manner not of a creature but of the Creator, acting on and through the prayers of the saints as means to bring about changes in the world. In this way, at least, prayer is a matter of real dialogue with the divine. Surely doubts will remain among many. In particular, some might question whether this really counts as *dialogue*, whether God really responds to prayer or simply incorporates prayer into a prior purpose established quite apart from prayer. We will delay looking at the fullest Christian word on the matter until our conclusion. But for now, when it comes to the general question of God's plan and our prayer, we can say that Scripture doesn't present us with an either–or. We are not forced to choose. Episodes like Isaiah 36–37 are given in Scripture to help us know how to think about such things—and, just as importantly, how *not to talk* about such things. With the help of the prayer of Hezekiah, we can see that the question "Why pray if God is sovereign in everything?" smuggles some wrong-headed assumptions that Scripture neither demands nor expects us to make about the nature of God, responsibility, and prayer. To get better answers, we must ask better questions.[5] This leads us to a second biblical prayer.

4 See the Westminster Confession of Faith 3.1.
5 Some differently stated and structured questions that get at similar concerns, but with less of a tendency to set up a false alternative, include "Why does the sovereign God invite us to

Jesus's Prayer in John 17

John 17 is sometimes referred to as Jesus's high priestly prayer. It is Jesus's extended prayer just prior to his arrest and crucifixion, a prayer for his disciples, for those who believe in him, for all who are in Christ today. It's a precious passage of Scripture where we see the love of Christ enacted in the form of prayer to the Father for our everlasting good. Here's how Jesus begins his prayer: "Father, the hour has come; glorify your Son that the Son may glorify you" (v. 1).

That statement requires clarification at two points. First, what is the "hour" to which Jesus refers? This language of a coming "hour" (or "time") appears in several other places in the Gospel according to John, helping us fill in what Jesus means in John 17.[6] An important instance is found in John 12: the "hour" is a time for Jesus to be "glorified" (12:23) and for the Father to "glorify" his own name as well (12:27–28). What's more, the Father sent the Son into the world with the express purpose of meeting this "hour" (12:27). This was the divine plan all along. So when Jesus says that "the hour has come" in John 17:1, he means something like this: "The appointed time for glorification is upon us." Or "the moment you've been eternally planning for has arrived, in which to glorify me and yourself."

In one sense, then, it's unsurprising that Jesus goes on to say, "Father . . . *glorify your Son* that *the Son may glorify you.*" This

---

pray?," and best of all, "*Who* is the sovereign God who invites us to pray? What is his name?" Many of the chapters to follow will touch on the first question. The conclusion will zero in on the second, and I think most important, question. Here I am simply trying to correct an important misstep in our conceptualization of God vis-à-vis human responsibility and historical change.

6 For a thorough treatment of the Johannine "hour," see Stefanos Mihalios, *The Danielic Eschatological Hour in the Johannine Literature*, LNTS 436 (London: T&T Clark, 2011).

glorification of Son and Father is exactly what this "hour" means and is about. It's almost as if Jesus is being redundant. But it's not mere repetition. The two statements address the same subject matter; but they are two different kinds of statements, two different speech acts. The first statement is an assertion or affirmation; the second statement is a request, a supplication, a prayer.

Here is where the second clarification becomes crucial. The logical relationship between Jesus's assertion ("the hour has come") and his prayer ("glorify your Son that the Son may glorify you") is not expressly stated. What's the link that Jesus must be assuming between the assertion and the prayer? How do these statements relate? What conjunctions might we add to clarify the implicit logical connection? Most likely, it is an inferential relationship. Jesus offers in the first statement a *reason* for the Father to act on his prayer: Father, *because* the hour has come, *therefore* glorify your Son that the Son may glorify you.

Let's pause to think about how odd this is. Jesus is saying, in effect, "Father, since the hour in which you have purposed to glorify me and yourself has come, therefore glorify me and yourself." Jesus prays that the Father would do what he has sovereignly purposed to do from eternity past!

Why pray if God is going to sovereignly do what he wills anyway? Jesus turns that sensibility on its head, stirring up a different question: How could we pray with enduring confidence, boldness, and fervor *without* awareness of and assurance about God's sovereign commitments, purposes, promises, pursuits, and power? On the heels of acknowledging God's sovereign plan to glorify him, Jesus prays that God would work out his purpose to glorify him. The sovereignty of God doesn't discourage Jesus from praying. It encourages him to pray. God's sovereign promises and purposes give him reasons to pray, reasons to offer to God for fulfilling his request, reasons to expect that God will respond favorably. The will of God made known to him informs what he prays for, freeing him to pray with boldness and eagerness, knowing that the things he is seeking in prayer are at the center of the heart and purposes of the sovereign God.

Prayer and the "Will of God"

At this point, we might think that Jesus has a leg up on us. Jesus knows God's eternal purpose, knows God's will to glorify the Son. He is the Son of God, after all! Of course, Jesus can pray with boldness and confidence about that. But we are different. We don't have the advantage of knowing what Jesus knows, of being privy to God's will, so we can't pray with confidence and fervency as Jesus prays.

This is muddled thinking. (It doesn't help that we often functionally operate with an unbiblical Christology that assumes that because Jesus is God, therefore he can do things or know things that we "normal humans" can't.)[7] To be sure, Jesus has a different personal experience and a different personal knowledge than we do, just as you have a different personal experience and knowledge than I have. But it is important to realize that, like Jesus, we too can know the will of God in a way that informs our prayers and strengthens our confidence in praying.

We must specify what "will of God" we are talking about. It is not the secret or hidden will of God, what theologians call the "will of decree," his sovereign, unbreakable plan wherein he ordains all that comes to pass (see, e.g., Dan. 4:35; Rom.

---

7   See, further, Thomas G. Weinandy, *Does God Suffer?* (Notre Dame, IN: University of Notre Dame Press, 2000), 199–206.

1:10). As Moses says in Deuteronomy 29:29, "The secret things belong to the LORD our God." It is not our responsibility, nor is it within our power, to try to divine the secret will of decree of our sovereign God. Access to *that* will is not the golden ticket to confident prayer. Access to *that* will of God would, in fact, be the death of prayer. But, as Moses goes on to add, "the things *that are revealed* belong to us and to our children forever." We are given access to and can know God's revealed moral will, what theologians call God's "will of command." God has spoken and revealed in his Word (living and written) what he "wills" for us to take up and heed, what he desires to see among the nations, what he is committed to with respect to the creation (see, e.g., Ezra 10:11; 1 Thess. 4:2–3).[8] We can and should inform our prayers according to *that* will of God. We can and should, for the sake of our prayers, attend to what God has revealed of himself and has already brought about in the world.

That Paul was in the practice of this is evident in the letter to the Ephesians. In chapter 1, Paul first *blesses God* for what he has already accomplished and revealed in Christ for the church (vv. 3–14), then he *prays to God* for the Ephesian church's continued growth and good (vv. 15–23). The relationship between the blessing and the supplication is instructive. These two speech acts (blessing and supplicating) are "about" the same stuff, have nearly identical "content." Table 1 shows some of the most significant parallels, indicating that Paul's thoughts in verses 15–23 have not strayed far from his thoughts in verses 3–14.

---

8   Importantly, *nothing* can thwart the accomplishing of God's will of decree (Dan. 4)—it is sovereign and invincible. By contrast, God's will of command can be thwarted—we can break God's commands, and we do every day. But both the will of decree and the will of command are rightly named "the will of God."

Table 1. Blessing and prayer in Ephesians 1

The Blessing in Ephesians 1:3–14	The Prayer in Ephesians 1:15–23
"the God . . . of our Lord Jesus Christ" (v. 3)	"the God of our Lord Jesus Christ" (v. 17)
"the praise of his glory" (vv. 12, 14; also v. 6)	"the Father of glory" (v. 17)
"Holy Spirit" (v. 13)	"the Spirit of . . ." (v. 17)*
"wisdom and insight" (v. 8)	"wisdom . . . in the knowledge" (vv. 17–18)
"making known . . . the mystery of his will" (v. 9)	"revelation" (v. 17)
"riches of his grace" (v. 7)	"riches of his glorious inheritance" (v. 18)
"inheritance" (vv. 11, 14)	"inheritance" (v. 18)
"that we should be holy" (v. 4)	"the saints" (v. 18)
"in the heavenly places" (v. 3)	"in the heavenly places" (v. 20)

* Though many English translations have a lowercase "spirit" here (and leave it indefinite: "*a* spirit"), almost assuredly Paul is referring to *the* Spirit, who grants wisdom and gives/ illuminates revelation. See Gordon D. Fee, *God's Empowering Presence: The Holy Spirit in the Letters of Paul* (Peabody, MA: Hendrickson, 1994), 675.

Paul was not a very creative pray-er. Which is precisely the point. Paul's prayer isn't an ex nihilo creation. Rather, it is informed by and conformed to what has preceded him. Apparently, Jesus is not the only one who can pray according to the will of God. Like Jesus's prayer in John 17:1 but at a greater length, which allows us to consider the matter in greater detail, Paul's prayer in Ephesians 1 is shaped by God's purposes already received, God's saving work for him and the church already experienced, the mystery of God's will already revealed in Scripture and in Christ. Paul's prayer is his answer to what God has first communicated to him.

It turns out that prayer is not only a real dialogue of responsiveness among God and his people but also, and first, answering speech, a word spoken aright when spoken in response to God's prior words and ways addressed to us: "Our Father in heaven, *thy will* be done." When we answer God with prayers in accord with his word first spoken to us, in accord with his will and ways and character and aims revealed therein—when we pray, in short, "in Jesus's name"—then we can pray with great confidence and boldness. For we can be sure that these things prayed "in Jesus's name" are the very things that the sovereign God, the almighty Maker of heaven and earth, *wants* and is *actively pursuing*. As our Lord himself said, "Whatever you ask of the Father in my name, he will give it to you" (John 16:23). Prayers of rightly ordered answering speech *will* come to fruition.

———

Heavenly Father, full of goodness and grace, as you are pleased to declare your holy will to your poor servants, and to instruct them in the righteousness of your law, so write and engrave it on our hearts, that we should seek to serve and obey you alone in our whole life. Do not impute to us the transgressions that we have committed against your law, so that as we sense your grace being multiplied upon us in such abundance, we would have cause to praise and glorify you, through Jesus Christ your Son, our Lord. So let it be.

PRAYER AFTER THE READING OF THE DECALOGUE,
STRASSBURG LITURGY (1545)[9]

9 In *Reformation Worship: Liturgies from the Past for the Present*, ed. Jonathan Gibson and Mark Earngey (Greensboro, NC: New Growth Press, 2018), 309.

It's enough to drive a man crazy; it'll break a man's faith,
It's enough to make him wonder if he's ever been sane—
When he's bleating for comfort from thy staff and thy rod,
And the heaven's only answer is the silence of God.

ANDREW PETERSON
"The Silence of God"

2

When the Dialogue
Seems One-Sided

RIGHTLY ORDERED PRAYERS raised in Jesus's name will come
to fruition. Except when they *don't*. Because, sometimes, they
won't.[1] The life of faithful answering speech inevitably stirs
up a very great existential anxiety and anguish. The anxiety is
intensified and, in fact, forced upon us when we take Jesus's
words about prayer seriously: "Whatever you ask of the Father
in my name, he will give it to you" (John 16:23). Herein lies
the trouble: Jesus's words seem patently *contrary to our experience*. Every one of us knows, or will know, the reality of "unanswered prayer." We lift up our voices to the God who invites
our answering speech, only to receive back silence. What do
we do with that?

There's an easy way out of this conundrum, which needs to
be noted but is insufficient. The primary burden of this chapter
is to acknowledge that things are not always so easy in the life
of prayer.

---

1   With apologies to Theodor Geisel.

The Problem of Unanswered Prayer

Whatever you ask, the Father *will* give it to you. Of course, it's not that simple. Jesus adds a condition: "whatever you ask in my name." All our supplications raised "in Jesus's name"—in accord with the character and mission of Christ, because of (and in) Christ and his priestly work on our behalf, for the honor of Christ[2]—Jesus expects every one of those prayers to be granted by the Father.

We can further clarify the point by considering Jesus's words to his disciples earlier in John 15:7. "If you abide in me," he says, "ask whatever you wish, and it will be done for you." Only those who abide in Jesus can expect to receive whatever they ask of the Father. Looking to the context, we can say that "abiding in Jesus" involves dependence on him and obedience to him. It involves a personal love of him as our Friend, Brother, and Comforter. It involves being pruned and fruitful, growing in holiness and reaping harvests of new disciples. If we abide in Christ, then we can ask whatever we wish, and the Father will gladly give it.

In John 15:7, Jesus states another condition for receiving from the Father: if Christ's words are in our pockets, accessible at the swipe of a finger, we can ask whatever we want of the Father. In fact, Jesus does not say, "If my word is *accessible to* you," but "If . . . my words *abide in* you." If, like bees gathering pollen in their hives, we gather the word in our souls through meditation and memorization, so that, like pollen, the word transforms into sweet honey, the honey of renewed logic and refurbished imaginations

---

2   For extended discussion of the phrase "in Jesus's name," see Craig S. Keener, *The Gospel of John*, 2 vols. (Peabody, MA: Hendrickson, 2003), 947–49. I incline toward a more maximal understanding of the phrase in John.

and transfigured wills and affections[3]—if Christ's word abides in us like that, then we can ask whatever we desire, confident that the Father delights in our requests and will give us what we seek.

It's clear from John 15 what faithful prayers consist of (the exaltation of Jesus's name) and where they come from (abiding in Christ and his word abiding in us). It's equally clear what Jesus expects the Father to do in response to such faithful prayers: "He will give it to you." "It will be done for you."

From this, there arises an easy answer to the problem of unanswered prayers: such prayers aren't faithful. Many of our prayers aren't lifted up in Jesus's name, in accord with his character and mission, for his glory alone. We often pray, in effect, "Our will be done," period. We often pray from a position not of abiding in Christ but of attachment to our idols, asking for our divine husband's checkbook, that we may spend on our false lovers (see James 4:3–4).[4] Ought we to expect God to be a contented cuckold? We pray for God to continue to provide for our pampered lives while we remain oblivious to our oppression of neighbors. Should we not expect such prayers to be hindered (see, e.g., Isa. 58; cf. 1 Pet. 3:7)?

The easy answer to the "problem of unanswered prayers" is that the problem is some moral defect in *us*. But reality is not always so easily explained or explained away. We would do a disservice to leave things simply at that, to bring no nuance to

---

3 The bee-and-pollen analogy for learning and intellectual or moral transformation goes back as far as Seneca (see *Letter* 84.2–5, to Lucilius) or further (Seneca cites, e.g., Virgil).

4 James writes to a collective body made up of both women and men. Normally, the masculine plural would be used in addressing a collective. But James addresses the church as "adulteresses" (James 4:4), purposefully using the feminine plural (this is obscured by many translations; see, rightly, NASB and the ESV marginal note). John J. Schmitt, "You Adulteresses! The Image in James 4:4," *NovT* 28, no. 4 (1986): 327–37, discusses several proposed interpretations of the image.

what actually gives in the life of prayer.[5] For experience tells us (as does Scripture; see below) that prayer doesn't always work that way. Sometimes we pray not obviously hardened in sin but making every effort to abide in Christ, with his word abiding in us as we lift up good, Christ-exalting prayers to God in Jesus's name as the desires of our hearts—but God does not apparently grant us what we seek.

That happens. Often. Months and years and decades of desperate, dependent, faithful prayer to the Lord for some good and Christ-exalting reality, giving way to growing anxiety and despair and the ache of disappointment at the sustained silence of God. We pray

- for the salvation of parents, siblings, children, spouses, yet they persist in unbelief;
- for the strengthening of the church's witness in the world, but here comes another sad church scandal;
- for preservation of life, only to witness the tragic victory of disease and death, even among our youngest;
- for victory over addictions to alcohol or pornography or some other besetting sin, which victory never seems to come;
- for openings into an unreached people group, and we encounter multiplying obstacles, increasing delays, one closed door after another;

5 To leave things simply at that would give quite the wrong impression about Jesus's words on prayer in the upper room. Jesus's "conditions" for answered prayer are not intended to give God an "escape valve" when it comes to our prayers. Jesus would not have confident prayer die a death by qualification. Rather, Jesus's intent is that we might have peace in him, take courage in him, and be filled with unshakable joy (John 15:11; 16:33; see also 14:1, 27, 29).

- for the preservation of a marriage that ends in divorce, or maybe for a godly husband or wife, but we face only decades of disappointment and loneliness;
- for rescue and redemption for the oppressed and helpless, while every year the number of those caught in human trafficking or foster care systems or systemic racism seems depressingly to increase.

There are hundreds of wonderful, Christ-honoring, neighbor-loving things we pray for in life, and there are seemingly just as many times when God doesn't do anything in response to them, or his response seems oh-so little and oh-so slow in proportion to what we are asking. Then the questions and doubts fall like hail upon our souls. *Are you cold or blind, God? What I am seeing down here is horrific, and you refuse to act! Why are you deaf to my prayers? Are you not good? Are you impotent? Are you lazy? Are you unjust? Unloving? Maybe you love others, but am I outside your love? Maybe you're just a figment of my imagination?*

What do we do with that? Jesus means for us to pray with zeal and expectancy. That's the point of him saying, "Ask whatever you wish and it will be done for you." We are to pray with expectancy that God will act for our good in response to our pleas to him in Christ. But how do we sustain such expectancy when faced with years of silence? How do we not become jaded by repeated and long-lasting disappointment in our supplication to God for seemingly good things? On a personal note, I have a well-formed habit of praying cynically, pessimistically. Nothing's really going to change here and now; maybe when Christ returns, but for now, I must just grin and bear it. I'm a sinner, we're all sinners, the world is broken—all we can expect is disappointment. And that's where I too often pray from.

But that is to give up on prayer at a deep heart level. So how do we battle that tendency in the face of unanswered prayer?

I don't have a silver bullet to slay all the angst and anguish in the blink of an eye. But I want to share four biblical insights that the Spirit has used in differing moments of need, each coming somewhat unexpectedly, to lift my flagging zeal, heal my diseased expectations, and keep me persevering in prayer.[6] It is my hope that they might do the same for you, so that you might not give up on the life of prayer but persevere.

Do Not Lose Heart

First, God knows we will face weariness and despondency in our prayer lives. He's well aware that persevering in expectant, hope-filled prayer will be a *battle*. Remember Jesus's parable from Luke 18? It's of a widow against whom some great injustice has been done. She persistently makes her plea before an unjust judge, who takes no action in response to her plea. Only after long-lasting, relentless begging does he finally enact justice for her. Jesus compares this widow's experience to the disciple's life in prayer. He shares this parable, Luke 18:1 says, so that we might "always . . . pray *and not lose heart.*"

Jesus *expects* that losing heart will be a prime temptation as we pray, which is why he tells us this parable. He knows that sometimes disciples will *feel* like the widow in the parable, like those knocking in vain on the door of an apathetic and unjust judge. He knows that, in the sometimes-hard life of prayer, we will be inclined to grow weary and give up. He expects us to have to *battle* these tendencies, not to be totally free of them.

---

6 Full disclosure: I have stolen three of the following four points from John Piper, having learned them under his teaching in various settings through the years.

Our weariness doesn't catch God off guard or offend his sensibilities. Knowing this certainly doesn't resolve all our frustration and remove all the ache, but there is some small reassurance in God's attentiveness to our existential plight. He's not oblivious to it but has compassion for us in it. He's not disappointed in our propensity to grow weary but determined to encourage us through it. When weariness creeps in, it helps a little to know that God's patience with us isn't so short as to give up on us for that reason.[7]

God understands the temptation to lose heart in the face of unanswered prayer. In fact, we can say with full theological integrity that God not only understands the disappointment of unanswered prayer as an object of detached scientific analysis but also sympathizes with it, having experienced it personally. For it was Christ himself who prayed to his Father, "Let this cup pass from me," only to have every last drop of the cup poured out on his head hours later.

"I Have Heard"

A second point, perhaps a bit more helpful, comes from the story of Abraham. In Genesis 17, God tells the ninety-nine-year-old Abraham that ninety-year-old Sarah will give birth to the son whom God has promised, who will be Abraham's heir. Laughing at the thought, Abraham offers up this plea: "Oh that Ishmael might live before you!"

Remember Ishmael? He was Abraham's son by the Egyptian slave Hagar, born of Abraham and Sarah's lack of faith. Nevertheless,

---

7 It helps also to know that the "hardness of prayer" is experienced by all the saints; see Timothy Keller, *Prayer: Experiencing Awe and Intimacy with God* (New York: Dutton, 2014), 24–25.

Ishmael was Abraham's beloved son. In Genesis 17:18, Abraham pleads for his son's good, essentially saying: "O God, please! Let the heir be Ishmael! Let him live and receive blessing from you! Don't let him pay for my sins! Please, be gracious to my son." That's a good prayer. That is a father's sincere, upright, earnest, loving prayer for his son's life and blessing. That's how God wants fathers to pray for their sons. And God says, immediately in 17:19, "No, but Sarah your wife will bear you a son," and "I will establish my covenant with him." Good prayer. Clear "no" in response. Abraham knows well the disappointment of unanswered prayer.

But the words that come next are stunning and precious. In Genesis 17:20, God says, "As for Ishmael, I have heard you; behold, I will bless him." God acts promptly to respond to Abraham—not giving him precisely what he asked for, but not ignoring altogether the heart of Abraham's request. In response to Abraham's prayer, God gives precisely what Abraham most needs for his deepest good and happiness, *and* what Ishmael needs, *and* what all nations need. For through Isaac, the son of Sarah, the son of promise, blessing will come to all nations. In his sovereignty, wisdom, and active concern, God responds to Abraham's prayer not with what Abraham feels he needs but with what Abraham and everyone else really need.

God responds in this way to every prayer prayed to him in faith through Christ. This assumes that God *hears* our prayers, listens attentively to them—every one of them, even the ones he does not grant, or does not grant in the way or timing we would want. Scripture doesn't leave that as an unstated assumption. God says to Abraham, "I have heard you."[8] He doesn't *need* to tell Abraham (and

---

8   God's "I have *heard* you [שְׁמַעְתִּיךָ]" involves a wordplay with the name *Ishmael* [יִשְׁמָעֵאל], which means "God hears" (see Gen. 16:11; cf. John Goldingay, *Genesis*, BCOT [Grand

us) that he hears Abraham's prayer. But God does tell him because it's good for him (and us) to know. We need to be expressly assured that God hears us. He doesn't turn a deaf ear to the longings of our hearts poured out to him in Christ. Whatever the cause of his seeming silence and apparent delayed response, it is *not* inattentiveness. He attentively listens to us, always. With equal loving attention, he will respond, and perhaps *already* is responding, for our best good, always. It might not be by giving the specifics that we, in the moment, think are most needed. But what God gives and does in real-time response to our prayers is, in fact, for our best good and his greatest glory.

The Gathered Prayers of the Saints

Third, we can turn our attention to the end of the biblical story in the Revelation of Saint John. In Revelation 8, God begins his end-time trumpet judgments on the earth. With the help of John, we're given a glimpse of what takes place in the throne room of heaven in preparation for the blasting of these trumpet judgments. In particular, we read in verses 3–5 that there is an altar before the Lord. What is on the altar? According to verse 3, it's "the prayers of all the saints." An angel comes with a golden censer to take what's on the altar, to add to it incense,[9] and to throw all of this holy mixture upon the earth, thus beginning the final judgments (vv. 4–5).

When God enacts the judgments of the last day, when he wins his eschatological victory over evil, when he sets to right all the earth and establishes full and final justice and peace and joy in the world, the means by which he does so is the prayers of the

---

Rapids, MI: Baker, 2020], 282). The listening God sets his attention specifically on the person at the center of Abraham's loving supplication.

9 Peter Leithart intriguingly argues that the added incense is the Spirit's intercessions that are united to, empower, and carry the prayers of the saints to accomplish God's purposes in the world; see Leithart, *Revelation 1–11*, ITC (London: Bloomsbury T&T Clark, 2018), 350–51.

saints.[10] *All* of the saints. The saints living today across the globe lift up their pleas to God, but they seem often to go unnoticed. The martyrs under the heavenly altar presently crying for the vindication of their blood must still wait for the answer to their prayers (see Rev. 6:9–11).[11] The saints who perished under oppressive, God-denying regimes of ages past never saw the full coming of God's kingdom for which they cried out. The saints lauded in Hebrews 11 all laid hold of God's promises by faith, earnestly seeking God for their fulfillment, and all of them died having not received what was promised (see v. 39). These prayers are not ignored or forgotten but gathered. Apparently, God purposes "something better" than acting to fully grant the prayers of his people individually and piecemeal, something involving the *whole* of the one, holy, catholic, and apostolic church, both militant and triumphant, together (see v. 40).

As John Piper puts it, we never pray in vain:

Hallowed be your name.
Your kingdom come,
your will be done,
   on earth as it is in heaven. (Matt. 6:9–10)

It might seem like God isn't acting in response to prayers for his kingdom's coming, his defeat of evil and death, the vindication of his people. But that's not true. He hears those prayers. He is storing them up on his heavenly altar. He is waiting in wisdom and

---

10   See, further, G. K. Beale, *The Book of Revelation*, NIGTC (Grand Rapids, MI: Eerdmans, 1999), 455.

11   On Rev. 8:3–5 as the fulfillment of the martyrs' supplication in 6:9–11, see Beale, *The Book of Revelation*, 454–55.

in the power of patience. One day he will pour out the full bowl of prayers and incense on the world and usher in the justice and peace and restoration we long for.

We will face disappointment in our life of prayer. But don't lose heart. Don't give up. God knows and sympathizes with our struggle. He hears and is acting even now upon our pleas, often in unexpected ways. And not a single prayer for his glory and the world's good will fall to earth utterly fruitless. Such prayers always arise as sweet incense to him. He is storing them up for the day of unimaginable glory and goodness, which is our sure hope in Christ. So, in the meantime . . .

The Silence of Holy Saturday

The trouble is with this "in the meantime," the time of so many seemingly unanswered prayers. It is important, then, to add a fourth and final point having to do with Holy Saturday, the day between Good Friday and Easter Sunday. That there is such a thing as Holy Saturday in the gospel is remarkable, if oft overlooked. Why wouldn't a simple movement from death one day to resurrection the next be sufficient? Why put a whole day, and a day of "rest" and inactivity at that, between cross and resurrection? Why might it be crucial to come to terms with not only the substance of the doctrines that we associate with Holy Week but also the three-day *shape of the drama* at its climax? A theology of Holy Saturday is of crucial importance for many things,[12] including sustained faithful, fervent prayer.

---

12 The most significant work in this respect is Alan E. Lewis, *Between Cross and Resurrection: A Theology of Holy Saturday* (Grand Rapids, MI: Eerdmans, 2001). While it is insightful, helpfully provocative, and an important launching point for the following thoughts, I am persuaded Lewis presses his observations of Holy Week into the service of unwarranted assertions about the immanent Trinity. For a forceful critique along these lines, see Thomas G. Weinandy, "Easter Saturday and the Suffering of God: The Theology of Alan E. Lewis," *IJST* 5, no. 1 (2003): 62–76; see also, more appreciatively, Keith L. Johnson's review of

Let us imagine ourselves in the shoes of the first disciples on that Sabbath between cross and resurrection. What would that day have been like?

- It was a day of anguished disappointment, regret, and failure. All their hopes were ruthlessly dashed upon the rocks of the previous day. They had hoped that Jesus would redeem Israel, but he was put to death.[13]

- It was a day of fear—their supposed King was dead, and the authorities who put him to death were alive and well and powerful all around.

- This means it was also a day when the idolatrous kingdoms of the world still apparently ruled the day. In Matthew 27:62–66, the rulers of the world plotted together (v. 62), self-assured that theirs was the only show in town.

- That Saturday was a day when it seemed that death had the last word. After all, the one claiming to be the Son of the God of life was buried, defeated by death. And this Son's people, the agents of his life, were isolated, alone, hiding away in fear for their lives.

- The Sabbath after the first Good Friday was, therefore, a day of ambiguity: What next? What hope could lie ahead? What kind of imposter or fool was the corpse lying in Joseph's tomb? The disciples likely still believed in the God

Lewis in *Perspectives in Religious Studies* 35, no. 3 (2008): 338–43. Also worth engaging, building on Lewis's magnum opus, is the more accessible and practically oriented work of Adam D. Tietje, *Toward a Pastoral Theology of Holy Saturday: Providing Spiritual Care for War Wounded Souls* (Eugene, OR: Wipf and Stock, 2018).

13 The words from the disciples on the Emmaus road in Luke 24:20–21, while spoken on Sunday morning, are nevertheless a clear window onto the disposition of the disciples on Saturday.

of Israel in a manner, but that faith didn't see a clear way
forward for God's people and mission and promise.

- It was a day of silence from God. In all this distress and
darkness and uncertainty, no word of direction or answer
was heard from the heavens.

Try putting that in your telling of the gospel! Amazingly, written into the God-inspired gospel climax is a day of ambiguity, of
the kings of the world still apparently ruling the day, of the fear
and uncertainty of God's people, of the seeming victory of death,
of the silence of God. The canonical telling of the one and only
"good news" is a telling that does not avoid Holy Saturday. This
is part of the divine author's message, part of his inscrutably wise
ways in the world.

It turns out that God not only *expects* the life of prayer to traverse
seasons of weariness but even *writes such seasons into the heart of
the story.* The sovereign God *grants* his disciples such experiences.
We may rightly assume that they are intended in some way for his
people's good. Again, that helps us, a little—not as an immuniza-
tion against anguish in the face of good prayers long left unanswered, but as a reassurance that such experiences are not pointless
but part of a drama with good ends and final beauty and peace.

So if we suffer seasons individually and corporately wherein the
life of prayer feels like a one-sided dialogue, this isn't necessarily a
result of our unbelief and sin. It's not an occasion for wallowing in
introspective self-pity, as if our moral defects were always to blame.
It isn't an indication that we are outlier Christians. It's not evidence
that we are outside God's will or attention. And it most assuredly
isn't a sign that things are ultimately spinning chaotically out of
control. Susceptibility to weariness in prayer and experiences of

the silence of God are, strange as it may sound, part of God-given normal life in Christ in the time between his first and second comings. The church age is, we might say, a Holy Saturday age: an already-and-not-yet "day" in between, an "as sorrowful yet always rejoicing" sojourn, an epoch during which ambiguity, confusion, unresolved tensions, and weeping go hand in hand with humble, bold, joyful confidence in God's sure promises.

But a theology of Holy Saturday opens the door to more than just a *little* help in our experiences of the silence of God. Looking intently at Holy Saturday from our vantage point, we discern nothing short of good news. On Holy Saturday, the disciples are suffering the apparent silence of God, but Jesus is dead. How is that good news? He's dead and buried on Holy Saturday because he himself has already gone through it all on Good Friday—anguish, loneliness, failure, rejection, abuse, silence from God. In fact, the silence from God that Jesus underwent was not just strong and intense like ours; his was absolute, which ours is not. And the good news is this: Jesus underwent this ultimate nightmare for us, in our place, for the life of the world. Jesus suffered God's silence not just *like us* but also and fundamentally *for us sinners*.

As a result, we can have full assurance of faith that though we may often meet with God's hiddenness and silence, it is not absolute for us. God's sometime silence toward us his praying people, being only a hint of the absolute silence endured by God-incarnate on our behalf, can be received from God as a strange, severe mercy for our good. What's more, we can also have great confidence that Jesus (who is no longer dead but lives) sympathizes with our plight and can even be present with us through it. Since Jesus has plumbed the utter depths, there is no depth or darkness that we can fall into where Jesus might not also be found.

In the words of Hans Urs von Balthasar, "He wanted to sink so low that in the future all falling would be a falling into him."[14] When life seems a living hell and our cries receive the seeming silent treatment, we can know that God himself has gone there first and thus can be found even there.

———

O God, Creator of heaven and earth: Grant that, as the crucified body of your dear Son was laid in the tomb and rested on this holy Sabbath, so we may await with him the coming of the third day, and rise with him to newness of life; who now lives and reigns with you and the Holy Spirit, one God, for ever and ever. Amen.

COLLECT FOR HOLY SATURDAY,
BOOK OF COMMON PRAYER (1979)[15]

---

14 Hans Urs von Balthasar, *Heart of the World*, trans. Erasmo S. Leiva (San Francisco: Ignatius, 1989), 43, quoted in Tietje, *Pastoral Theology of Holy Saturday*, 38. See, further, 47–48.
15 Episcopal Church in the United States of America, *The Book of Common Prayer* (New York: Church Publishing, 1979), 283.

Culture is the gesture people make toward the good life.

KEVIN J. VANHOOZER
"What Is Everyday Theology?"

All beginnings are hard.

CHAIM POTOK
In the Beginning

*If a man should give me a diamond worth one hundred
thousand dollars, I think I would make bold to ask him
for a little piece of brown paper to carry it away in.*

DWIGHT L. MOODY
"The Eighth Chapter of Romans"

The End and the Beginning of Prayer

"URGENT PRAYER REQUEST! [name] was just in a terrible car accident. We need as many prayer warriors as possible pleading with God for the preservation of his life. Please forward this along to others." Many of us have likely received an email or text message to this effect, a recruitment letter of sorts enlisting people for what sometimes goes by the name of a "prayer chain." The apostle Paul also wrote such letters, seeking to stir up as many partners in prayer as he could, seeking to grow his "prayer chain." It can be useful to compare the present-day practice with the Pauline.

Prayer Chains, Popular and Pauline

A particularly clear and helpful passage for this task comes in what we know as Saint Paul's Second Letter to the Corinthians. In 2 Corinthians 1:8–11 we read:

> We do not want you to be unaware, brothers, of the affliction we experienced in Asia. For we were so utterly burdened beyond our strength that we despaired of life itself. Indeed, we felt that we had received the sentence of death. But that was

to make us rely not on ourselves but on God who raises the dead. He delivered us from such a deadly peril, and he will deliver us. On him we have set our hope that he will deliver us again. You also must help us by prayer, so that many will give thanks on our behalf for the blessing granted us through the prayers of many.

Paul recalls a personal experience of being delivered by God (vv. 8–10a). He gives few if any specifics, but the hardship was so extreme that he "despaired of life itself." It seems that this hardship was given by God. At least, that is Paul's conviction, for he says, "We had the sentence of death within ourselves *so that* we would not trust in ourselves, but in God who raises the dead" (v. 9 NASB). Paul speaks in terms of *purpose*.[1] Who could send such a death sentence, and who would do so purposing to wean Paul and his partners off self-reliance and to grow *God*-reliance in its place? The answer, of course, is God. Paul's sufferings were God-ordained for the end of bringing more glory to God in his people's full reliance upon him.

All of that is background to the invitation Paul gives in verses 10b–11. Here Paul shifts his attention from the past to the future. In particular, he enters recruitment mode, calling the Corinthian church to join him in prayer for the future. Paul explains in verse 10b that he has set his hope on God for further deliverance, which I think must mean, at least, that Paul resolves to pray to God for deliverance in every hardship to come. Then he tells the Corinthians that they, too, "must help us by prayer." Paul is starting a prayer chain. He's getting

---

1 As is recognized by most interpreters, the ἵνα in v. 9 indicates not merely result but purpose.

as many voices as possible to join his voice lifted to God in supplication.

But here is where Paul's prayer chain likely differs from many contemporary efforts to recruit as many prayer warriors as possible for an urgent need. We might say that Paul operates by a different kind of intercessory math than is common today. For most prayer chains today, the implicit logic of the recruitment effort seems to go something like this:

> my prayers
> + <u>your prayers</u>
> God granting our request

Or to shift to a different field of math having to do with probabilities: the more voices we add to the mix, the higher the likelihood that God will hear us and grant our request. The Gentiles think that they will be heard for their many words (Matt. 6:7); the implicit logic of many prayer-chain movements seems to be that we will be heard for our many voices. The longer the prayer chain, the better our chances of reaching God and tugging him into action for our good. Additionally, we should note that the *end goal* of prayer chains, popularly conceived, is apparently attaining what we ask for. God's action for our good is uncertain, and assembling a great army of prayer warriors boosts our confidence that God will so act.

But this is quite different from Paul's disposition in 2 Corinthians 1. We could portray Paul's intercessory math like this:

> my prayers
> + <u>your prayers</u>
> *more thanksgiving* when God acts for our good

Importantly, the action of God to deliver is *not* the uncertain variable, not what more prayer "adds up to." Before Paul ever calls the Corinthians to pray, and before he himself determines to set his hope on God for deliverance, he *asserts* in verse 10 that God "will deliver us." Prayer is, for Paul, answering speech. It's Paul's response to the word of God already spoken, to promises already made, such as the promise that God *will* save everyone who calls upon his name (Joel 2:32).[2] "He will deliver." Paul does not seem at all uncertain about that.[3]

What's uncertain for Paul is how many will recognize God's activity for what it is when it comes, and how many will be prepared at that time to choir the proper praise. So Paul stirs up the Corinthians to join him in prayer as an act of preparation. He spells out his purpose expressly: "You also must help us by prayer, *so that many will give thanks on our behalf for the blessing granted us through the prayers of many.*" Paul's aim in making the prayer chain as long as possible is not to increase the odds of reaching God and commanding his attention. Rather, Paul pursues more links in the chain to heighten the joyful jingling sound of thanksgiving to God when he answers prayers. More pray-ers now means more thankers then (at the time God wisely appoints for our deliverance). Paul's mustering of an army of prayer warriors to raise supplications to God is actually a mobilizing of the army for its most proper and glad function: to praise God. Paul wants

---

2 As Scott J. Hafemann notes, Paul's conviction likely also is tied to the experiential evidence of God's past works of deliverance in his own life and especially in the death and resurrection of Christ (Hafemann, *2 Corinthians*, NIVAC [Grand Rapids, MI: Zondervan, 2000], 64–65).

3 At the same time, Paul's phrasing indicates that he does not presume upon the manner or timing of God's deliverance. See, rightly, Mark A. Seifrid, *The Second Letter to the Corinthians*, PiNTC (Grand Rapids, MI: Eerdmans, 2014), 43–44.

the Corinthians to "help us by prayer" because he wants in the end the greater glorifying of God.

The End of Our Supplications

I have said that Paul's intercessory math and his purposes in prayer *might* be different from those at work in many popular prayer-chain initiatives. There might be a fundamental difference, and I think there likely is, but we can't be certain, for the simple fact that many of our prayer chains remain mum on the fundamental purposes driving them. Many prayer requests and prayers offered are not as forthcoming about their ultimate ends as Paul's prayer request is in 2 Corinthians 1. It is worth asking: *Why* do we want God to do such and such? *To what end* do we want many to join us in supplication to God for this or that?

The same "stuff" can be prayed to very different ends. It's good to pray for the Holy Spirit, whom the Father gladly gives to those who ask (Luke 11:13). But it's possible to ask for the Spirit and power while serving the god of money; in so doing, we will be condemned (see Acts 8:9–24). It is good to pray boldly for the Lord's mercy, patience, and forgiveness toward us. But it's possible to come into God's presence seeking amnesty not with the intention of turning from idolatry, oppression of the weak, and exclusion of ethnic outsiders but with the intention of keeping up such evils scot-free (see Jer. 7:1–11). "Behold, I myself have seen it," declares the Lord, "I will cast you out of my sight" (Jer. 7:11, 15). Surely, it's good to pray theologically well-ordered prayers. But some do so with the goal of being admired by others (Matt. 6:5). Truly, they already have all the reward they can expect. Similarly, we pray publicly for our uncle's neighbor's son's healing from the flu. Sometimes we do so because our hearts are earnestly aimed at magnifying God's glory through Christ-won resurrecting power over sickness (see John 9:3; 11:4). But maybe more often we do so to the social end of saving face when it's our turn to share prayer requests—we have to say *something*.

The end for which we ask for this or that proves to be just as important as, if not more important than, *what* we specifically request of the God who hears. G. K. Chesterton once remarked, "The test of all happiness is gratitude."[4] Transposed into the key of prayer, we can say that the test of all truly happy (in the sense of "blessed" and "felicitous") prayers is whether they express gratitude to God and are aimed at still more thanksgiving to him. So important is this test that we do well to get into the wise and well-ordered habit of expressly naming in our prayers the aims of our supplications: "Father, accomplish this or that *in order that* we may give you thanks and praise." For the ends we are after in praying are what we most love and most serve and are most committed to.

Our hearts are always pointing toward something we imagine to be ultimate. Our historical-cultural actions always lean toward that ultimate, hoped-for kingdom. And as a form of culture, prayer, too, always gestures toward some final hoped-for vision of "the good life." Sometimes our desired ends in prayer are expressly stated, as in Paul's prayer in 2 Corinthians 1; often they are unstated and assumed. But our prayers always logically end somewhere. And where our prayers end reveals what our hearts bow down to and hope for. When we pray, what are we ultimately after? Are we praying in the service of the gods of comfort and physical security and temporal life and romantic love and personal fulfillment and optimization and our tribe and nation and bank

---

4   G. K. Chesterton, *Orthodoxy* (1909; repr., Peabody, MA: Hendrickson, 2006), 50.

account? Or are we praying, like Paul, to the end that many voices would give the God who raised Christ from the dead much glory in thanksgiving?

The Beginning of Our Supplications

So we can identify our ultimate end and goal of asking God to grant this or that, since where our prayer ends reveals the worship of our hearts. But there's a grammatically simpler way to get at the same point. We can identify *what we most desire*, what we want God to do above all else, our first and fundamental prayer request that orders every other thing we are asking for. Not just the end (goal) of our prayer, but also the *beginning* of our prayer—what we regularly ask God for *first* and want from him most of all—is an important indication of our hearts before God and the health (or lack thereof) of our prayer lives.

Our Lord Jesus Christ himself instructed us to begin our prayers in this way:

> Our Father in heaven,
> *hallowed be your name.* (Matt. 6:9)

The first and fundamental thing we are to seek from God is the spreading of his fame, the exaltation of his character and worth, the shining forth of his glory. According to our Lord, this is to be the first desire of our hearts, the request that precedes and rightly orders all the other good things we ask of the Father's hand, whether bread or forgiveness or protection or life itself. Do we pray "hallowed be your name" as our first and driving prayer, or are our prayers first and last and throughout in the mode of "give us bread"? Is our praying a reflection of loving what God loves, seeking what God seeks, yearning for the honor and respect due him as we would for a beloved father?

Prayer is, above all, a relational activity, a form of communion, a communicative form that answers to someone who addresses us. That someone, God, is personal. God is not an impersonal power or resource to help us get things we might want—health, success, material provision, romantic fulfillment, temporal or eternal security, inner peace, good standing in our community, long life—regardless of whether we treasure a relationship with him. Rather, God is someone who speaks to us in love, telling us what's on his heart and what he is zealous for. God's ultimate passion and pursuit is nothing less than *his exaltation to the ends of the earth* (which happens to be, at one and the same time, our best good and happiness as his creatures[5]).

> For my own sake, for my own sake, I do it,
>> for how should my name be profaned?
> My glory I will not give to another. (Isa. 48:11)

What is our most felicitous response? "Whether you eat or drink, or whatever you do, do all to the glory of God" (1 Cor. 10:31), including prayer.

Prayer expresses to God what we think of his heart and zeal and pursuits and loves. It's our opportunity to experientially join with him in our longings and leanings in seeking his glory in our lives and among the nations. What both the beginning and the end

---

5 See esp. Jonathan Edwards, *A Dissertation on the End for Which God Created the World*, in *The Works of Jonathan Edwards*, ed. Sereno E. Dwight, rev. and corr. Edward Hickman, 2 vols. (Edinburgh: Banner of Truth, 1974), 1:94–121; and Edwards's contemporary popularizer John Piper, *Desiring God: Meditations of a Christian Hedonist*, rev. ed. (Colorado Springs: Multnomah, 2011).

of our supplications to God reveal is our relational orientation to God in prayer.

The Beginning of Prayer

But what about *God's* relational orientation toward us? Many of us struggle with uncertainty over this dimension of prayer.

In each of the preceding two chapters, I have referred to John 16:23: "Whatever you ask of the Father in my name, he will give it to you." Now consider the context in which that verse appears, for it gives us a crucial insight into the heart of God toward us in Christ.[6] In the context leading up to John 16:23, Jesus tells the disciples of his coming departure (his death) and return to his Father, and of the benefit that will come to them through this—specifically, another Helper, the Holy Spirit, will be sent to them (see, e.g., John 16:7). Then Jesus says:

> In that day you will ask nothing of me. Truly, truly, I say to you, whatever you ask of the Father in my name, he will give it to you. Until now you have asked nothing in my name. Ask, and you will receive, that your joy may be full.
>
> I have said these things to you in figures of speech. The hour is coming when I will no longer speak to you in figures of speech but will tell you plainly about the Father. In that day you will ask in my name, and I do not say to you that I will ask the Father on your behalf; for the Father himself loves you, because you have loved me and have believed that I came from God. (John 16:23–27)

6 The following discussion is an adaptation of Daniel J. Brendsel, "The Spirit after Pentecost: Three Facets of His New-Covenant Glory," Desiring God, January 28, 2022, https://www .desiringgod.org/.

Asking Nothing, Asking Everything

Notice how strange, seemingly contrary, the statements in John 16:23 are. Jesus first says that a day is coming when we will *ask* nothing of him. Then with his next breath he speaks the sentence we have noted repeatedly: whatever we *ask* of the Father in his name will be granted to us. Indeed, ask with all boldness, Jesus says, "that your joy may be full" (John 16:24). On a dime, Jesus seemingly turns from "ask nothing" to "ask everything."

The oddity is resolved, I believe, by understanding Jesus to be referring to two different *kinds* of asking. When he says in verse 23a that someday we will "ask nothing of him," he is referring to *inquiry*, to raising questions because of a lack of knowledge, to seeking explanations and clarifications of things that confuse. That's what the disciples do throughout the Gospel according to John. They are confused; they misunderstand; they ask questions from ignorance. Jesus promises that, by the Spirit, they will move from misunderstanding to understanding. They will no longer make inquiries to remedy ignorance. In contrast to verse 23a, we can interpret verses 23b–24 as referring not to inquiry but to *supplication*, asking for good gifts in Jesus's name from the Father. Asking for gifts is different from asking for answers and explanations. According to Jesus, inquiry will give way to supplication.[7]

7 In Koine Greek, and in John's Gospel in particular, the verbs ἐρωτάω (16:23a) and αἰτέω (16:23b–24) can be used more or less synonymously to refer to supplication/request (in contrast to classical Greek, where the former is generally used to refer to inquiry). However, as C. K. Barrett points out, "John always uses αἰτεῖν with the meaning 'to ask for something' (see 4.9f.; 11.22; 14.13f.; 15.7,16; 16.23f.,26) and does upon occasion use ἐρωτᾶν with the meaning 'to ask a question' (see 1.19,21,25; 9.2,19,21; 16.5,19,30)" (Barrett, *The Gospel according to St. John*, 2nd ed. [Philadelphia: Westminster, 1978], 494). More importantly, Barrett notes that this distinction marks "the prevailing usage in this chapter [i.e., chap. 16]" (494). Additionally, while it is well known that John is in the practice

The same movement occurs in John 16:25–26. Jesus says in verse 25 that what now seems mysterious and "figurative" will soon become "plain," indicating a deepened understanding, in particular, about the Father ("I . . . will tell you plainly *about the Father*"). And he goes on to say in verse 26 that asking in his name will then become possible. It's the same movement that occurs in verses 23–24—a new understanding will lead to freedom to ask the Father for good gifts in Jesus's name.

Jesus's reasoning seems to go like this: since disciples soon will gain some new understanding about the Father, therefore they will confidently ask the Father for things that their joy may be full. A new Spirit-empowered understanding will render certain inquiries obsolete, freeing us up for a life of bold and blood-earnest supplication to the Father in Jesus's name.

New Understanding about the Father

What exactly about the Father will we come to understand that might embolden us to pray? The key clue in John 16 rests in the connection between verses 26 and 27. In verse 26, Jesus says again that we can pray to the Father in Jesus's name, and he immediately clarifies what he does and does not mean. By saying that we can appeal to the Father "in my name," Jesus is not suggesting that the Father doesn't want anything to do with us, that he'll only deal with us at arm's length, as though he welcomes Jesus but can't stand us. Reading verse 26 with an emphasis on the pronouns illumines the point: "In that day *you*

---

of using rough synonyms more or less interchangeably for variety, nevertheless, "when they are used in close proximity (especially in the same verse) there is usually a carefully nuanced distinction or comparison intended between them" (Edward W. Klink III, *John*, ZECNT 4 [Grand Rapids, MI: Zondervan, 2016], 689).

will ask in my name, and I do not say to you that *I* will ask the Father on your behalf."[8] *You yourselves*, Jesus underscores, will be able to make requests directly to the Father "in my name." For the Father is not disgusted with us, but the very opposite. Jesus says it unmistakably in verses 26–27: "Ask in my name," he encourages us, *"for the Father himself loves you."* That's what Jesus's "name" and especially his departure (his death) prove once and for all. Indeed, God so loved the world that he gave his only begotten Son to perish in our place, to forgive us of our sins, and to open the pathway to his throne, where we can present our supplications to him knowing that he delights to answer them and that he even delights over us. That we can entreat the Father in Jesus's name is an indication not of the Father's disapproval of us but of his overflowing love for us.

The asking of inquiry gives way to the asking of supplication because Jesus's death, and the Spirit's illumination of its meaning, answers for us the most important of questions: What is God's disposition toward us? Toward me? Is he angry with me? Is he disgusted with me? How could the holy God possibly approve of me, a sinner? Jesus's death demonstrates that God's heart toward us is infinite and overflowing love, and the Holy Spirit, whom the risen Jesus sends us, seals upon our minds and hearts confidence and joy in that reality—namely, that God loves us in Christ. Knowing that, in Christ, God loves us infinitely, we are freed to enter boldly and joyfully into the Father's presence, asking him, in Jesus's name, to do good things and to grant good gifts for our good and for the

---

8 Perhaps it goes without saying, this is not to deny or obviate Jesus's intercessory ministry on our behalf, as the following chapter in John's Gospel makes clear (see also Rom. 8:34). In John 16:26, Jesus isn't denying that he has an intercessory ministry but is emphasizing a point about our privilege of supplication.

good of our neighbors, for the spread of God's kingdom, and for the glory of Jesus.

The Beginning, and before the Beginning

In this light, prayer is not offered in uncertainty about God's orientation toward us; rather, it flows *from confidence in his orientation toward us* rooted in the knowledge of Christ's finished and glorious work. We lift up prayer in Jesus's name not in an effort to twist God's arm to love us and give us good gifts but because we know that he who gave his Son for us did so in love. And if he "did not spare his own Son but gave him up for us all, how will he not also with him graciously give us all things?" (Rom. 8:32). We pray to God not under a shadow of doubt about his relation to us but secure in it. Indeed, *the* beginning of most any prayer—that is, the very first words of most prayers, not simply the first requests in them—should alert us to the identity of the one with whom we would speak and the relation of those in Christ to him: "Our *Father*."

Praying this way is something we must be taught (Luke 11:1). Indeed, nothing we have addressed in this chapter comes naturally. If left to ourselves, none of us would make thanksgiving and glory to God the beginning and end of our supplications. Even at the very beginning of all our prayers, none of us, if left to ourselves, would know to address God *as Father*, much less have confidence about his fatherlike posture toward us. It is rather more likely that, left to our own lights, we would hedge our bets and simply cast about to "the unknown god" (see Acts 17:23). It turns out that beginning in the right place in prayer is no simple matter, given our unrefined tastes, urges, and reasonings. Rather, we must *learn* the right things to seek in prayer. We must *learn* the right ends of our lives toward which to aim in prayer. We must *learn* with whom we have to do. We must *learn* what a properly ordered communicative relationship with our Creator and Savior and King looks like.

It turns out that the theological beginning of true prayer precedes any word we speak. Prayer is answering speech, our word spoken to God after hearing from him a truthful revelation of our lives and words. Thus, we turn in part 2 to Scripture.

———

We praise Thee, O God; we acknowledge Thee to be the Lord.
All the earth doth worship Thee, the Father everlasting.
To Thee all angels cry aloud, the heavens and all the powers therein;
To Thee cherubim and seraphim continually do cry:
Holy, Holy, Holy, Lord God of Sabaoth;
Heaven and earth are full of the majesty of Thy glory.
The glorious company of the Apostles praise Thee.
The goodly fellowship of prophets praise Thee.
The noble army of martyrs praise Thee.
The holy Church throughout all the world doth acknowledge Thee:
The Father of an infinite majesty;
Thine adorable true and only Son;
Also the Holy Ghost, the Comforter.
Thou art the King of Glory, O Christ.
Thou art the everlasting Son of the Father.
When Thou tookest upon Thee to deliver man,
Thou didst humble Thyself to be born of a virgin.
When Thou hadst overcome the sharpness of death,
Thou didst open the kingdom of heaven to all believers.
Thou sittest at the right hand of God in the glory of the Father.

We believe that Thou shalt come to be our Judge.
We therefore pray Thee, help Thy servants,
Whom Thou hast redeemed with Thy precious blood.
Make them to be numbered with Thy saints in glory everlasting.

"TE DEUM"
LATIN HYMN FROM THE FOURTH CENTURY,
OFTEN USED IN MORNING PRAYER SERVICES[9]

9 The text is taken from my grandmother's tattered old copy of *The Lutheran Hymnal* (St. Louis, MO: Concordia, 1941), 35–36.

PART 2

SCRIPTURE

The differences between "Here I am" and "I see" are obvious. In the one, I place myself at the disposal of the covenant Lord, submitting to his Word; in the other, I am in possession. . . . The God of Scripture dwells in the midst of his people, speaking, not in front of them, as an object of gaze.

MICHAEL S. HORTON
The Christian Faith

Consider that the first time someone spoke of God in the third person and therefore no longer with God but about God was that very moment when the question resounded, "Did God really say?" (cf. Genesis 3:1). This fact ought to make us think.

HELMUT THIELICKE
A Little Exercise for Young Theologians

4

Praying in Response to Scripture

IT MAY BE HELPFUL TO OFFER two clarifications. The first is long overdue. Throughout the preceding pages, I have used the word *prayer* without clearly specifying what I'm referring to. As A. A. Hodge explains:

> The word "prayer" is used constantly in a more general and a more specific sense. In its more specific sense it is equivalent to supplication, the act of the soul engaged in presenting its desires to God, and asking God to gratify them and to supply all the necessities of the supplicant. In its general sense, prayer is used to express every act of the soul engaged in spiritual intercourse with God. In this sense the main elements it embraces are—(1.) Adoration, (2.) Confession, (3.) Supplication, (4.) Intercession, (5.) Thanksgiving.[1]

Our reflections on prayer thus far have slid back and forth between the "specific sense" of supplication (esp. chaps. 1–2) and

1 A. A. Hodge, *The Westminster Confession: A Commentary* (1869; repr., Edinburgh: Banner of Truth, 2002), 275.

the more "general sense" of communicative communion with God (chap. 3). It's the more general sense that we'll be focusing on here.

But before directly addressing the practice of general prayer, some important preliminaries are necessary. This is the second clarification: this chapter is something of a ground-clearing exercise. I would like eventually to consider the ways in which the Bible governs, guides, forms, and informs healthy and earnest prayer. That is, I would like to explore, as we noted at the conclusion of part 1, how we learn to pray from Scripture. But before we can consider that, we need to come to a proper understanding of what Scripture *is*. And for that, we must first highlight a central attribute and activity of God Almighty.

God's Word of Address

God speaks. He speaks to his people, addressing them with words. Let that sink in. Unlike the idols of the nations, which have mouths but cannot talk, the God whom the church of Christ serves is not silent. Rather, he is a communicative God, a personal Creator who converses, a King who declares his will and ways and summonses, a Lord who relates to his people through speech. The biblical writers are confident, consistent, and clear in this conviction:

> He who has an ear, let him hear what the Spirit *says* to the churches. (Rev. 2:7, 11, 17, 29; 3:6, 13, 22)

> As the Holy Spirit *says*,
>
> > "Today, if you *hear his voice*,
> > do not harden your hearts as in the rebellion." (Heb. 3:7–8)

> Working together with him [i.e., God], then, we appeal to you not to receive the grace of God in vain. For he *says*,

"In a favorable time I listened to you,
 and in a day of salvation I have helped you."

Behold, now is the favorable time; behold, now is the day of
salvation. (2 Cor. 6:1–2)

The Lord *has commanded us, saying,*

"I have made you a light for the Gentiles,
 that you may bring salvation to the ends of the earth."
 (Acts 13:47)

From such statements, three apostolic sensibilities regarding
God's activity of speaking are worth highlighting for how they
help us understand the nature of Scripture. First, the speaking of
God is clearly identified as—or takes place in, by, and with—the
sacred writings, the written word of God. We now know that word
to be the sixty-six books of the Old and New Testaments. But for
the New Testament authors quoted above, we may say that God's
written word was basically identified with the Old Testament writings.[2] According to Hebrews 3:7–8, "the Holy Spirit says" what
he says *in and by* Psalm 95, which the author quotes. Similarly,
in 2 Corinthians 6, Paul quotes Isaiah 49:8 as being what "God
says." With respect to what the Spirit "says" to the churches in
Revelation 2–3, while here the speaking is not directly from the
Old Testament Scriptures, nevertheless it is a speaking of the Spirit
by way of *written* letters (see Rev. 2:1, 8, 12, 18; 3:1, 7, 14) that

---

2   This is not an uncontroversial point. For discussion, see John Wenham, *Christ and the Bible*,
    3rd ed. (Grand Rapids, MI: Baker, 1994).

are collected in the larger written letter known as the Apocalypse (Rev. 1:11). God speaks through written Scripture.

Second, the divine speech that takes place by and with the sacred writings is spoken to us, God's people, in the here and now. Hebrews 3 takes its cue from what "the Holy Spirit says," present tense. Remarkably, Psalm 95, written hundreds of years before the book of Hebrews, is for the author the Spirit's speaking and being heard "today." When Paul quotes the words of the eighth-century-BC prophet Isaiah in 2 Corinthians 6:1–2, it is what God "says," present tense, a word for the "now." For the New Testament writers, God's presence and activity by speech have not ceased, being lost to ages long past, but continue today by the written word.

Third, God's speech continuing in the present by way of Holy Scripture is a word of *address* to the people of God. A word from the prophet Isaiah is understood by Paul and Barnabas in Acts 13 not merely as teaching principles that loosely apply to their situation; rather, they regard Isaiah 49:6 as a *command from the Lord to them*. God somehow addressed them through Isaiah. Still more clearly, Hebrews 12:5 (not cited above) asks, "Have you forgotten the exhortation that *addresses you as sons*?" The exhortation then quoted comes from Proverbs 3:11. An ancient document, originally addressed to an Israelite aristocratic son,[3] is somehow discerned to be addressing the church of Christ today as "sons."

Of course, this is not a matter of straightforward grammar and syntax. Isaiah 49:6 is neither in the imperative mood (it's not a command), nor directly addressed to Paul and Barnabas;

---

3   On the royal context and address of Proverbs, see Christopher B. Ansberry, *Be Wise, My Son, and Make My Heart Glad: An Exploration of the Courtly Nature of the Book of Proverbs*, BZAW 422 (Berlin: de Gruyter, 2011).

rather, in its original context, it is a report about something God said to the enigmatic "servant of the LORD." Some kind of biblical-theological "translation" or larger frame of reference must be at work in how Paul and Barnabas, together with other early Christians, read Scripture.[4] Scripture as a whole comes argu-ably in the form of a covenant document given by the covenant Lord to his covenant people. It addresses the church in a way analogous to an ancient king's address to his kingdom through a written treaty.[5] Spelling out exactly how that works in specific Scripture passages, rightly receiving Scripture's intended address to us as God's covenant people, is a complex matter requiring careful nuancing.

But with such nuancing in place, we can and should under-stand Scripture—writings of ancient origin, ostensibly about his-tory long past, initially addressed to ancient peoples—as a word that is theologically addressed to us, the church. At least, we can understand Scripture in this way if we take the New Testament writers' sensibilities as our cues. As Paul puts it in Romans 15:4, "Whatever was written in former days was written *for our instruc-tion*, that through endurance and through the encouragement of the Scriptures we might have hope."

4 See, e.g., Daniel J. Brendsel, *"Isaiah Saw His Glory": The Use of Isaiah 52–53 in John 12*, BZNW 208 (Berlin: de Gruyter, 2014), 37–64, for a proposal with respect to the figure of the Isaianic "Servant."

5 I am persuaded that this is the most precise and proper answer to the question "What is the Bible?" Indeed, the entire process of canonization was arguably initiated by God's establishing a covenant with a people. See Meredith G. Kline, *The Structure of Biblical Authority*, 2nd ed. (Eugene, OR: Wipf and Stock, 1997). We will see below that the Bible can be likened, in a limited way, to a love letter. But Scripture does not come in the literary form (genre) of one long letter from God. Neither does it come in the form of a manual or advice book specifying all the areas of advice needed in each individual's life. In its literary form, in the way in which it means what it does, and in the manner in which it addresses its readers, the Bible differs from such writings.

Problematic Postures toward the Word

The early Christian convictions and sensibilities surveyed above are important for coming to a proper understanding of what Scripture is—namely, the covenant address of God to the church of Christ. At the same time, these apostolic convictions provide needful corrections of a couple of common problematic postures toward Scripture that hinder us from fervently responding to God's word in prayer.

On the one hand, there are those who pay little to no attention to Scripture, assuming it to be a dead artifact, helpful for a primitive age perhaps but not well fitted to the problems and possibilities of the modern world, and certainly not addressed to it. Typically for such Christians, it is not that God no longer speaks today for guidance and enrichment of individual life; it's just that we must go elsewhere besides Scripture to discover his "voice" and relevant "truth"—perhaps at conferences with gurus, or in mystical experiences and trances, or through individual intellectual-philosophical labor. Stripping a line of a famous Christian hymn from its proper Christian context, some think, "He speaks to me everywhere," so they feel little burden to pay attention to the written words of ancient prophets and apostles. The widespread sensibility is that we can hear God speaking, to our personal delight, on a walk through the woods just as much as, if not more than, we could by slogging through Leviticus. Yet, in striking contrast, the apostle Peter hears in Leviticus a call to the adopted children of God today to live lives of holiness (1 Pet. 1:14–16). For Peter and the other New Testament writers, "hearing" God today does not mean ignoring Scripture but requires carefully attending to it all the more—indeed, it means hearing it in real time in the public assembly (see 1 Tim. 4:13).

Another common posture toward Scripture in the contemporary church seems the opposite of disinterest in Scripture (though there may be more overlap between the two than meets the eye). We can depict it with the help of nineteenth-century philosopher Søren Kierkegaard. Kierkegaard once offered this invitation: "Imagine a lover who has received a letter from his beloved. I assume that God's Word is just as precious to you as this letter is to the lover." But we all know that the Bible was originally written not in our mother tongue but in Hebrew, Aramaic, and Greek. So, strange love letter that it is, we must *translate* Holy Scripture. Kierkegaard asks us to assume the same about the letter our imagined lover received from his beloved:

> This letter from the beloved is written in a language that the lover does not understand. But let us also assume that there is no one around who can translate it for him. . . . What does he do? He takes a dictionary, begins to spell his way through the letter, looks up every word in order to obtain a translation.

When a friend finds the lover at this labor, the friend says, "So, you are reading a letter from your beloved." What, asks Kierkegaard, will be the lover's response?

> He answers, "Have you gone mad? Do you think this is reading a letter from my beloved! No, my friend, I am sitting here toiling and moiling with a dictionary to get it translated. At times I am ready to explode with impatience; the blood rushes to my head, and I would just as soon hurl the dictionary on the floor—and you call that reading! You must be joking! No, thank God, as soon as I am finished with the translation

I shall read my beloved's letter; that is something altogether different."[6]

There is all the difference in the world between "studying a text" and *receiving a beloved's word to us*. Not infrequently, at least in certain Christian circles, talk of "knowing what it says in the original" or ably using interlinear Bibles, of really "digging into historical backgrounds," of doing our "personal Bible study" with commentaries and lexicons open on the table, and the like, is thrown about as if these things were in themselves badges of honor and virtue. We can be beguiled into thinking that such "study" is simply identical with reading and responding to the Bible for what it is. The point here is not to denigrate study but to clarify that it is preliminary to our chief privilege and engagement.

As Dietrich Bonhoeffer once observed, "You would not dissect and analyze the word spoken by someone dear to you," pulling out your notebook to take notes over supper, pausing to reconstruct the historical background from which each statement arose, flipping through a dictionary to define every word.[7] Those may be, in some circumstances, necessary preliminaries to loving communication, but they are only preliminary. The desired end would be to *hear* the word actually spoken, to give all your attention to *it*, not the background out of which it came—indeed, to give all your attention to the beloved speaker with gladness and gravity, and to respond to his or her word with your own fitting word. If our posture when it comes to Scripture is only or predominantly

6   Søren Kierkegaard, *Provocations: Spiritual Writings of Kierkegaard*, comp. and ed. Charles E. Moore (New York: Plough, 2011), 80–81.

7   Dietrich Bonhoeffer, *Meditating on the Word*, trans. and ed. David McI. Gracie, 2nd ed. (Lanham, MD: Cowley, 2000), 24. Bonhoeffer thinks that such study, while having an appropriate place, "will only reveal the surface of the Bible" (35).

a posture of "study," we may be getting our signals crossed on what Scripture *is*.

The sensibilities of the apostles surveyed above, sensibilities about God's speaking to the church by and with Scripture, help to correct a wrongheaded posture toward Scripture that would rest satisfied treating it as an artifact to analyze and from which to extract "principles," or as a textbook full of "content" to master. Holy Scripture is, much more, a word of address inviting our proper relational and communicative response. "I love you" calls for a response not of "I see" or "I understand" but of "I love you, too." The former is a matter of passing an exam or mastering content; the latter is a fitting relational reply and, when it comes to reading Scripture, properly a part of prayer. A mere "I understand" treats God's word as if it were ultimately information about things, and treats the God who speaks the word as an object of detached contemplation for mastery. "I love you, too" recognizes God's word for what it truly is, a relational word of address speaking the love of God made known in Christ to the church, and it recognizes the God who speaks the word to be not an object for disinterested inspection and mastery but a person who invites us by the word into loving communion with him.

The Word and Prayer, the Word *Then* Prayer

This begins to make sense of why God's word and prayer are frequently joined at the hip in the pages of Scripture. The apostles, for example, determined to devote themselves "to prayer and to the ministry of the word" (Acts 6:4). The earliest church likewise consistently gathered in order to devote themselves to, among other things, the apostles' teaching and prayer (Acts 2:42). Everything created by God, according to the apostle Paul, can be a gift received with thanksgiving, if it is sanctified "by the word of God and prayer" (1 Tim. 4:4–5). And the command to take up "the sword of the Spirit, which is the word of God" in Ephesians 6:17, is directly and immediately modified by an adverbial participle of manner in verse 18.[8] How ought one to take up the sword of the Spirit? In the manner of "praying at all times in the Spirit, with all prayer and supplication."

The word and prayer are something of an expected pairing, like lightning and thunder, like Minneapolis and St. Paul, like peanut butter and jelly. But, *unlike* peanut butter and jelly, the pairing is not simply the association of two more or less self-standing realities, things that have only some loose taxonomic relationship (they are both "food"), or that may go well together when so desired (it's a great combo if you're okay with a meatless sandwich), but have no *necessary* relationship. Peanut butter and jelly go well together, but they're also both fine on their own. That's not what the pairing of the word and prayer is like. They go together not simply for both being generically matters of piety and religion. Rather, they go together like "I love you" goes together with "I love you, too." They go together the way "I promise you" goes with "I trust you." They go together like "Who will go for us, and whom shall we send?" goes with "Here I am, send me!" They go

---

8 Some commentators argue that the participle προσευχόμενοι ("praying") in Eph. 6:18 modifies not the command δέξασθε ("take") in v. 17 but the command στῆτε ("stand") in v. 14 (e.g., Clinton E. Arnold, *Ephesians*, ZECNT 10 [Grand Rapids, MI: Zondervan, 2010], 463). But (1) the distance between v. 14 and v. 18 makes it implausible to think that v. 18 directly modifies the verb στῆτε (so, rightly, Frank Thielman, *Ephesians*, BECNT [Grand Rapids, MI: Baker, 2010], 432–33); and (2) the presence of a new imperative δέξασθε after the chain of participles in vv. 14–16 separates the participle in v. 18 from the chain. Additionally, there is a verbal and conceptual link tying v. 18 directly to v. 17: one properly takes up the sword *of the Spirit* in the manner of praying *in the Spirit*.

together the way a personal verbal invitation goes with a fitting personal verbal reply.

There is a relational-communicative logic to the pairing of the word and prayer, so that "studied" knowledge of the content of Scripture that doesn't awaken prayer is no virtue but a relational breakdown and a failure to hear the word. Similarly, a prayerful spirituality that is inattentive to Scripture is like demanding the goods that come from relationship without any of the relational commitment or attentiveness. It's like expecting someone to listen to us when we haven't the time of day to listen to them. Proverbs rightly warns,

> If one turns away his ear from hearing the law
>   even his prayer is an abomination. (Prov. 28:9)[9]

The juxtaposition of the word and prayer in Scripture makes most sense when we understand the word of God for what it is—God's verbal address to us, his people. But the word and prayer not only are fittingly paired; they also relate in a theologically meaningful order. It is first the word, then prayer. Prayer rightly *follows* the reading/hearing of the word. Scripture is God's word addressed to us, and prayer is answering speech. God's word initiates the dialogue, and our prayers are, by the power of the Spirit, one of the first forms of fitting response.

Daniel is stirred to offer a prayer of representative confession of sin *after and by* reading "the word of the LORD to Jeremiah the prophet" (Dan. 9:2–20). And prayerful repentance (a "plea for mercy") was also the response hoped for from the Davidic house

9   See also Zech. 7:8–14.

to the reading/hearing of Jeremiah's scroll, the inscribed word of the Lord (Jer. 36, esp. vv. 6–7). However, in this latter instance, the hoped-for consummation of the communicative event in prayer was spurned.

Likewise, it seems no accident that many New Testament letters wrap things up (often signaled with the adverb "finally") by way of bullet-point practical exhortations that include the express command to pray (Phil. 4:6; Col. 4:2; 1 Thess. 5:17; 2 Thess. 3:1; 1 Pet. 5:7; 1 John 5:14–15; Jude 20), or with direct appeals for prayer for the author or one another (Rom. 15:30; Eph. 6:18–20; Heb. 13:18; James 5:13–18; cf. Philem. 22). In the context of early Christian practice, these New Testament letters would have been read at the public assembly (see, e.g., Col. 4:16; 1 Thess. 5:27; cf. Rev. 1:3). We may rightly assume that the concluding exhortations to prayer in the Epistles would have had an immediate, and intended, practical effect—namely, churches were stirred to pray as the enacted sequel to the public reading of these letters, which are the written word of God. Indeed, this is how the Bible as a whole ends in Revelation 22:17, 20. There is a call to prayer, "Let the one who hears say, 'Come,'" followed by obedient response to the call: "Come, Lord Jesus!" The early church recognized that Scripture was not fundamentally a textbook to master or a sourcebook of eternal principles to gather for safekeeping until we might have use for them; rather, these inspired writings were God's word to them that awaited their communicative response.

It is, therefore, important to ask a few questions in conclusion. On the one hand, where do we turn to "hear God's voice still speaking today"? Is our "spirituality" largely a matter of inattentiveness to what God says, or is our prayer life properly cleaved to Scripture?

On the other hand, for those of us who are more inclined to "be Bereans," who study up on Scripture, to what are we devoting ourselves in this "study"? Do we recognize the word of God for what it is? Perhaps the clearest test to diagnose the health or lack thereof in our posture and sensibility toward Holy Scripture, and our relationship with the God who speaks it, comes down to a simple matter of grammatical person. After reading Scripture, are we led to talk *about* God (third person), or *to him* (second person)? Does our engagement with the word find regular consummation in prayer?

———

O Lover of the loveless,
It is thy will that I should love thee
  with heart, soul, mind, strength,
  and my neighbour as myself.
But I am not sufficient for these things . . .
May thy Spirit draw me nearer to thee and thy ways.
Thou art the end of all means,
  for if they lead me not to thee,
  I go away empty.
Order all my ways by thy holy Word
  and make thy commandments the joy of my heart,
  that by them I may have happy converse with thee.
May I grow in thy love and manifest it to mankind.

PURITAN PRAYER[10]

10 In *The Valley of Vision: A Collection of Puritan Prayers and Devotions*, ed. Arthur Bennett (Edinburgh: Banner of Truth, 1975), 137.

For most of church history, Christians understood prayer not primarily as a means of authentic self-expression, but as a learned way of approaching God.

TISH HARRISON WARREN
"By the Book"

How sweet are your words to my taste, sweeter than honey to my mouth!

PSALM 119:103

Understanding comes to fruition only in the response.

MIKHAIL BAKHTIN
"Discourse in the Novel"

5

Praying Scripture

IT IS A FUNDAMENTAL ANTHROPOLOGICAL TRUTH: being human involves not first knowing but being known. Similarly, we are not first speakers but spoken to, and only in being spoken to do we thus receive our "own voice." "Before we could talk or 'make up our own mind,'" observes Peter Leithart, "we were addressed, talked to, kissed, smiled at."[1] We are not fundamentally "blank slates," autonomous and uninfluenced "individuals," sovereignly "free" choosers of our identity and language and voice. To *be* is to be in relationship and to have already received much from outside us, much that shapes and identifies us and gives us voice. To be able to speak, we must be spoken to.

The anthropological truth is nested within a theological truth: we are *spoken into existence* by a speaking Creator (see Gen. 1:3–27). We are ever and always first addressed and known by God, which address and knowing reveal our truest identity (cf. Gal. 4:9) and pull out from us our proper verbal response, our answering speech, our prayer. To be able to pray, we must be

---

1 Peter J. Leithart, *Against Christianity* (Moscow, ID: Canon, 2003), 85.

addressed. Prayer can be voiced only because the word of God has preceded us.

In the last chapter, we applied this twin anthropological-theological insight to a proper understanding of what Scripture *is*—namely, God's covenantal word of address that awaits our answering speech. But we can press the matter a step further in suggesting crucial things that Scripture *does* in and for a healthy life of prayer. In this and the following chapter, I will suggest seven ways in which we can engage the word of God by answering speech. (We'll cover only one in this chapter; the remaining six will be addressed in chap. 6.) I explore these seven modes of responding to Scripture in prayer in the hope that we will actively put them into practice. But throughout we will find that it is, in fact, *the word that is acting upon us.* The word of God is living and active, powerful to shape our prayers and us even as we seek to engage it prayerfully.

Imitation of the Word

The first and most basic facet of a prayerful responsiveness to Scripture is, quite simply, *praying Scripture*—praying its prayers, repeating its language, mimicking its cries, its cadences, its syntax, its logic, its idioms. Imitate God's word with your words in prayer. I should underline that I don't simply mean making sure our prayers are "biblically informed" and in harmony with biblical truths. Without a doubt, Scripture should generally inform our prayers,[2] and we will return to this matter in the next chapter. But Scripture is also more specifically a kind of script with lines for us to speak. Let us take the words of Scripture

---

2 See also Andy Naselli, "12 Reasons You Should Pray Scripture," *Themelios* 38, no. 3 (2013): 417.

on our lips as our first (though not only) form of prayerful response to God.[3]

It is so elementary an exhortation that it might not seem worth saying. But I think it needs to be addressed overtly and at length, if for no other reason than this: our present cultural moment would incline us to assume that prayer is "authentic" only when it springs from the depths of our own raw, unformed emotional life. Prayer that counts, we're socialized to think, is a "heartfelt," spontaneously formulated individual expression, just "our own words" uninfluenced by anything outside us. In our contemporary context, "simply being real" is the measure of the truth and worth of all things, including prayer. So the exhortation to mimic the words of Scripture as one of our first forms of prayer might seem to cut at the root of a sincere and feeling prayer life. Why would *I* pray *someone else's* expressions? What if I don't *mean* them? Isn't it fraud to take an ancient author's words for *my own* words?

The illusion here is that "*my own* words" somehow materialized out of nothing in my heart of hearts, as though we came from our mothers' womb (and the womb of our new birth by the Spirit) as fully formed speaking subjects. On the contrary, "my own words" became my own only by way of my taking the words of others on my lips. Only by maturation beginning in mimicry, and through practice and patience along that path, did you and I and everyone become fluent, skillful, relationally aware, and truthful speakers. We first learned to talk by mimicking the sounds our parents made, sounds we hardly understood. We learn to talk *meaningfully and politely* by repeating expressions given to us by others. In John Witvliet's helpful words:

---

3   It bears mentioning that the call to imitate Scripture in our prayers can be taken in pedantic ways by thoughtless critics and complacent Christians alike, as if the be-all and end-all of prayer were *merely* repeating verbatim the words we find on the pages of Scripture.

Young children need to learn to say "thank you," "I'm sorry," and "please." Parents need to prompt and reinforce these basic conversational moves. Eventually they become part of the way toddlers see the world and navigate relationships. Indeed, there are few moments quite as sweet as hearing a sudden, unprompted "Thanks, Mommy and Daddy."[4]

In the life we are given by our Creator, there is no other way to "unprompted" or so-called spontaneous expressions of gratitude (or love or trust or confession or whatever), except the path that begins in prompting and structured imitation, leading to the development of what Witvliet calls "good communication habits."

So it is with Scripture in the life of prayer. The covenantal word of address teaches and guides us in how to pray, which is good news, since, as someone has testified somewhere, we do not know how to pray as we ought. Knowing the danger of our ignorance, Athanasius of Alexandria encouraged Christians not to shy away from taking the very words of Scripture for our uttered prayers. The word of God offers not merely teaching *about* the life of prayer "but also a fit form of words wherewith to please the Lord on each of life's occasions . . . so that we fall not into sin; for it is not for our actions only that we must give account before the judge, but also for our every idle word."[5] In a sense, healthy, well-ordered praying is not merely instinctive, something that "just comes naturally." Rather, praying is something we must *learn*.[6] And the beginning of our path

---

4   John D. Witvliet, *The Biblical Psalms in Christian Worship: A Brief Introduction and Guide to Resources* (Grand Rapids, MI: Eerdmans, 2007), 11.

5   Athanasius, "The Letter of Athanasius to Marcellinus on the Interpretation of the Psalms," in *On the Incarnation*, trans. and ed. anonymously, 2nd rev. ed. (Crestwood, NY: St. Vladimir's Orthodox Theological Seminary Press, 1953), 107.

6   See, further, chap. 9 below.

of learning is imitation. Scripture prompts and reinforces—yea, provides the very words of—proper, polite, and passionate prayer. If we want to develop "our own voice" in prayer, it will come about by putting the words of another into our mouths.

A "Taste" for the Word

The psalmist delights in the taste of God's words. They are, he says, "sweeter than honey to my mouth" (Ps. 119:103). Might this be no merely artful reference to an abstraction, like the value of God's word or its satisfying quality? Might the psalmist, rather, refer to his embodied practice of putting God's word into his mouth? I submit that Scripture's honey sweetness is indeed to be experienced on our tongues—that is, in the recitation of it in our prayer life.

It perhaps goes without saying that such a practice is not always milk and honey. Taking the word of God into us so that it might verbally pour forth from us can, instead, produce bitterness (see Rev. 10:8–11; cf. Ezek. 2–3). The words of God sometimes are bitter words of confession of sin or terrible judgment or lament. But sometimes the recitation of Scripture tastes bad to us because our palate has been consistently cultivated to crave only the flavors of our own spontaneous and self-wrought words. We are averse, and sometimes dogmatically opposed, to putting someone else's (even God's) words into our mouths in prayer. But according to Dietrich Bonhoeffer, in a slim but significant book,

> It is a dangerous error, surely widespread among Christians, to think that the heart can pray by itself. For then we confuse wishes, hopes, sighs, laments, rejoicings—all of which the heart can do by itself—with prayer. . . . If we are to pray aright, perhaps it is quite necessary that we pray contrary to our own heart.

Not what we want to pray is important, but what God wants us to pray. If we were dependent entirely on ourselves, we would probably pray only the fourth petition of the Lord's Prayer. But God wants it otherwise. The richness of the Word of God ought to determine our prayer, not the poverty of our heart.[7]

Praying Scripture exposes us to different experiences, emotions, and pursuits in prayer than we individually and locally/culturally/historically might be familiar with and inclined toward. We might think it strange to pray for the prospering of Israel's king, and might never think to petition for such a thing before the divine King. We might not currently suffer under the weight of overt oppression and injustice and thus might be disinclined to raise, and may even blush at, the vehement laments of many psalms. We might think it silly and primitive to pray that the trees and mountains sing for joy, and so refrain from such prayers as upstanding citizens of the modern scientific age. We might think prayer is about securing our health and prosperity, not about seeking God's kingdom and glory. Many of the prayers found in Scripture are likely to be foreign territory for us, and we might habitually retreat into familiar forms and our felt needs and wants. Praying Scripture forces us, says Witvliet, to enact "forms of faithful speech to God that we are not likely to try on our own."[8] And this is for our good and growth.

We need to be stretched by Scripture's strangeness, fighting the tendency to reduce prayer to mere individual self-expression and reflex and the comfort of familiarity, while working doxo-

7 Dietrich Bonhoeffer, *Psalms: The Prayer Book of the Bible*, trans. J. H. Burtness (Minneapolis: Augsburg Fortress, 1970), 9, 14–15.
8 Witvliet, *The Biblical Psalms in Christian Worship*, 12.

logical and intercessory muscles that may be underdeveloped. We need, for the sake of maturation in prayer, to allow the diversity of concerns and modes in the prayers of Scripture to guide us. We need to cultivate our palate and tastes, so prone are they to spiritual junk food; and that begins by trying a new (actually a very old, but not quite a paleo) diet. To pray Scripture is to be *impacted and shaped* by Scripture, to put into our mouths and hearts more than what we would have in them if left to our own devices and desires. It opens our eyes to new vistas of reality that we miss in the parochial confines of our personal concerns and experiences.

In Acts 4:24–31, the earliest church, led by the apostles, gathered for corporate prayer. And, strange people that they were, they offered *their* prayer by way of *the prepackaged words of Psalm 2* (see Acts 4:25–26). As a pastor, I have frequently been asked why we have so many responsive readings from and recitations of Scripture in our church gatherings. To many, it seems cold, lifeless, and perfunctory, and it supposedly detracts from "genuine outpouring of my heart." But in Acts 4, the early church didn't seem worried that praying someone else's words was "inauthentic," or led to "mindless parroting," or promoted coldly "formal, unfeeling" prayer. *Rote* was not a four-letter word for them, and *repetition* was not synonymous with "perfunctorily going through the motions." The early Christ followers repeated the word of God as their prayer because they apparently liked the taste of God's word in their mouths. The rote was for them, arguably, a wisely ordered part of cultivating palates that can better appreciate good flavors. Taking the very words of Scripture on their own lips was a crucial facet of their prayer life, and it proved to be fuel that fed the flames of Spirit-empowered transformation (see Acts 4:31).

The Prayer Book of the Bible

Of course, some passages in Scripture are easier and more fitting to mimic than others. It is much easier (though not entirely uncomplicated), and it is more verbally fitting, to pray Psalm 69:1,

Save me, O God!
For the waters have come up to my neck,

than it is to pray 2 Kings 2:23, "Some small boys came out of the city and jeered at him, saying, 'Go up, you baldhead!'" To take the simplest and most obvious difference: the former is a word of address to God, the fitting form for prayer; the latter is a historical report and not directly answering speech. Praying Scripture—that is, speaking its words as our words of address to God—will understandably zero in on certain portions of Scripture.

Taking the earliest church in Acts 4 as a model, praying Scripture will especially revolve around the Psalter. Psalms has long been called the prayer book of the Bible, the prayer book of the church. The psalms are nothing if they are not prayers—many of them individual prayers of David and others, and all of them intended as prayers to be read and heard, recited, sung, and responded to in corporate worship.[9] It is remarkable that the Spirit-inspired word *from God to us* includes a whole book (the longest

9 There are several indications that the psalms are meant to be enacted in the public assembly. Here are three chosen at random: (1) Many psalms have directions for choir directors in the superscription, the implication being that they were intended for and used in corporate enactment. (2) Several psalms are addressed in part or entirely to the gathered people of God, calling them to praise and trust in the Lord, which indicates that the psalms were for reading in the assembly (see, e.g., Ps. 130, addressed below; also Ps. 95). (3) Many psalms evidence the expectation for antiphonal (call-and-response) enactment, the most outstanding example being Ps. 136.

book of the Bible, to boot) filled with Spirit-authorized words *for us to speak to God.* That's how important helping us pray, even forming our actual prayers, is to the Lord. By extension, we can receive in the same way many other prayers in Scripture (praises, supplications, laments, confessions, professions of faith, thanksgivings), whether we find them in the Law (e.g., Ex. 15:2–18), the Prophets (e.g., 1 Sam. 2:1–10; Hab. 3:2–19), the Writings (e.g., Neh. 1:5–11; Job 42:2–6), the Gospels (e.g., Matt. 6:9–13), or the Epistles (e.g., Eph. 1:15–23; 3:14–21). We can speak and sing these words as the beginning of our prayer to God.[10]

The point is not "mindless repetition," that great evangelical bogeyman. The imitation of biblical prayer that is enacted by the church in Acts 4, and that the faithful praying church has engaged in and matured by throughout the ages, is a thoughtful repetition, an attentive repetition, a humbly submitted repetition that at the same time asks questions and seeks to understand. Indeed, I have found that praying the words of Scripture has consistently produced in me a better understanding of the word of God, in part, because it forces me to ask some critical questions of the text that are otherwise easy to leave unasked.

Consider praying the familiar words of Psalm 130. It is a powerful plea for mercy and a declaration of patient confidence in the Lord's merciful love.

---

10 Those Christian traditions committed to *singing or chanting* biblical psalms and canticles—not merely paraphrases of Scripture but the biblical word itself—may have a leg up on many. They are accustomed to setting Scripture in their mouths in a much more regular and extended manner than is typical in contemporary churches. And they realize that this practice can take place not only in earnest speech but also in lively and earnest song. For a helpful survey of various "options for singing" the Psalter, including suggested resources, see Witvliet, *The Biblical Psalms in Christian Worship*, 94–130. For several musical settings and chant modes, see Joyce Borger, Martin Tel, and John D. Witvliet, eds., *Psalms for All Seasons: A Complete Psalter for Worship* (Grand Rapids, MI: Brazos, 2012).

Out of the depths I cry to you, O LORD!
    O Lord, hear my voice!
Let your ears be attentive
    to the voice of my pleas for mercy!

If you, O LORD, should mark iniquities,
    O Lord, who could stand?
But with you there is forgiveness,
    that you may be feared.

I wait for the LORD, my soul waits,
    and in his word I hope;
my soul waits for the Lord
    more than watchmen for the morning,
    more than watchmen for the morning.

O Israel, hope in the LORD!
    For with the LORD there is steadfast love,
    and with him is plentiful redemption.
And he will redeem Israel
    from all his iniquities.

Most of this psalm addresses God in the first person singular. It's an individual praying for forgiveness and deliverance. Deliverance from what? When we pray this psalm thoughtfully, with ears and eyes open, it is almost impossible *not* to ask, "What 'depths' is the psalmist in, and do they have any meaningful connection to 'depths' I find *myself* in?" But this psalmist concludes the psalm by addressing *Israel* in verses 7–8. Why conclude a prayer to God with a word to Israel? What does that suggest about the psalmist's prayer life, about *where* it takes place and *with whom*? As we pray Psalm 130 today, where are we, and with whom? Might there be a disconnect with Psalm 130 because our praying today is alone in our prayer closet, with no "Israel" to address or communicate with? Or maybe the disconnect is more theological: can we, the church of Christ, a large portion of which is Gentile, pray this prayer so directly meant for Israel? These important questions are forced upon us as we try to take up these words in prayer. Uttering Scripture's prayers in our prayers presses us to ask interpretive questions (and I think the best questions) about what these prayers mean and how we, God's praying people here and now, relate to the words and forms of Scripture.

But praying the psalms can help us better understand our Bibles in a second way. In Psalm 105, the psalmist rehearses the exodus story. He is, in effect, praying (or calling others to prayer; see v. 1) in response to what he reads in his Bible. But he makes some strange moves in his handling of Scripture. In describing the exodus plagues, the psalmist surveys only eight plagues (see vv. 26–36), not all ten narrated in Exodus. More oddly, he moves the plague of darkness, appearing ninth in Exodus, to the beginning of his list (v. 28). Why does he do this? How must he be reading his Bible?[11] As we've seen at various points, biblical characters consistently pray in response to Scripture, filling their prayers with biblical content and expectations and aims, as seems to be the case in Psalm 105. But the biblical characters, the psalmist of Psalm 105 being an outstanding example, frequently seem to read and handle the Bible in ways

---

11 For discussion, see Archie C. C. Lee, "Genesis I and the Plagues Tradition in Psalm CV," *VT* 40, no. 3 (1990): 257–63.

that differ notably from the contemporary Western church's habitual and unofficially sanctioned ways of reading the Bible.[12]

Taking scriptural prayers on our lips is, then, a way of exposing ourselves to and directly engaging *a different way of reading and responding to the Bible than we're used to*. But however new to us such a mode of biblical interpretation and engagement may seem, it is not in itself novel. As early as the sixth century, monastic leader Cassiodorus modeled and promoted what Matthew Swale calls "*prayerful, formational* biblical interpretation" especially of the Psalms.[13] As Swale shows, a special concern of Cassiodorus's three-volume *Explanation of the Psalms* is to demonstrate that in order to understand the Bible, one must pray it; and as one prays it, one is formed by it. These are not stages that follow the completion of our interpretive work but part of properly realizing the meaning and intent of the Psalms. I believe that Cassiodorus's strange (to us) example is much needed. We may find that following him, with the help and illumination of the Spirit, our own reading of and responding to the Bible is shaped for the better.

At its best, praying the Bible's words serves a hermeneutical function, in that such a practice raises pointed questions about the meaning of what we are praying, about how we as pray-ers might have a theological relation to the prayers and pray-ers of the Bible, and about how the biblical pray-ers themselves read and respond to the Scriptures. In this way, at least, praying Scripture can and ought to be a far cry from mindless repetition or cold formalism.

12 I have tried, in an introductory way, to spell this out in Daniel J. Brendsel, "Scripture in Scripture: Reading the Old Testament with the Apostles," Desiring God, September 8, 2020, https://www.desiringgod.org/.

13 Matthew Swale, "Power for Prayer through the Psalms: Cassiodorus's Interpretation of the Honey of Souls," *Themelios* 44, no. 3 (2019): 495, emphasis original.

Multifaceted Praying of Scripture

But we can say still more. Here we are helped by *Psalms for All Seasons: A Complete Psalter for Worship*. The editors of this excellent resource have suggested not a rigid, one-dimensional recitation of biblical psalms in our prayer lives. Rather, they advise a multifaceted approach. We can pray the psalms (and other biblical prayers) in several modes and orientations. We can recite the prayers of Scripture

- "as an expression of our own experience"—for example, praying Psalm 22 to formulate our lamentation and longing in the midst of persecution;
- "as a text which we do not yet experience fully, but which we are growing into"—for example, praying Psalm 116 "as a way of stretching ourselves toward the kind of thanksgiving and dedication to God we desire to exhibit as God's covenant people";
- "as a way of praying in solidarity with those whose experience is quite different from our own"—for example, praying psalms of lament to identify with and "remember those in prison, as though in prison with them" (Heb. 13:3);
- "as a way of entering into or responding to a particular biblical narrative"—for example, praying the psalms of David to better enter David's story and world;
- "as a way of contemplating or wrestling with a given text without committing to a particular way of understanding our relationship to it"—for example, praying Psalm 41 in order to challenge ourselves with the meaning of betrayal in God's world and growing in our understanding of reality.[14]

14 Borger, Tel, and Witvliet, *Psalms for All Seasons*, iii–iv.

And there are still other ways to pray the Psalms thoughtfully.[15] Some of these suggestions piggyback on things we've already covered above; many introduce further facets of our prayerful engagement with Scripture to be addressed in the next chapter. The point here is that praying Scripture is not necessarily mindless parroting. But it *is* necessary for a healthy life of prayer. We may at times sound like parrots who repeat sounds and words. But our repetition is part of a well-ordered culture and cultivation; part of our personal maturation into understanding, wise speech, and warmhearted adulthood; and part of enacting and entering more fully into our variegated identity as the people of God.[16] God wants us to grow into such things. God wants us to learn how to pray. And as our Creator, God knows how we his creatures mature in such skill. Therefore, he has given us a word to pray, full of model prayers to speak forth in imitation. Isn't it a wonder and a great *kindness* that God has not left us to our own lights in the life of prayer? The word of God proves to be not only God's covenantal word of address properly awaiting and inviting our prayerful response, but also our first teacher in what that response can sound like.

"Teach Us to Pray"

We need a teacher in these things, as the first disciples well knew. In the four canonical accounts of the one true gospel, the disciples are recorded to have ever asked Jesus to teach them just one thing: "Lord, teach us to pray" (Luke 11:1). Not "teach us how to raise

---

15 Borger, Tel, and Witvliet add one further possibility: "As a way of distancing ourselves from the text, in light of our wrestling with another part of Scripture"—e.g., praying Ps. 109 as a purposeful contrast to Jesus's response to his murderers while hanging on the cross, to stir up wonder and trembling before God crucified (*Psalms for All Seasons*, iv).

16 Cf. Cassiodorus, as discussed by Swale, "Power for Prayer through the Psalms," 493.

our kids." Not "teach us how to steward our money." Not "teach us how to manage our time well." Not "teach us how to develop better friendships." Not "teach us the secret of a happy marriage." Not "teach us how to make an impact on the culture and change the world." Not even "teach us how to fight sin" or "teach us the meaning of the Bible." Teach us to *pray*. Of all the things they could have asked Jesus to teach them, and likely did ask him to teach them, this is the one request the evangelists saw fit to include in their accounts of the good news of Jesus. It might be because learning how to pray is the single most important life skill worth acquiring, a starting point of sorts for lives that honor Christ and flourish in God-intended ways.

In keeping with this possibility, the Bible doesn't have anything close to a how-to manual for financial security, or child-rearing, or healthy twenty-first-century dieting (that's *not* what the Levitical food laws are), or thrilling sex lives (a sex manual is emphatically *not* what the Song of Solomon is). But the Bible does have a prayer book filled with forms for prayer—the Psalms—and numerous other model prayers and songs. Let us not leave them on the page unvoiced and untasted.

———

I will extol you, O Lord, for you have drawn me up
　and have not let my foes rejoice over me.
O Lord my God, I cried to you for help,
　and you have healed me.
O Lord, you have brought up my soul from Sheol;
　you restored me to life from among those who go down to
　　the pit.

Sing praises to the LORD, O you his saints,
 and give thanks to his holy name.
For his anger is but for a moment,
 and his favor is for a lifetime.
Weeping may tarry for the night,
 but joy comes with the morning.

As for me, I said in my prosperity,
 "I shall never be moved."
By your favor, O LORD,
 you made my mountain stand strong;
you hid your face;
 I was dismayed.

To you, O LORD, I cry,
 and to the Lord I plead for mercy:
"What profit is there in my death,
 if I go down to the pit?
Will the dust praise you?
 Will it tell of your faithfulness?
Hear, O LORD, and be merciful to me!
 O LORD, be my helper!"

You have turned for me my mourning into dancing;
 you have loosed my sackcloth
 and clothed me with gladness,
that my glory may sing your praise and not be silent.
 O LORD my God, I will give thanks to you forever!

PSALM 30

For as the Jews of old by God's command
Travelled, and saw no town:
So now each Christian hath his journeys spanned:
Their story pens and sets us down.
A single deed is small renown.
God's works are wide, and let in future times;
His ancient justice overflows our crimes.

GEORGE HERBERT
"The Bunch of Grapes"

The Bible does not tell stories that illustrate something
true apart from the story. The Bible tells a story that is
the story, the story of which our human life is a part.
It is not that stories are part of human life, but that
human life is part of a story. It is not that there are
stories that illustrate "how things are"; it is that we
do not begin to understand how things are unless we
understand how they were and how they will be.

LESSLIE NEWBIGIN
The Open Secret

6

Praying (in the Story of) Scripture

THE DRIVING CONVICTION OF PART 2 is that a holy, healthy, and happy—if sometimes hard—life of prayer will be one that is tethered to the written word of God. If we would pray aright, we must pray, so to speak, with our Bibles open. To put it differently, we must pray with our "eyes" on Scripture—all seven of them.

I propose seven *i*'s of biblically attuned prayerfulness. We've already considered one at length in the last chapter—namely, *imitating* Scripture. But biblically attuned praying also involves *invoking, informing, inducing, identifying, illuminating,* and *imagining*.

Praying with Our *I*'s on Scripture

Invoking

Prayer is a word of address, a relational word spoken *to* God, not merely *about* God. But a breakdown in relationship has occurred or is bound to occur when we forget God's name and fail to address him by it, like Jerry Seinfeld forgetting his girlfriend's name: "Oh *you!*" In prayer, we do not merely cry out, "Hey *you*, hear

93

me!" Rather, we address God by name. The fancy word for this is *invocation*. In prayer, we invoke or call upon the name of the Lord.

But how do we come to know God's name that we might call upon it? None of us knows God's name unless God himself speaks and reveals it to us. We have such a revelatory word in Holy Scripture. Prayer tethered to the word is empowered to address God properly and confidently by his revealed names. They include

- the Maker of the heaven and the earth and the sea and everything in them (Ex. 20:11; Neh. 9:6; Ps. 146:6; cf. Acts 4:24);
- my rock and my fortress (Deut. 32:4, 15, 18, 30–31; cf. 2 Sam. 22:2–3);
- the great and awesome God, who keeps covenant and steadfast love with those who love him and keep his commandments (Ex. 34:6–7; cf. Dan. 9:4);
- the "LORD God," or our "Lord GOD" (the small capitalization of GOD or LORD in English versions denotes the use of the covenantal name YHWH, which was first revealed in Ex. 3:14; cf. Josh. 7:7);
- the God who drives back the sea (Ex. 14–15; cf. Ps. 74:13);
- the helper of orphans and widows (Deut. 10:17–18; cf. Pss. 10:14; 68:5);
- the King of the nations (Ps. 22:27–28; cf. Jer. 10:7; Rev. 15:3);
- the God of Abraham, Isaac, and Jacob (Ex. 3:6; cf. 1 Chron. 29:18);
- the God of maternal kindness and care (Isa. 66:13; Hos. 11:3–4; cf. Num. 11:12);
- the Father from whom every family is named (Gen. 1–10; cf. Eph. 3:14–15);

- the Father of our Lord Jesus Christ (Mark 1:9–11; John
  1:14–18; cf. 1 Pet. 1:3);
- Father, Son, and Holy Spirit (Matt. 28:19; cf. Gal. 4:6).

This is just the tip of the iceberg of the many biblically revealed
names, titles, or appellations of God, which bespeak the variegated
glory of his identity and character. Calling upon God's name is
a kind of humble, loving attentiveness to who God is. As our
understanding of God's character grows, our confidence deepens
that God is able and willing to act on our supplications for good,
all of which leads to a supremely happy result (see Joel 2:32). So
let us pray always with our Bibles open, so that we may invoke
God by name.

Informing

As I've already emphasized, we need to *learn* to pray. My children need to be taught what is best to feed their bodies, lest,
left to themselves, they consume only candy, cookies, and soda
pop, stunting their growth (and causing my dentist bills to
skyrocket). Similarly, we children of God need to be taught
what should come out of our lips in prayer. We need proper
instruction in prayer.

I assume that something like this is what first comes to most readers' minds when thinking about how the Bible and prayer relate:
Scripture *informs* us about prayer, and we should offer "biblically
informed prayers." I don't disagree. But being "biblically informed"
can mean a dozen different things to a dozen different people.
More importantly, speaking only of being "informed" by Scripture
makes it too easy to imagine that Scripture is merely a repository of
principles and truths, often inconveniently dressed up in narrative

and historical garb. In this view, Scripture is a source of inert but potentially useful spiritual information

- that we can collect and store away for use at our sovereign discretion (like being well informed about a vehicle we may or may not purchase);
- or before which we stand as uncommitted and detached analyzers (like being well informed about the candidates we may or may not vote for);
- or that might make us good at Trivial Pursuit while we have little sense of its overarching unity or meaning, so that it doesn't translate into practical wisdom, skill, and gracefulness ("he knows a lot but doesn't have a lick of 'common sense'");
- or with which, so we assume, we can gain more control of our lives and mastery over others, whether neighbor or God ("knowledge is power").

Yes, we need to be well informed biblically to grow in prayer. But saying that does not go far enough and is not specific enough to be of help. We need also to articulate *how* Scripture properly informs our praying. Think of the *i*'s of biblically attuned prayer as so many attempts to specify what biblically informed praying properly consists of. We can learn from Scripture proper forms and patterns and rhythms for prayer, the name and character of the one we address in prayer, the (theo)logic of holy argumentation in prayer, the types of things we must seek and desire and pray for in the here and now through prayer, and much, much more. Let us pray with our Bibles open, so that our praying becomes ever more biblically informed.

Inducing

Admittedly, *inducing* is not the most felicitous descriptor. But I promised seven *i*'s of biblically attuned praying, and a six-*i*'d creature would be weird. I have in view *reasoning*—indeed, *arguing*—with God to induce him to act on our supplications.

Of great importance for growing in the life of prayer is seeing how biblical pray-ers argue with God. They provide implicit and explicit reasons for God to respond favorably. In the wilderness, when God speaks of destroying the Israelites for their rebellion, Moses intercedes, saying, "If you kill this people as one man, then the nations who have heard your fame will say, 'It is because the LORD was not able to bring this people into the land that he swore to give to them that he has killed them in the wilderness'" (Num. 14:15–16). That's a theological-missional *reason* for God to spare the Israelites: *God, think of your reputation among the nations!* Moses goes on: "Please let the power of the Lord be great as you have promised, saying, 'The LORD is slow to anger'" (Num. 14:17–18). Moses gives God another reason for showing mercy: *God, act "as you have promised," in accord with what you have committed yourself to and revealed of your character!* The psalmist of Psalm 88 also argues with God, by way of a rhetorical question:

> Is your steadfast love declared in the grave,
>> or your faithfulness in Abaddon? (v. 11)

Essentially, the psalmist says: "Dead people can't sing your praise. You care that your praise be heard in the earth, don't you, Lord? *Therefore*, don't abandon me to death, but deliver!" Our Lord himself reasons with his Father, praying for unity among his people "so that the world may believe that you have sent me" (John 17:21). It's theological reasoning, holy argumentation. Indeed, for Christians, every prayer is to be raised "in Jesus's name," which is at minimum a basis, the best and fundamental reason, for the holy Father to act for our good in response to our supplications.

Daniel, too, reasons with God in prayer. In Daniel 9, he pleads with God to forgive exiled Israel, and he states the standard by which this ought to be done—namely, "according to all your righteous acts" (v. 16). This instance of reasoning is head-scratching in context, since Daniel acknowledges in the preceding verses that the devastation of exile happened "for the LORD our God is righteous" (v. 14). God punishes covenant breakers with exile because he is "righteous," yet apparently Daniel is convinced that God may also mercifully deliver from exile because he is "righteous" (which raises the question "What *is* God's righteousness?"[1]). Daniel's path of persuasion is a clear example of how holy argumentation is sometimes surprising and counterintuitive to our common ways of thinking. The Bible has its reasons, and they often expose the poverty of our reasoning. We need Scripture to help us think and reason aright, to teach us the dynamics of godly reasoning rooted in God's character, his mighty deeds, his purposes and goals, his promises, his commitment to be glorified in the world.

So let us pray with our Bibles open, that our minds may be renewed and our reasoning transformed. Let us join Moses, the psalmist, Daniel, Jesus, and many, many others in Scripture in offering compelling reasons to persuade God to act for his name's sake in the world.

---

1   I was first alerted to Daniel's seemingly self-contradictory appeal to God's "righteousness" by John Piper, *The Justification of God: An Exegetical and Theological Study of Romans 9:1–23*, 2nd ed. (Grand Rapids, MI: Baker, 1993), 113–14. For an introduction to the interpretive debate surrounding the "righteousness of God," see Richard N. Longenecker, *The Epistle to the Romans*, NIGTC (Grand Rapids, MI: Eerdmans, 2016), 169–76.

Identifying

"Remember those who are in prison, as though in prison with them, and those who are mistreated, since you also are in the body" (Heb. 13:3). How do we who are not in prison, and may not fear imprisonment for the faith, act "as though in prison" with the persecuted? "Weep with those who weep" (Rom. 12:15). How can we seek to obey this exhortation if we don't *feel* like grieving in the moment? A needed beginning is to pray Scripture.

Prayer must be tethered to Scripture. But we need to pray a healthy and full complement of Scripture. If we turn only to our "favorites" and "greatest hits," our "life verses," we'll miss a lot that is crucial. If, rather than submitting ourselves to be *shaped by* Scripture, we only seek to *use* Scripture—for example, popping a verse or two "as an antidepressant"[2] to uplift us—we will avoid or be unaware of the dark and despairing words of Psalm 88's lament. If we only ever want the things that resonate with us and express what we feel in the moment, we will likely neglect Scripture's anguished pleas for justice on behalf of oppressed orphans (e.g., Ps. 10), and its many raging and confused cries of saints persecuted as though they were sheep in a butcher's shop (e.g., Ps. 44), and its plethora of despairing groans from the refugee and exile who have none of the protections of home and voice (e.g., Ps. 137; Lamentations). Scripture is full of such anguish and lamentation, especially in the Psalms. It's there in abundance, because this *is* the present experience of the people of God in our present Holy Saturday waiting.

Even when we (e.g., we in the relatively affluent and stable West) don't completely avoid such sections, we are still susceptible to some missteps with them. Wanting to apply these Scriptures, we

2 Eugene H. Peterson, *The Pastor: A Memoir* (New York: HarperOne, 2011), 85.

are tempted to *de-concretize* the images, treating them as so many illustrations of our personal inner life: in one psalm, we read pleas of imprisoned persons and think less of actual prisoners and more of how the psalm represents feelings of bondage in our souls; in another psalm, we read of the plight of orphans and widows and think less of actual orphans and widows and more of how the psalm symbolizes our personal sense of helplessness. Or, with attention limited to the details of our own immediate circumstances, we are tempted to *reduce* the scope of these lamentations: we apply Scripture's laments of injustice and oppression to our having political freedoms or rights threatened in the West; or we equate our experience of cultural marginalization with the psalmist's experience as "a sheep for slaughter."

There are varying degrees of appropriateness to such spiritualizing and applicational moves. But the fact is that there are actual orphans and widows being oppressed right now among God's people across the globe. There are those who are actually and wickedly imprisoned and butchered among the saints. There are kingdom citizens in the actual throes of refugee and exilic life. The dark portions of Scripture allow *their* voices to be heard. And we need to pray those Scriptures, even if we aren't feeling in the moment what such sections express.

In prayer, *I* pray, but never alone. Even in my prayer closet, I am not alone in lifting up praise, confession, petition, thanks, and lament to God. For I always pray as part of a *we*, which is to say, in Christ my identity is never less than a citizen in God's kingdom, a brother or sister of God's other children, a member of a body. This is the logic at work in the exhortation of Hebrews 13:3 to identify with those wracked with suffering: do so, "since you also are in the body." We are ever and always part of a constantly praying body scattered across the globe, a "holy catholic church," as the creed has it. So prayer can never be only about expressing what *I* feel in the moment, or finding verses to use for self-expression. Prayer is also a crucial opportunity for realizing our identity as members together with others, for stirring up sympathy and empathy for siblings, for showing solidarity with them. At least, prayer can be this when bound to Scripture. Let us, then, pray with our Bibles open, that we may identify with our brothers and sisters.

Illuminating

Still, praying remains an intensely personal activity, a word *I* do speak to the God who loves and cares for me. In love, this God invites me to know my truest identity. And when I pray with the Bible open, I begin to learn just that.

John Calvin called the Psalter "An Anatomy of all the Parts of the Soul,"

> for there is not an emotion of which any one can be conscious that is not here represented as in a mirror. Or rather, the Holy Spirit has here drawn to the life all the griefs, sorrows, fears, doubts, hopes, cares, perplexities, in short, all the distracting emotions with which the minds of men are wont to be agitated.[3]

3 John Calvin, *Commentary on the Book of the Psalms*, vol. 1, trans. James Anderson (Edinburgh: Calvin Translation Society, 1845), xxxvii. The image of a mirror appears in several places in Christian reflection on the Psalms (e.g., Athanasius, "The Letter of Athanasius to Marcellinus on the Interpretation of the Psalms," in *On the Incarnation*, trans. and ed. anonymously, 2nd rev. ed. [Crestwood, NY: St. Vladimir's Orthodox Theological Seminary Press, 1953], 104–14; Martin Luther, "Preface to the Psalms," in *Martin Luther: Selections from His Writings*, ed. John Dillenberger [New York: Anchor, 1962], 40–41]; and on Scripture more generally (see esp. Søren Kierkegaard, *For Self-Examination and Judge for Yourselves!*, trans. Walter Lowrie [Princeton, NJ: Princeton University Press, 1944], 39–74).

Scripture is the Spirit's flashlight for illuminating our souls, which our naturally darkened vision sees dimly at best. Praying Scripture is like shining the flashlight on our souls. Left to our own lights, we do not know ourselves aright. Praying Scripture, especially the Psalms, gives us words to name our experiences and emotions truthfully.

Let's take just one example. When things go badly in life, when we're frustrated and face hardship, what do we often do in response? What I typically do is point my finger: it's my wife's or children's fault; it's your fault for being so demanding; it's the fault of the conservatives or the liberals for ruining our nation; it's my boss's fault for being so greedy; it's the church's fault for not taking care of me. I complain. I gripe. I blame. But rarely is my first instinct to take my complaints to God.

In contrast, the psalmists constantly turn to God with their protests and complaints. In even more astounding contrast, the psalmist in Psalm 88 blames *God* for his troubles:

> *You* have put me in the depths of the pit. . . .
> *You* have caused my companions to shun me. (Ps. 88:6, 8)

This means, at least, that he acknowledges God's sovereign control over his life, which is a world of difference from blaming our problems on everyone else. Psalms of lament help us to name our problems and frustrations as fundamentally problems lived out before a sovereign God. They help us to name our anxiety as a yearning for God to act with power and goodness.

As we pray Scripture, we find our emotions illumined. What's more, praying Scripture also helps us mature into more well-rounded human beings and citizens of God's kingdom. Again, if it were up to us, we'd pray only what we feel like praying as a "pick-me-up." That might help us feel good in the moment, but it won't much *stretch* us and thus help us to grow. The whole Psalter will stretch us, filled as it is with many unfamiliar emotions, experiences, and rhythms of praying. So, lest we remain immature, narrow, stunted, and oblivious in our emotional life,[4] let us pray with our Bibles open, with the result that our souls are illuminated, our emotions rightly named,[5] and our character matured.

Imagining

The Bible is a single grand narrative or drama, beginning in Genesis and culminating in Revelation. The variety of literary genres in Scripture certainly extends far beyond just narrative. The Bible is more than narrative. But it is not less.

Importantly, the biblical narrative isn't an indirect, second-class way of talking about literal truths and eternal principles. The stories of Scripture are, in Todd Billings's words, "not inferior attempts at declarative sentences, but they provide a possible world for readers to inhabit: the narrative lens makes readers' own contexts appear

---

4   Peter J. Leithart, *Against Christianity* (Moscow, ID: Canon, 2003), 74; John D. Witvliet, *The Biblical Psalms in Christian Worship: A Brief Introduction and Guide to Resources* (Grand Rapids, MI: Eerdmans, 2007), 11–12.

5   Defining what an emotion *is* has caused no small amount of debate in philosophical, psychological, and theological scholarship. I have found two writers to be of particular help: Robert Roberts, *Emotions: An Essay in Aid of Moral Psychology* (Cambridge: Cambridge University Press, 2003), who proposes that emotions are "concern based construals"; and Kevin J. Vanhoozer, *Remythologizing Theology: Divine Action, Passion, and Authorship*, CSCD 18 (Cambridge: Cambridge University Press, 2010), 398–416, who translates Roberts's conceptual category into the language of theological discourse, speaking of "covenantal concern-based theodramatic construals." Emotions are dramatic construals of our concerns or stakes in a situation. Scripture provides the authoritative dramatic context in which to properly name and narrate our emotional life to God in prayer. In this light, Scripture's role in helping us name our emotional life before God is directly tied to Scripture's role in shaping our imaginations addressed below.

in a different light. Narratives do not simply present us with new information, but with a new way to perceive the world around us."[6] The narratives of Scripture aren't wrappers to be safely ignored once the candy of eternal truths is accessed "within" them. Rather, the narratives of Scripture form a world for us to inhabit, a drama for us to enact.[7] And this has everything to do with prayer.

The conjunction of the biblical *drama* with the labor of *prayer* is displayed in the prayer lives of biblical characters. Biblical pray-ers pray to God with an awareness of where they are in the drama, what "act" they are in, as it were. And they pray in keeping with that (f)act.

For example, in 1 Kings 8, at the dedication of the temple, King Solomon's prayer exults in the fruition of God's "good promise" of "rest" given "by Moses his servant" (v. 56). Solomon is praying with his eyes on Scripture. In prayerfully consecrating the temple, Solomon has in view God's promises made in Deuteronomy (see, e.g., Deut. 12:1–12). Moreover, the king recognizes that, in the prophetic timeline set forth by Moses (see esp. Deut. 27–30), this great moment of covenantal blessing still awaits the coming curse of exile.[8] So Solomon prays in a way that looks forward to that dread expectation (see 1 Kings 8:46–53).

6 J. Todd Billings, *The Word of God for the People of God: An Entryway to the Theological Interpretation of Scripture* (Grand Rapids, MI: Eerdmans, 2010), 44.
7 For a discussion of the difference between drama and narrative, emphasizing the importance of rightly identifying Scripture with drama, see Kevin J. Vanhoozer, *The Drama of Doctrine: A Canonical-Linguistic Approach to Christian Theology* (Louisville: Westminster John Knox, 2005), 48–49, cf. 273–74. See also, more generally, Vanhoozer, *Faith Speaking Understanding: Performing the Drama of Doctrine* (Louisville: Westminster John Knox, 2014), to fill out further the following emphasis on our performative, speaking part in the drama.
8 More specifically, the petitions of 1 Kings 8:31–53 are keyed to the covenantal curses set forth in Deut. 28. Matthew H. Patton, "Searching for a Truly Penitent Israel: Ezra-Nehemiah and Restoration Prophecy" (unpublished paper presented at the Wheaton College PhD Colloquium, February 4, 2010, 10–11).

Similarly, in Daniel 9, Daniel confesses sin not only for himself personally but *representatively for the nation of Israel.* Why does he do such a thing at such a time? It's because he has been reading the prophet Jeremiah (Dan. 9:1–2), who revealed God's intention to punish Israel with a seventy-year exile (see Jer. 25:11–12; 29:10). Daniel realizes that Israel has been exiled for about that long and begins to think, *According to God's purposes in history—according to the revealed storyline—now is the time for us to return!* But Daniel also knows from Scripture that return from exile *comes only through confession and repentance.* This is made clear, for example, in Leviticus 26 and Deuteronomy 30, and also in 1 Kings 8, considered above. So, what does Daniel do? As God's servant representing the people,[9] as their liturgical head, he confesses and repents of Israel's sins. Daniel's prayer is well fitted to his place in the biblical drama.

We, too, can and ought to pray with awareness of our place in the biblical storyline, in accord with our "act" in God's drama. What's our place in the storyline? We are at a time in the story when all the great promises to Israel about God's reclaiming a cursed world from the clutches of oppressors are beginning to be fulfilled—after the promised second exodus secured in the death and resurrection of Christ; after the ascension and the beginning of Christ's rightful rule; after Pentecost and the giving of the Spirit, the bounty of the kingdom, for the life, mission, and building of the church; during a new kind of exile awaiting Christ's second coming and the consummation of new creation. Praying with the Bible open and offering biblically attuned supplications will be guided by questions like the following: What

---

9 I have a hunch that the servant from Isaiah plays a major role in Daniel's prophetic self-understanding, and on the book of Daniel that he has written.

prayers might be appropriate for and flow fittingly from our place in the story? What has God revealed of his committed pursuits in this act of the drama? How might we by prayer get in on that work? In this way, our part in the drama is realized. By prayer, we enter the drama in a practical way.

It turns out that what is penned in the Bible is also *our* drama: we are characters in it, cast with speaking parts, given a script. Praying Scripture and praying from our place in the scriptural storyline both arise from and contribute to a different vision of reality than many of us might be familiar with. The narrative of Scripture is, in fact, the real world and true drama that we still inhabit today, the proper perceiving of which leads to more truthful life. When we pray to the divine protagonist of the biblical drama, according to what we discover of him in the story, we can measure and move our pursuits in the light of his. When we pray the Psalms, we find that the workings of our souls are given names, more truthful and explanatory names than we tend to give our "emotional life." When in prayer we seek to construe our personal, local dramas as nested within the biblical drama, recognizing that we pray from a particular place in the overall plotline of Scripture, we can begin to recognize the many parallels between the shapes and movements of our narratives and the biblical narratives and overall drama.

Apart from Scripture, we fall prey to the myriad idolatrous narratives and construals of reality on offer in the world. Scripture is the mirror that helps us see ourselves, and the reality of which we are a part, as we truly are, as God sees us. Let us think of praying Scripture as a *doing* (an enacting) of the word that helps us to not forget (cf. James 1:22–25). Prayer with seven *i*'s on Scripture is an opportunity to purge our imaginations of the idolatrous and reductionistic ways in which we have been socialized to narrate reality.[10] Praying Scripture can shape our imaginations to envision reality differently, to perceive reality as it really is, so that we might go with its grain and not against it, playing our proper part in the drama. It is, then, of utmost importance that we pray with our Bibles open.

Prayer with the Bible Open as Formation

It is good for us to get into the habit of opening our Bibles and paying attention to it as we pray, praying more intentionally and proactively in accord with Scripture. To the naked eye, this can look like *we* are the primary actors *using* the Bible to enhance our prayer life. Thankfully, we have seven *i*'s with which to see in proper focus the truth of praying Scripture. Praying Scripture is just as much, if not more, about allowing Scripture to act on us, to give us voice, to name our inner life, to reveal our identity as a part of God's kingdom, to refurbish our imaginations, to properly narrate our lives, to transform how we perceive and inhabit the world. We open our Bibles to pray, and in doing so we lay ourselves open for the Spirit to cut, pierce, kill, and make us new with his sword.

Praying is much more than an opportunity for honest self-expression. When we answer God according to the word with which he addresses us, we find that we are shaped and transformed into a new people who may inhabit the world in a new way. To make such a statement is also to suggest that the life of prayer is a public and political life. It is civic life. That might at first sound surprising to many. But how could it be otherwise, since praying implicates us in the use of language?

10 On the "purging" of the Christian imagination, see Richard Bauckham, *The Theology of the Book of Revelation*, NTTh (Cambridge: Cambridge University Press, 1993), 17.

———

O Lord Jesus Christ, Word of life, speak peace unto Thy people; speak peace to those who are far off, and to those who are near. Fill us with reverence, I pray Thee, for Thy most holy written Word: give us grace to study and meditate in it, with prayer and firm adoring faith; not questioning its authority, but obeying its precepts, and becoming imbued by its spirit. Teach us to prostrate our understandings before its mysteries; to live by its law, and abide by its promises. Amen.

PRAYER OF CHRISTINA ROSSETTI
BASED ON I JOHN I:I (1874)[11]

———

11 In *Selected Prose of Christina Rossetti*, ed. David A. Kent and P. G. Stanwood (New York: St. Martin's, 1998), 215.

PART 3

LANGUAGE

How *we see our situation is itself, already, a*
moral activity, and one which is, for better as
well as worse, "made" by linguistic process.

IRIS MURDOCH
Metaphysics as a Guide to Morals

There was a young couple strolling along half a block ahead of me.
The sun had come up brilliantly after a heavy rain, and the trees
were glistening and very wet. On some impulse, plain exuberance,
I suppose, the fellow jumped up and caught hold of a branch,
and a storm of luminous water came pouring down on the two of
them, and they laughed and took off running, the girl sweeping
water off her hair and her dress as if she were a little bit disgusted,
but she wasn't. It was a beautiful thing to see, like something from
a myth. I don't know why I thought of that now, except perhaps
because it is easy to believe in such moments that water was made
primarily for blessing, and only secondarily for growing vegetables
or doing the wash. I wish I had paid more attention to it.

JOHN AMES
in Marilynne Robinson's *Gilead*

Let not the blessings we receive daily from God make us not to value,
or not to praise him because they be common. . . . What would a
blind man give to see the pleasant rivers and meadows and flowers
and fountains, that we have met with since we met together? . . . This,
and many other like blessings, we enjoy daily. And for most of them,
because they be so common, most men forget to pay their praises; but
let not us, because it is a sacrifice so pleasing to Him that made the
sun and us, and still protects us, and gives us flowers and showers,
and stomachs and meat, and content and leisure to go a-fishing.

PISCATOR
in Izaak Walton's *The Compleat Angler*

7

Naming and Receiving
Reality Aright

WHEN I OFFICIATE WEDDINGS, I often tell the bride and groom something to this effect: "Today, God is doing a work of new creation. Today, you become something you have never been before. Today, you receive new names: husband and wife." The new names and the new creational work of God are not unrelated. The names change everything. Similarly, should the Lord one day lead the married couple to adopt a baby boy, that too would be a matter of uttering a world-transforming new name: *our son*. Nothing "inside" the boy would change. No unseen substance would be added to his heart or mind. Nothing about his visible or invisible makeup per se would be altered. Yet he would become completely new, called by a new name.

For anyone cultivated in the material and social conditions of modernity, the notion of names, of "mere words," changing everything is hard to grasp. We who have been socialized on the playground by chanting, "Sticks and stones may break my bones, but words will never hurt me," presume that "mere words" are small-fry, relatively nonimpactful in the big scheme of things. But let us consider: *What is a word?* Despite first impressions, this is a philosophically challenging question. Recently, Michael Sacasas discussed the matter with helpful simplicity:

> When you think of a word, what do you think of? I'd be willing to bet that if you were asked to think of the word "cat," for example, you would almost certainly think of the three letters C-A-T (or whatever the equivalent might be in your native tongue). Now ask yourself what would be the answer to that question in the era before writing was invented? Clearly not a set of symbols.
>
> When you think of a word as a set of letters, you're thinking of the word as an inert, lifeless thing. Before the introduction of writing, the word was not a thing but an event. It was powerful and effected irreversible change. Nothing better illustrates these different attitudes to the word than when modern readers encounter the biblical narrative of Isaac and his two sons, Jacob and Esau. When Jacob deceives his father into conferring his spoken blessing on him rather than Esau, the eldest son, a modern reader is likely to ask, well, why not just take it back, they're just words. But when the word is an event rather than a thing, you can't just take them back just as you can't undo an event.[1]

As Sacasas rightly observes, words can (should!) be thought of as *events*, not mere lifeless artifacts. As anyone who has unleashed his or her tongue hurtfully toward another well knows, you cannot just "take it back" and say, "I didn't *mean* it," or, "It was *just a word*." The event has happened. One can only respond in new ways, speak new words, inaugurate new events ("I was wrong; I'm sorry") to rectify the damage

---

1 L. M. Sacasas, "The Material Sources of Free Speech Anxieties," *The Convivial Society*, July 9, 2020, https://theconvivialsociety.substack.com/p/the-material-sources-of-free-speech.

done. This example also underlines that the events which are words are fundamentally *relational* in nature. Words are *relational events*. Words embody the relationships we understand ourselves to have or desire to pursue with reality around us. What we name and call a thing is an enactment of our relationship to it, of how we imagine it to be, of what we might expect of it, of our sense of responsibility before it. This is why I believe prayer is crucial for well-ordered, happy life.

We have been reflecting on prayer as answering speech. In recognition that Christian answering speech assumes a certain dialogue partner, part 1 considered different angles on the identity and character of the God who first addresses his people by his word. Part 2 moved on to explore how the word God speaks to us, Holy Scripture, both calls for and shapes our verbal response, our answer in words of prayer. Now in part 3, we narrow our focus to the linguistics of answering speech. What might prayerful speech, the language that we, God's people, address to God, say about us and the God whom we address? What might it indicate about the world God has made, his activity in it, and our privilege and responsibility as a part of it? Why might the *language* that is prayer be important, and what must take place for us to learn it?

Praying for Spring Rains and Daily Bread

For a launching point, we can take a curious verse tucked away in the curious book of Zechariah. Zechariah 10:1 is a call to prayer:

> Ask rain from the LORD
>> in the season of the spring rain,
> from the LORD who makes the storm clouds,
>> and he will give them showers of rain,
>> to everyone the vegetation in the field.

What's so curious about this invitation? Here's what seems strange to me. God gives rain, and he gives it in its due season. Scripture is clear about this (see Lev. 26:4; Deut. 11:14; 28:12). God has done this (i.e., provided rain in its due season) time out of mind. In fact, he has done it with such consistency that we can, in a sense, *count on* rain in the spring without praying at all—all farmers, whether believers or unbelievers, have known this and have banked on rain in the spring year after year. Yet God calls his people in Zechariah 10:1 to pray for rain in the rainy season.

Why does God command prayer for something apparently automatic and "natural," something that seems to us to occur regardless of whether we pray?[2] Is it because he isn't aware that we need spring rains? Surely that's not the case, "for your Father knows what you need before you ask him" (Matt. 6:8). What if it's because the Father doesn't *want* to grant us our needs, isn't disposed to such benevolence, and won't grant it until we grovel before him? Again, that is surely incorrect. As just noted, God has for long ages caused rains to come in the spring regularly and indiscriminately, on the good and the bad, on those who ask for it *and* on those who do not (cf. Matt. 5:45). These false trails founder on the assumption that prayer is a tool of our devising to manipulate God to do something. But this is to ignore the unmistakable point that Zechariah 10:1 is *God's invitation* to pray. Prayer is not our strategy to effect a change in God but activity-in-speech to which God summons us. He doesn't

---

2　The phrase "seems to us" is crucial. It seems to us, individually, that God gives rain regardless of whether we, individually, pray. And it seems to us, culturally enlightened as we are, that rain is simply the product of meteorological forces detachable from prayer. But even if this is to us *apparently* the case, that does not *necessarily* mean that God gives rain apart from prayer. It might just mean that our present individual praying isn't the be-all and end-all of God's working through prayer in the world (see, further, chaps. 8 and 11 below), and that meteorology might not be so detachable from theology.

call us to pray because he is strapped for any other way to deliver the goods to us, as it were. And he doesn't ordain prayer (I speak in human terms) for his own benefit. As John Calvin observes, God "ordained it not so much for his own sake as for ours."[3]

It will greatly help us to unpack what Calvin means. To do so, I will draw liberally on the most helpful guide in this that I have come across, Matthew Myer Boulton in his remarkable book *Life in God: John Calvin, Practical Formation, and the Future of Protestant Theology*. Boulton directs our attention to the paradigm prayer, the Lord's Prayer. Specifically, he considers the fourth petition, the request for bread for the day.

> We make this request not to inform God of our hunger, or to rouse God into action, but rather the better to experience— in and through the reception, touch, taste, enjoyment, and sustenance of whatever bread may subsequently come our way—the tangible reality of God's providential love for us. We ask for bread, then, not only so that we might receive it, but also and principally so that when we receive it, we might actually experience it as it is: a divine gift to us, and even more, an answer to our prayers. For in truth, Calvin insists, God does provide for us every day, precisely as our active, loving, attentive parent. But just as with human parents and children, we come to know and trust this kind of truth only through repeated experiences of asking and receiving, needing and enjoying, vulnerability and love.[4]

3 John Calvin, *Institutes of the Christian Religion*, ed. John T. McNeill, trans. Ford Lewis Battles (Louisville: Westminster John Knox, 1960), 3.20.3.

4 Matthew Myer Boulton, *Life in God: John Calvin, Practical Formation, and the Future of Protestant Theology* (Grand Rapids, MI: Eerdmans, 2011), 168.

According to Boulton, God ordains that we pray not only as a means of accomplishing or providing the things we pray for "but also and principally" for our experiential training and maturation. God summons us to pray for daily bread and for spring rains—and for life and breath and everything—because he wants us to experience them *as they truly are*. There are two central characteristics of bread and rain, and the like, as they truly are: first, they are "divine gift"; second, they are "an answer to our prayers." Let's consider both characteristics in turn.

Gracefully Receiving Divine Gifts

"Awake, O sleeper!" (Eph. 5:14). Too often we go about our lives sleepwalking, perceiving and receiving reality at best drowsily and at worst obliviously and idolatrously. We don't know rain for what it is, and we don't speak about it or receive it truthfully, if we take it to be merely the necessary result of so-called "laws of nature,"[5] or if we simply presume upon it as automatic and thus unworthy of notice and comment. We don't know our daily bread for what it is or eat it truthfully if we take it as a mere commodity we purchase with our money, or as something to stockpile in cupboards so that, at least for the next two weeks, we don't need to *depend* on anything or anyone besides ourselves and our storehouses for daily sustenance. We don't know such things aright if we don't know them, receive them, and experience them as gifts from a loving giver.

Strange as it may sound, receiving aright the gifts God benevolently and abundantly bestows—that is, receiving them *as gifts*—

---

5 Such language, so often assumed to be "literal," "scientifically precise," and "just the way things are," is, as C. S. Lewis has pointed out, thoroughly *metaphorical*. See Lewis, *The Discarded Image: An Introduction to Medieval and Renaissance Literature* (Cambridge: Cambridge University Press, 1964), 92–94.

requires activities of prayer. It requires, at least, the verbal practice of *thanksgiving*. Boulton explains:

> Part of gracefully receiving a gift is receiving it gratefully; indeed, to a significant extent, gratitude constitutes the reception itself, since if no gratitude arises, we may well ask whether the gift was received as a "gift" at all. Analogies abound in human affairs: If you generously give me bread to satisfy my hunger, and I simply devour it thoughtlessly, or conceive it as a *quid pro quo* for a favor I did for you yesterday, or as the front end of a bargain that tomorrow obligates me to "return the favor," as we say—then have I actually received the bread as a gift, that is, as a living symbol of your care for me? By no means. I have received it as plunder, windfall, or merchandise. But in the case of God's gifts to humanity, practices of prayer can help remind us that our daily bread finally "comes from God's hand," and so may help stimulate our thanksgiving not only to the "ministers," as Calvin calls them, through whom God makes the bread available (the shopkeeper, the baker, the farmer), but also and ultimately to God.[6]

To experience reality aright, we must at least fill our lives with prayers of thanksgiving. Every good gift and every perfect gift is from above, coming down from the Father of lights—always. What's more, our lives are literally chock-full of God's good gifts, from the bread set on our tables every day, to the rain falling so persistently every spring, to our moment-by-moment existence being sustained continually, as a gift, in Christ (Col. 1:17). This is true even when we don't recognize such things as gifts or acknowledge their source. So it is not without reason that Scripture commands us

6   Boulton, *Life in God*, 170–71, emphasis original.

to be "giving thanks always" (Eph. 5:20). But "what makes gratitude appropriate," notes Nicholas Wolterstorff, "is not first of all that it is commanded (although, of course, it is), but simply that it is right and proper."[7] In the *Sursum Corda*, a liturgical dialogue for the eucharistic table, the minister bids the congregation, "Let us give thanks to the Lord"; the people respond, "It is meet and right to do so." It is fitting and truthful to give thanks always because it fits with how reality always is—we are always the recipients of benevolence and gifts.

Prayer is the beginning of our realizing what is always true. It's practice in naming (and learning to name) reality aright. It's experiencing and receiving reality properly. It's how we grow in our most fundamental relationship with the generous giver of gifts. Our Father desires that we know and receive spring rains and daily bread *truthfully*, as gifts of his love, which is why he invites us to give thanks always, even for something as seemingly "natural" and automatic as spring rain. Boulton comments:

> The point is that in fact, every good [disciples] receive is a divine gift, and through practices of prayer the Spirit makes them more mindful of this, their true situation. Thus they may live and act in ways more in tune with reality. In other words, through the daily prayer cycle, the Spirit accustoms disciples to turn toward God for all their needs, and so forms them toward a more humble, lively awareness of their daily reliance on what God provides, which is to say, their ongoing relationship to God as God's beloved children. At their best, practices of prayer clarify this relationship, and at the

7 Nicholas Wolterstorff, *Until Justice and Peace Embrace* (Grand Rapids, MI: Eerdmans, 1983), 14.

same time draw disciples toward deeper, more fully conscious participation in it.[8]

God would have us grow more fully attuned to the nature of the world and our position in it as constant recipients of his benevolence. So he calls us to pray.

The Father's Answers to Our Answering Speech

But prayer not only awakens us to the gift-like nature of our existence. Second and more significantly, to return to Boulton's comments that we began with a few pages back, God summons us to a life of prayer—prayer for even mundane things like bread and rain—in order that we might receive each of God's good gifts as "an answer to our prayers." That might seem, at first, like too obvious and pedestrian a point to highlight, but in fact it is of life-transforming significance.

To give thanks at day's end for the day's good gifts—be it bread or rain or whatever—is one thing. It's a needful thing. It helps us better engage such realities as they truly are. But God not only expects us to give *thanks* for good gifts; he also invites us to voice *petitions* for spring rains and to pray every morning, "Give us this day our daily bread" (Matt. 6:11). The life of prayer includes, in addition to the speech act of thanksgiving, the speech act of *supplication*.

The psalmist says, "In the morning I will present my prayer to You and be on the watch" (Ps. 5:3 NASB). Consider what effect such a beginning to the day has on the thanksgiving raised at day's end:

8 Boulton, *Life in God*, 170.

1. At the break of day, we pray, "Give us today our bread for this day."
2. At breakfast, lunch, and dinner, by the hand of our almighty and most merciful Father, bread is set on our table for us to feast on.
3. Thus, as we lie our heads on our pillows, for what can we give thanks?

When we begin with number 1, we can end with number 3 in thanksgiving for much more than the good gift of bread from God. It is true enough that each day we are recipients of God's lavish goodness, and we rightly give regular thanks to him for it. But God's goodness is more specific, more personal, more near and relationally vibrant than we might be accustomed to perceiving. So we can give thanks for the gift of bread, and, much more importantly, we can give thanks for *God's answer to our morning prayer*. We can give thanks that God is as he is, and come to know his character and heart more truly: he is an attentive, responsive Father, who is ever present for our life and good. In this light, God commands the Lord's Prayer and morning prayer more generally, in Jonathan Edwards's words, "so that we may be prepared to glorify his name when the mercy is received."[9]

The conditions of modernity incline us to think of God as, at best, only distantly related to things like rain and bread. We may admit that God is ultimately responsible for their existence, but functionally he is to our thoughts and perceptions no more practically and personally near to such things—and to *us* who depend

---

9 Jonathan Edwards, "The Most High a Prayer-Hearing God," in *The Works of Jonathan Edwards*, ed. Sereno E. Dwight, rev. and corr. Edward Hickman, 2 vols. (Edinburgh: Banner of Truth, 1974), 2:116.

on them—than a watchmaker is to the ticking of the watch he made. This is a way of understanding that, according to Alexander Schmemann, is lived into "so consistently that it has become something that is 'in the air.' It seems natural for man to experience the world as opaque, and not shot through with the presence of God."[10] However "natural" it might seem to view rain and bread in this way, it is a falsehood. However apparent God's absence from our lives may be, it is a false and anxiety-producing perception. Our situation may be likened to childhood anxieties and fears that must be grown out of under the watchful care, protection, and shepherding of a loving parent. To help her children, to guide them in growth out of childish anxieties into the maturity of strong relational confidence, "what does a present, active, loving parent do for her children?"

> She provides for them, yes, but even more iconically, and therefore more reassuringly and persuasively, she hears their cries. She responds to them. She interacts with her children, relating and communing with them in freedom, familiarity, and love. She may very well know exactly what they need, and she may already have decided to provide it, but for their sake, so that they might even more vividly experience her care, she encourages them to ask for what they require. That way, her gifts may be seen and received for what they are. Thus she not only anticipates her children's needs, or provides for them in general, as if from afar. She also invites their requests, listens to them, and answers them, not always with the answers they expect or want to hear, but with kind-hearted answers nonetheless. And she does all

---

10 Alexander Schmemann, *For the Life of the World: Sacraments and Orthodoxy*, rev. and exp. ed. (Crestwood, NY: St. Vladimir's Seminary Press, 1997), 16.

this for the sake of comforting, assuring, and delighting her sons and daughters, and so finally for the sake of her ongoing relationship with them.[11]

If we, being evil, know how to relate in such good, wise, patient, benevolent, communicative, and pedagogical ways with our children, how much more our heavenly Father? What does this Father do for us who are prone to oblivion about his care and anxiety about his absence? What does the Father do for the young boy Samuel in 1 Samuel 3? Recall that Samuel had been dedicated to serve the Lord with Eli the priest in days when "the word of the LORD was rare" (v. 1). It is a great surprise when God comes calling Samuel, who mistakes God's call for Eli's, running to find out what Eli wants. This happens not once, not twice, but three times, before Eli catches on and counsels Samuel, "Go, lie down, and if he calls you, you shall say, 'Speak, LORD, for your servant hears'" (v. 9). The next time God calls, "Samuel! Samuel!," Samuel is ready and says, "Speak, for your servant hears" (v. 10). That is, Samuel *answers*. And *only then* does the Lord reveal to Samuel his purposes for Israel and the house of Eli. The narrator takes care to clarify that, prior to Samuel's answering speech to God, "the word of the Lord had not been revealed to him" (v. 7). We might criticize God's methods, thinking the more "efficient" route of divulging his word from the get-go to be better than all the runaround of waiting for Samuel's word of response. But that would be to show confusion about the nature of the word of God and the love of the Father who speaks it. And it would be to miss what Samuel, the child

11 Boulton, *Life in God*, 172.

of God, most needs to learn and grow into. For Samuel, as for us, that most important lesson cannot come about but through answering speech.

So our God says, "Pray for spring rains."[12] He commands us to supplicate every morning, "Give us this day our daily bread." He invites us not to one-off prayers to see if they work, not to spectacular events and spiritual highs, but to a practiced *life of prayer* (hence the subtitle of this book) that disciples us experientially in reality, the most significant facet of which is our relationship with our Father. "Without this kind of experiential training, left to our own dull devices," says Boulton,

> we may well regard our daily bread as little more than just that: the same old daily bread, a humdrum prop in a bland or harried or thoughtless routine, or a more or less pleasing occasion for ungrateful satisfaction. Far too often, Calvin maintains,

12 Returning to Zech. 10:1, we can note that Yahweh's invitation through the prophet to pray for rain overturns Yahweh's earlier rejection of supplications in the days of the prophet Jeremiah (see Jer. 14:10–12; 14:22–15:1). More specifically, Zechariah's words are a reversal of Yahweh's rejection *and* a response to his judgment against false prophets (note Jer. 14:13–18; see Rex Mason, "The Use of Earlier Biblical Material in Zechariah 9–14: A Study in Inner Biblical Exegesis," in *Bringing Out the Treasure: Inner Biblical Allusion in Zechariah 9–14*, ed. M. J. Boda and M. H. Floyd [London: T&T Clark, 2003], 63–69). Covenantal blessing (of which rain is a part; see Lev. 26:4; Deut. 11:14; 28:12) does not come apart from awareness of and fidelity to covenantal responsibility and relationship to the Lord. But throughout Israel's history, false prophets assured Israel of the former without reference to the latter. By contrast, the prophet Zechariah does what no false prophet does: he directs the people to responsive, relational reliance upon the covenantal Lord for everything, even spring rains. He takes up the responsibility of a true "shepherd" (cf. Zech. 10:2) by calling for what Mason describes as "a proper response to Yahweh who alone is the giver of the blessings of the new age, a response which is, therefore, the essential condition of experiencing it" (66). In this light, the present chapter can be seen to be part of a prophetic-pastoral labor and responsibility to help the people of God recognize that blessedness comes not around but through, and indeed just *is*, covenantal relationship with and filial reliance upon a Father who is present and responsive in everything.

our attention lags or wanders this way; we lose track of our actual situation as God's beloved children; and consequently our desires are anxious, paltry, self-absorbed, or unwise. We are anemic, and so need to be reminded. We are worried, and so need to be reassured. We are oblivious, "sleepy or sluggish," bogged down by "such great dullness," and so need to be awakened and revived. . . . And so we need to pray, Calvin contends, not only for our daily bread but also for all our needs and the world's needs besides, the better to remember, calm down, and wake up.[13]

The Transformation of the World

At the end of the day, a life that is attentively, earnestly, and rhythmically devoted to prayer does not result merely in the reception of the things we ask for. Prayer is no thin technique for getting what we want. The effects of a well-ordered life of prayer are nothing less than cosmic in scope, for the universe is thick with love awaiting consummation. Prayer transforms the world. On the one hand, the stuff of this world is itself transformed into, or fulfilled as, the relational reality it was meant to be, being finally received as a gift, "for everything created by God is good, and nothing is to be rejected if it is received with thanksgiving, *for it is made holy by the word of God and prayer*" (1 Tim. 4:4–5).

But on the other hand, how we perceive the world is also transformed for the better. Whereas we used to think that ours was a reality where God was distant, by the daily cycle of prayer we discover that God is ever near to us. Whereas the structures of modern industrial societies incline us to think of ourselves as forgotten and interchange-

13 Boulton, *Life in God*, 168–69, quoting Calvin, *Institutes* 3.20.3, 5.

able nobodies,[14] the rhythms of prayer illuminate that we are, in fact, personally the objects of a good Father's care, a Father who is attentive to us, who listens to us, who responds to us. Whereas the world once felt like a cold machine operating by unchanging rules and natural laws, by supplication and thanksgiving our hearts are trained to name what strikes us as automatic and unchangeably persistent in creation not as dull mechanism but as the radiating glory of God's ubiquitous love for us. "Wherever you turn your eyes," muses John Ames in the novel *Gilead*, "the world can shine like transfiguration. You don't have to bring a thing to it except a little willingness to see. Only, who could have the courage to see it?"[15] Prayer is the beginning step in that willingness. Prayer is holy attentiveness, transforming perception and experience. By prayer in Jesus's name, the people of God begin to live into nothing less than a new creation.

———

Lord, in Thy Name Thy servants plead,
And Thou hast sworn to hear;
Thine is the harvest, Thine the seed,
The fresh and fading year.

Our hope, when autumn winds blew wild,
We trusted, Lord, with Thee:
And still, now spring has on us smiled,
We wait on Thy decree.

---

14 See, e.g., the perceptive discussion of Wendell Berry, "Men and Women in Search of Common Ground," *Sunstone*, July 1987, 10.
15 Marilynne Robinson, *Gilead* (New York: Farrar, Straus and Giroux, 2004), 245.

The former and the latter rain,
The summer sun and air,
The green ear, and the golden grain,
All Thine, are ours by prayer.

Thine too by right, and ours by grace,
The wondrous growth unseen,
The hopes that soothe, the fears that brace,
The love that shines serene.

So grant the precious things brought forth
By sun and moon below,
That Thee in Thy new heav'n and earth
We never may forego. Amen.

PRAYER OF JOHN KEBLE (1856)[16]

16 John Keble, hymn 165, in *Hymns Ancient and Modern*, hist. ed. (London: Clowes, 1909), 235.

*A higher grammar must reinstate the reality of speaking
and listening people in the place of the nightmare of a
speechless thinker who computes a speechless universe.*

EUGEN ROSENSTOCK-HUESSY
Speech and Reality

*The church is a social fact as well as an eschatological
sign. It draws its citizens into a shared public life with
its distinctive language, rituals, calendar, practices,
institutions, architecture, art, music, in short with
its culture. . . . The church is not an instrument
to achieve other ends than fellowship with God. It
serves society by being unapologetically itself and
by bearing witness to the justice that alone makes
human community possible, the justice due God. The
greatest gift the church can give society is a glimpse,
however fleeting, of another city, where the angels
keep "eternal festival" before the face of God.*

ROBERT L. WILKEN
The Spirit of Early Christian Thought

8

The Language of the City of God

IN 2002, THE INDEPENDENT, low-budget rom-com *My Big Fat Greek Wedding* was released.[1] It was low on star power. It had little by way of plot originality. It never reached number one in the box office. It enjoyed mostly lukewarm critical reception, being located somewhere between palatable prime-time sitcom and guilty pleasure baklava style. In view of all this, what *My Big Fat Greek Wedding* went on to become is amazing—namely, the highest grossing romantic comedy of all time in North America.[2]

I am persuaded that this surprise success owes a lot to Windex—more specifically, the main character's entertaining and Windex-wielding father, Gus Portokalos. Gus sprays Windex on everything, from psoriasis to poison ivy to pimples, confident in its panacean powers. But this is just the tip of the iceberg of his amusing quirks. He loves his children with a loyal, protective, clumsy, and condescending love. He has an un-self-conscious old-world paternalism. And his house, in "a normal middle-class Chicago neighborhood

---

1 Directed by Joel Zwick (New York: IFC Films, 2002).
2 This is as of 2022, according to Box Office Mojo, https://www.boxofficemojo.com/genre /sg2111762689/.

of tasteful modest homes," is modeled on the Parthenon. Gus is the source of much laughter and groaning.

If you didn't know Gus, you could probably guess his citizenship by looking at his house. But political-cultural identity is not only marked architecturally; it's also marked linguistically. Hearing Gus speak in Greek, or even just hearing him laud the Greek language, tells us much about him: "Give me a word, any word, and I'll show you how the root of that word is Greek. Okay. How about 'arachnophobia'? 'Arachna,' that comes from the Greek word for spider, and 'phobia' is a phobia, it means 'fear.' So, 'fear of spiders.' There you go." How about "kimono"? It's from the Greek *cheimonas*, meaning winter; and in the winter one wears a robe. Or the name "Miller"? From the Greek *milo*, meaning "apple." So there you go.

Etymological fallacies aside, Gus illustrates a fundamental truth: citizenship and cultural identity are bound to language. One speaks a language because one is a part of and has received the ability to speak it from a *people*.[3] In speaking a dialect or a tongue, one is civically marked out. Gus's pride and identity as a Greek cannot be separated from his mother tongue. Believe it or not, we are but a short step from prayer and its public and political implications. But to begin to make some sense of this, a brief lesson in civics is in order.

Civic Speech: The Praying City of God

Near the beginning of the letter to the Philippians, Saint Paul gives a paradigmatic exhortation: "Only let your manner of life be worthy of the gospel of Christ, so that whether I come and see you or am

---

3   Cf. Walter J. Ong, *The Presence of the Word: Some Prolegomena for Cultural and Religious History* (New Haven, CT: Yale University Press, 1967; repr., Minneapolis: University of Minnesota Press, 1981), 141.

absent, I may hear of you that you are standing firm in one spirit, with one mind striving side by side for the faith of the gospel" (Phil. 1:27). The sense and significance of this verse is, unfortunately, obscured in most English translations, but the ESV clarifies with a footnote after the word "worthy." The verb translated as "let your manner of life be" (*politeuesthe*) could also be translated "behave as citizens." The word Paul uses is decidedly civic and political in nature (note the *polit-* root of *politeuesthe*), almost always used elsewhere to speak of citizenship, of one's identity, privilege, and responsibility as a member of a *polis*, a city.[4] Paul is telling us to be good citizens, to be politically wise, to seek the flourishing of the city as befits the gospel.

But it's crucial to ask, "What city?" Later, in Philippians 3:20, Paul identifies the place of our truest citizenship, using the noun form of the word used in 1:27: "But our citizenship [*politeuma*] is in heaven, and from it we await a Savior, the Lord Jesus Christ." When in 1:27 Paul commands, "Behave as citizens," he means "citizens of the city of heaven." Our citizenship is of the City of God. That city's life goes public here and now in the life of the church, a society that bends the knee to "a Savior, the Lord Jesus Christ" (3:20), a people of "one spirit" and "one mind" distinguishable from surrounding political unities and entities (1:27). The church is an outpost or an embassy of the City of God, finding itself called to faithful presence among the cities of the earth.

---

4 In Acts 23:1, the Lukan Paul uses the verb, arguably with its political-citizenry aspect in full view. See also LXX Est. 16:15; 2 Macc. 6:1; 11:25; 3 Macc. 3:4; 4 Macc. 2:8, 23; 4:23; 5:16. When we look to external Greek sources, we find that the word is used consistently for citizenship in a city-state and activity under a government and law. See Henry George Liddell, Robert Scott, and Henry Stuart Jones, *A Greek-English Lexicon*, 9th ed. with rev. suppl. (Oxford: Clarendon, 1996), ad loc., and compare related terms.

The church has, like any city, what Robert Wilken calls "a shared public life," which includes, at least, a "distinctive language, rituals, calendar, practices, institutions, architecture, art, music." In a word, the church is a culture. Wilken refers to several features of the culture that is the church, each worthy of considerable attention, but it is his reference to the church's "distinctive language" that most interests us.[5] The church has, as it were, its own language, the Christian's mother tongue. And I propose that the life of prayer is a crucial training ground for fluency in the distinct language, the mother tongue, of the City of God.

The bulk of this book so far could be mistaken as addressing the life of prayer only on what we could call "the individual level." Here we need to make explicit something that has been more or less implicit throughout—namely, that prayer is always a civic activity. Prayer, so intensely personal, is not for that reason solely or fundamentally individual, nor a matter of private and parochial concern. The life of prayer is ever a shared life of the whole City of God. To pray to the Father in the name of the Son by the power of the Spirit manifests our political identity, as speaking Greek manifests Gus Portokalos's Greek identity. It is necessarily to be part of a praying *people*. What's more, the life of prayer is part of our properly political service and witness to the cities of the earth among which we sojourn as aliens. Attentive concern for the good of the nations is part of what it means to be the praying people of God. Language exercised by prayer in the City of God reverberates outward far beyond the walls of our personal interest.

5   For Wilken, it is chiefly Scripture that "formed Christians into a people and gave them a language" (Robert Louis Wilken, *The Spirit of Early Christian Thought: Seeking the Face of God* [New Haven, CT: Yale University Press, 2003], 52; see, further, 43, 69, 76–77). We might say that "Bible" is the true mother tongue of the church of God. My point here (esp. in light of part 2, above) is that prayer is how the City of God begins to speak and learn the language.

(E)vocative Speech: Relational-Covenantal Language

Let us return to Zechariah 10:1, to which I appealed in the preceding chapter. If we accept God's invitation to pray for spring rains, how might we articulate such a prayer? How would the wording go? An obvious and incredibly important observation about the *grammar* of such a prayer is that it will be uttered with the vocative case, the case of direct address to a "you." Prayer says, "Lord, give us the spring rains," not "May the Lord give us spring rains." We pray aright when we address God, "Our Father who is in heaven, give us this day our daily bread," not when we think a thought about him or state a conviction, "Our daily bread comes from the Father." Prayer is language in the vocative case, language of personal address.

The language of prayer teaches us a critical lesson about the gift and the proper functioning of language more generally in God's world. Language is first and foremost a means of relationship and intimacy with others. It is not only or chiefly about expressing or transferring content. It is no mere tool to get things done. It is not bits of data stored privately in our minds. "Language is not private," says Walter Ong, "but communal."[6] At root it is how we, as the communicative and covenantal creatures we are, live into and live out our defining relationships—with God, neighbor, and the rest of creation. This is true of all language, even statements that aren't apparently spoken to anyone in particular. In "The Lord comes to his temple," Peter R. Hallock's plainchant arrangement for Candlemas, the choir asks Simeon, "To whom do you address your words: 'Now

---

6 Ong, *The Presence of the Word*, 221. Cf. Hans Urs von Balthasar, *Prayer*, trans. G. Harrison (San Francisco: Ignatius, 1986), 14.

I can depart in peace, for I have seen my salvation'?"[7] They recognize that Simeon's words, though without any overt vocative case, are at bottom spoken *to* someone.

Eugene Peterson has especially emphasized the proper status of language as a means of enacting and experiencing communion:

> The language of intimacy and relationship . . . is the first language we learn. Initially, it is not articulate speech. The language that passes between parent and infant is incredibly rich in meaning but less than impressive in content. The coos and cries of the infant do not parse. The nonsense syllables of the parent have no dictionary definitions. But in the exchange of gurgles and out-of-tune hums, trust develops. Parent whispers transmute infant screams into grunts of hope. . . . For all its limited vocabulary and butchered syntax, it seems more than adequate to bring into expression the realities of a complex and profound love.[8]

So important is this central feature and purpose of language that Peterson has somewhat artificially but still instructively distinguished "the language of intimacy and relationship" from "the language of information," which instructs *about* things, and "the language of motivation," which seeks to persuade and get things accomplished. The point, as I understand him, is less to suggest that we can make clean separations of these ways of speaking[9] and

---

7   "The Lord comes to his temple," by Peter R. Hallock, track 17 on *What Hand Divine?*, Compline Choir Recordings, 2015, Apple Music, https://music.apple.com/.

8   Eugene H. Peterson, *The Contemplative Pastor: Returning to the Art of Spiritual Direction* (Dallas: Word, 1989), 98.

9   While Peterson admits that "all the languages blend together in actual use," he believes that the language of intimacy and relationship is "not exclusively . . . but mostly" the language

more to single out the importance, and the alarming contemporary eclipse, of the former:

> Informational language and motivational language dominate our society. We are well schooled in language that describes the world in which we live. We are well trained in language that moves people to buy and join and vote. Meanwhile . . . the language of intimacy, the language that develops relationships of trust and hope and understanding, languishes. Once we are clear of the cradle, we find less and less occasion to use it. There are short recoveries . . . in adolescence when we fall in love and spend endless hours talking on the telephone using words that eavesdroppers would characterize as gibberish. . . . When we are new parents, we relearn the basic language and use it for a while. A few people never quit using it—a few lovers, some poets, the saints—but most let it slide.[10]

Peterson's reference to "the saints" is not accidental. For saints are set apart for the constant activity of prayer (1 Thess. 5:17). Their language fills God's altar with incense (Rev. 5:8; 8:3–4). The saints, of all people, should be those who have not fallen out of the practice of relational, vocative speech. Their linguistic ministry is

---

of prayer. Eugene H. Peterson, *Answering God: The Psalms as Tools for Prayer* (San Francisco: Harper & Row, 1989), 39.

10 Peterson, *The Contemplative Pastor*, 99. Cf. Kevin J. Vanhoozer, "From Speech Acts to Scripture Acts: The Covenant of Discourse and the Discourse of the Covenant," in *After Pentecost: Language and Biblical Interpretation*, ed. Craig G. Bartholomew, Colin Greene, and Karl Möller (Cumbria, UK: Paternoster; Grand Rapids, MI: Zondervan, 2001), 27–28, who contrasts a "strategic" with a "communicative" use of language; and Charles Taylor, *A Secular Age* (Cambridge, MA: Harvard University Press, 2007), 615, who observes the modern Western reduction of "human linguistic-communicative activity" to "prose, descriptive language."

desperately needed today. In a society that treats language as a blunt tool for manipulating and gaining mastery over others, or a mere conduit for the transfer of information from one container to another, the saints by prayer can evoke a forgotten world in which language is practiced otherwise, a world filled not with problems to solve or resources to exploit but with personal relationships and the possibility of communion. Indeed, the early twentieth-century polymath Eugen Rosenstock-Huessy went so far as to assert that restoring "vocatives and imperatives" to a primary and central place in our speech "would do more toward the elimination of atheism and cynicism than all pious tracts together."[11] Would that this mission be accomplished in no small part through the City of God's devotion to its proper civic speech. It may just be the greatest gift, the truest political service, and the best starting point for kingdom witness that we can offer to the nations. For the good of the cities among which we sojourn, for the cultivation of our better speech among and with them, let us devote ourselves to prayer.

Priestly Speech: Intercession and Mediation

By a circuitous route, we have begun to recognize that the life of prayer has reverberations beyond an individual's experience and sphere, beyond even the experience of the corporate people of God in their gatherings to engage in their civic speech. Fulfilling our properly civic and political responsibilities as the outpost of the City of God, including growing in fluency in our mother tongue

---

11   Eugen Rosenstock-Huessy, *Der Atem des Geistes* (Frankfurter am Main: Verlag der Frankfurter Hefte, 1951), 89, quoted in George Allen Morgan, *Speech and Society: The Christian Linguistic Social Philosophy of Eugen Rosenstock-Huessy* (Gainesville, FL: University of Florida Press, 1987), 81.

by prayer, is no ignoring of or withdrawal from the cities among which we sojourn as aliens. Rather, it is precisely so that we might properly engage them with our own distinct and ever-fuller witness as a different city.

Intercessory Prayer

A much more direct route to showing that the life of prayer reverberates outward to the ends of the earth is to spotlight the practice and responsibility of intercessory prayer.[12] There is, in the life of prayer, not only a "me and mine" concern but also attention turned outward in concern for strangers. The Spirit poured into our hearts is unceasingly interceding for us with groans too deep for words, and the risen and ascended Christ is at the right hand of God interceding for us (Rom. 8:26–27, 34). In like manner, in conformity with Christ, as his Spirit-filled body on earth, we too are called to a ministry of intercession for the good of others. I mean this not only individually but also ecclesially. And I mean it civically—that is, our civic labor as the outpost of the City of God is to intercede on behalf of the neighborhoods and nations around us. Anything less than this falls short of the proper and full life of prayer.

It is nearly impossible to miss in Scripture this expectation for outward concern in the life of prayer. King Solomon's dedicatory prayer at the temple includes petitions for the "foreigner, who is not of your people Israel" (1 Kings 8:41–43). While exiled in pagan Babylon, the people of Israel are commanded to "seek the welfare of the city where I have sent you into exile, and pray to the LORD on its behalf, for in its welfare you will find your welfare" (Jer. 29:7).

---

12 This section leans heavily on Hughes Oliphant Old, *Leading in Prayer: A Workbook for Ministers* (Grand Rapids, MI: Eerdmans, 1995), 175–83.

Similarly, the apostle Paul famously urges that "supplications, prayers, intercessions, and thanksgivings be made for all people, for kings and all who are in high positions" (1 Tim. 2:1–2). More stunningly, Jesus commands, "Love your enemies and pray for those who persecute you" (Matt. 5:44), clearly people not in our fold. The Lord himself taught his disciples to pray,

> Your kingdom come,
> your will be done,
>> on earth as it is in heaven. (Matt. 6:10)

The Lord would have us seek by prayer nothing less than the fullness of the kingdom, known and experienced everywhere and all the time.

Clearly, the life of prayer is to be anything but a merely private and parochial exercise, a gazing at inner, invisible goods or at the good of only us and those of our ilk. So clear and frequently expressed in Scripture is the expectation that the people of God's kingdom pray for public life and palpable renewal beyond the walls of their household concern, as it were, that we might well ask if our actual practice reflects a corresponding percentage of such intercession. Is there ample space in our life of prayer for the neighborhoods and nations around us?

Consider, for example, the litany closely bound to the service of morning prayer in the 1662 Book of Common Prayer.[13] Here we find supplications for God to "have mercy on us miserable sinners," to "remember not . . . our offenses, nor the offenses of our forefathers" but to "spare thy people" and deliver them "from all

---

13 The 1662 Book of Common Prayer is available at https://www.churchofengland.org/.

blindness of heart; from pride, vainglory, and hypocrisy; from envy, hatred, and malice, and all uncharitableness" and "from lightning and tempest; from plague, pestilence, and famine; from battle and murder, and sudden death," and all for the sake of the finished work of Christ. We find prayers for the Lord God "to rule and govern thy holy Church universal in the right way," for him to strengthen and illumine church officers "with true knowledge and understanding of thy Word," and for him to give his people a "heart to love and dread thee, and diligently to live after thy Commandments." This is just a sampling to show that, for the church of the early and later English Reformation, the life of prayer concentrated on things that we today might associate especially with "the good of the church." This is to be expected, and it is entirely appropriate.

But equally in abundance are prayers for the Lord

- "to bless and keep" *all* magistrates, and endue them with "grace to execute justice, and to maintain truth";
- "to give *all* nations unity, peace, and concord";
- "to bring into the way of truth *all* such as have erred, and are deceived";
- "to succour, help, and comfort *all* that are in danger, necessity, and tribulation";
- "to preserve *all* that travel by land or by water, *all* women labouring of child, *all* sick persons, and young children; and to show thy pity upon *all* prisoners and captives";
- "to defend, and provide for, the fatherless children, and widows, and *all* that are desolate and oppressed";
- "to forgive our enemies, persecutors, slanderers, and to turn their hearts";

• indeed, "to have mercy upon" nothing short of "all men," and what's more, "to give and preserve to our use the kindly fruits of the earth, so as in due time we may enjoy them."[14]

These are not inwardly curved prayers but prayers bent outward by the word of God, seeking God's mercy, peace, justice, and life for all tribes and tongues and for the ends of the earth. We have abundant scriptural exhortation, and ample historic precedent,[15] to prod us toward liberally populating our prayers with priestly intercession for the nations. Indeed, this is part of what it means to be an outpost of the City of God: it means being "a royal priesthood" and a "holy nation" (1 Pet. 2:9) set apart from the kingdoms of the world, a people whose first responsibility among those kingdoms is to make priestly intercession for their good.

And the Lord hears, weighs, and answers such intercessions. It is not just that our Father stores the prayers of the saints on the heavenly altar, awaiting the day when he will pour them out on the earth (Rev. 8:3–5; see chap. 2 above). It is also that God's constant sustaining mercy and common grace to one and all is in answer to the prayers of the saints lifted up every Lord's Day in churches across the globe, and every day in the practices of individual "prayer warriors" and communities engaged in daily prayer. To recall a point made earlier, it can *seem* to us that God will give spring rains regardless of whether we pray or not. But that doesn't mean that the coming of rain is not a *gift* of God and, what's more, an *answer* to the cries of his children. Even if *we* don't voice such a prayer regularly, the church global, in many different places and times, is not silenced. While King Saul silently slept, David was committed

14 "The Litany," Book of Common Prayer (1662), emphasis added.
15 See, further, Old, *Leading in Prayer*, 177–81.

in song and supplication to "awaken the dawn" (Ps. 57:8; cf. 108:2). What if that were more than just a fancy equivalent to the prosaic proposition "I will get up early to pray"?[16] What if the sun also rises, even upon the likes of King Saul (cf. Matt. 5:45), because God answers the praise and prayer of the people made righteous in Christ?[17] What a weighty calling and privilege the City of God has, to lift up priestly intercession for the world!

Voicing Creation's Praise

But there is another way in which the City of God wields its civic speech to minister as priests in the world. In commenting on Saint Peter's identification of the church as a "royal priesthood" in 1 Peter 2:9–10, George R. Beasley-Murray notes that as a priesthood, the church is "called to offer sacrifices of praise for the whole creation in virtue of the one great sacrifice of Christ."[18] In Christ, empowered by his Spirit, our language voiced in praise of God can be representative "for the whole creation." The City of God is that people who with speech (and with much more) mediate the creation's praise of the Creator.

According to David in Psalm 19, "the heavens *declare* the glory of God," "the sky above *proclaims* his handiwork," and "day to day pours out *speech*" (vv. 1–2). Yet David seems to recant with his very next breath:

16 Equally, it is a misstep to read "dawn" (שַׁחַר) adverbially, as the LXX does (ὄρθρου); rather, "dawn" in Ps. 57:8 is the direct object of the *hiphil* אָעִירָה. The LXX seems to have had an undue influence on many early Christian interpreters (e.g., Augustine). But early Jewish interpretation, as reflected in Midrash Psalms, is correct in its insistence: "David said: 'I will awake the dawn, the dawn shall not awake me'" (*The Midrash on the Psalms*, 2 vols., trans. William G. Braude, YJS 13 [New Haven, CT: Yale University Press, 1959], 1:501–2).

17 This possibility was first suggested to me by Peter Leithart.

18 G. R. Beasley-Murray, *The General Epistles: James, 1 Peter, Jude, 2 Peter* (London: Lutterworth; New York: Abingdon, 1965), 60–61.

There is no speech, nor are there words;
Their voice is not heard. (v. 3 NASB)

What do we make of this apparent contradiction? It may be that the NASB exhibits a translational infelicity,[19] but I think rather that the solution comes to light when we take into consideration the priestly and verbal vocation of the people of God. The creation's proclamation is meant to be heard, but it will only be heard intelligibly when we human creatures, who have tongues and voices and the word of God to guide us (note how the second half of Ps. 19 zeroes in on the gift of the law), put into truthful words what the heavens would declare. The heavens exist to declare God's glory, though without audible speech. Similarly, the beasts of the earth exist to revel in the provision of their King, though their reveling sounds forth in no words (see, e.g., Ps. 104:10–11, 14, 21, 27). The mountains and hills exist to sing for joy to the Lord, but of course their music is not accompanied by lyrical articulation joyfully naming God as the Creator (see Ps. 98:8; cf. 1 Chron. 16:33; Pss. 65:13; 96:12).[20] "Even the birds as they rise in the morning," Tertullian observes with wonder, "wing their way up to heaven, and make an outstretched cross with their wings in place of hands, and utter something that seems a prayer."[21] It

---

19 There are dissenters to the NASB rendering of Ps. 19:3; see, e.g., ESV; NIV; John Goldingay, *Psalms 1–41*, BCOT (Grand Rapids, MI: Baker, 2006), 288. But בְּלִי, introducing v. 3b, might in poetry be expected to be a simple negative adverb parallel to אֵין (see Bruce K. Waltke and M. O'Connor, *An Introduction to Biblical Hebrew Syntax* [Winona Lake, IN: Eisenbrauns, 1990], 660n58).

20 For a helpful table of over fifty Old Testament texts referring to nature's praise of God (mostly from Psalms and Isaiah), see Terence E. Fretheim, *God and World in the Old Testament: A Relational Theology of Creation* (Nashville: Abingdon, 2005), 267–68.

21 Tertullian, *Concerning Prayer*, in *Tertullian's Treatises: Concerning Prayer, Concerning Baptism*, trans. Alexander Souter (London: SPCK, 1919), 45 (§29).

seems a prayer. But the "prayer" of birds can be translated into words, and the "prayers" of the trees and the mountains can be rendered audible and intelligible, when human voices express the glory of the Creator on the rest of creation's behalf.

Our priestly identity and responsibility involve, in Jeremy Begbie's words, "a double movement."

> *On behalf of God*, as God's image bearers, humans are to mediate the presence of God *to the world* and in the world, representing his wise and loving rule. But this is so that *on behalf of creation* humans may gather and focus creation's worship, offering it back *to God*, voicing creation's praise.[22]

This, too, is part of the life of prayer. When we wield our words for the cosmic call to worship, "All creatures of our God and King, lift up your voice and with us sing!"; when we respond to the beauty and grandeur of heavenly bodies by verbally praising the wisdom and power and glory of the Creator of sun, moon, and stars; when we pray with the Book of Common Prayer for the preservation of "the kindly fruits of the earth"—when our prayer life enfolds nothing less than all creation, we are fulfilling a crucial part of our calling as priestly citizens of the City of God. We are fulfilling a crucial role that language was meant to play in God's world. We are joining, and bringing to verbal realization,

---

22 Jeremy S. Begbie, *Resounding Truth: Christian Wisdom in the World of Music* (Grand Rapids, MI: Baker, 2007), 203, emphasis original. Cf. Alexander Schmemann, *For the Life of the World: Sacraments and Orthodoxy*, rev. and exp. ed. (Crestwood, NY: St. Vladimir's Seminary Press, 1997), 14–16. See Begbie, *Resounding Truth*, 344n65, for a response to critics of the supposed hubris of thinking the nonhuman creation needs our priestly mediation; cf. Christopher J. H. Wright, *The Mission of God: Unlocking the Bible's Grand Narrative* (Downers Grove, IL: InterVarsity Press, 2006), 332.

the exuberant praise the rest of creation renders to the worthy Creator.[23] We are demonstrating the wondrous, indeed cosmic, expansiveness of the life of prayer.

———

Almighty God, Creator of heaven and earth . . . since you desire to rule us also in this life by the hand of our government, your servants, we ask you, who have their hearts in your hand: may you grant grace and unity to all of them. . . . Grant, that they may order their whole rule in such a way, that our Lord Jesus Christ, to whom you have given all power in heaven and on earth, may reign over them and their subjects, so that the poor people, who are the creatures of your hand and the sheep of your fold, for whom the Lord Jesus has also shed his blood, may be ruled in all holiness and righteousness; and that also we may render them all due honor and loyalty for your sake, and lead an honorable, peaceful and Christian life under them. Grant also your blessing and benediction for the fruit of the earth, that by it we may know you as a Father and fountain of all mercy and good things. Moreover, we implore you not only for ourselves, but also for all men in the whole world. . . . Comfort and strengthen all the poor, imprisoned, sick, the widows and orphans, pregnant

23 I am saying something more than that scriptural reference to "creation's praise" is a mere cipher or metaphor for human praise—as if all that these texts indicated were *human impressions* about the Creator's glory upon perceiving the nonhuman creation, and not also something about what the nonhuman creation itself is "groaning" for. The matter is fraught with difficulty. For a helpful introductory treatment, see Mark Harris, "'The Trees of the Field Shall Clap Their Hands' (Isaiah 55:12): What Does It Mean to Say That a Tree Praises God?," in *Knowing Creation: Perspectives from Theology, Philosophy, and Science*, ed. Andrew B. Torrance and Thomas H. McCall (Grand Rapids, MI: Zondervan, 2018), 287–304.

women and the distressed and anxious hearts. Grant them peace through our dear Lord Jesus Christ, who has given us this firm promise: "Truly, truly, I say to you, whatever you will ask of the Father in my name, he will give it to you."

PRAYER AFTER THE SERMON IN THE
PALATINE CHURCH ORDER (1563)[24]

---

24 In *Reformation Worship: Liturgies from the Past for the Present*, ed. Jonathan Gibson and Mark Earngey (Greensboro, NC: New Growth, 2018), 613.

Authoritative guides teach us to notice what otherwise we would not even see. They teach us, through word and through example, the unformalizable skill of appraisal. . . . Truth is personal; all truth is known in personal relationships. A teacher, not some theory, is the living link in the epistemological chain. In fact, truth is troth, *a pledge to engage in a mutually accountable and transforming relationship, a relationship forged of trust and faith in the face of unknowable risks.*

ESTHER L. MEEK
"Learning to See"

Provide thyself with a teacher and get thee a fellow[-disciple].

PIRKE ABOTH 1.6

9

Learning the Language

IN HARPER LEE'S CLASSIC *To Kill a Mockingbird,* Miss Caroline Fisher is surprised to discover on the first day of school that Jean Louise "Scout" Finch can already read. Out of healthy pedagogical conviction, and perhaps protection of professional turf, Miss Fisher counsels Scout to tell her father to end the home teaching lest it interfere with the school's curriculum. The precocious Scout, stunned, replies, "Teach me? . . . He hasn't taught me anything, Miss Caroline. Atticus ain't got time to teach me anything." Miss Fisher is incredulous. But Scout, reflecting to herself further on the matter, is all the more sure of it: "I never deliberately learned to read. . . . Reading was something that just came to me. . . . I could not remember when the lines above Atticus's moving finger separated into words."[1]

That's how the notion of "learning to pray" may strike many— to wit, we never *learned* per se. It just came "naturally," the way it comes to all true Christians. Just as Scout (so she thought) became a reader in an instantaneous, punctiliar conversion—apart from

1 Harper Lee, *To Kill a Mockingbird* (Philadelphia: Harper & Row, 1960; repr., New York: Warner, 1982), 21–22.

any process or means or instruction—so also Christians don't learn to pray so much as they "naturally," without process or means or instruction, pray from the womb of new birth. Isn't prayer, after all, simply being transparent, vulnerable, "real" with God? What could be more instinctive than "pouring out our hearts"?

There's an echo of truthfulness, and there are some healthy impulses, in such questions. Prayer is certainly a matter of being honest before God. And something is perverted in our understanding of both God and ourselves if we are convinced that we must pray perfectly, as it were—to have all our t's crossed and our i's dotted theologically—before God will listen to our prayers. "Anything large enough for a wish to light upon," George MacDonald comments, "is large enough to hang a prayer upon: the thought of Him to whom that prayer goes will purify and correct the desire."[2] While we might not locate the correcting, purifying power quite so much on *our thought* of God, nevertheless there's much to be said for simply "getting started" in the life of prayer wherever our hearts and understandings are, not dragging our feet and refusing to pray unless and until we have become the mythical "well-informed person."

Still, contrary to Scout's self-perception, she did indeed learn and was taught to read. And contrary to what might be common Christian self-perception, however odd and perhaps offensive it may sound to our modern and populist sensibilities, we too must learn and be taught to pray—to whom we pray, how to pray, what to pray, when to pray, why to pray. Truthful prayer isn't something that is natural or instinctual to any of the sons and daughters of Adam. And none of us will attain to *mature* prayer unless we are

2   George MacDonald, *Unspoken Sermons*, 2nd ser. (London: Longmans, Green, 1885), 90.

discipled. Or to put it in the terms we're using here in part 3, no one becomes fluent in the Christian's mother tongue without a process of language acquisition.

Knowing via Tradition and Ritual

When you look at the following, what do you see?

כְּכֶלֶב שָׁב עַל־קֵאוֹ
כְּסִיל שׁוֹנֶה בְאִוַּלְתּוֹ

Likely, the vast majority of us see a jumble of unintelligible scribbles, perhaps having a vague awareness that this is some non-Latin script representing words of a non-Germanic language. Perhaps a good number of readers recognize these as Hebrew words, though like the previous folks, they have no idea *what* Hebrew words. With some translational fumbling, I see above my life verse, Proverbs 26:11:

Like a dog that returns to his vomit
  is a fool who repeats his folly.

Still others see the same thing differently from me, not as signs to be decoded into English words—they see their mother tongue or a tongue in which they are fluent signified on paper; they don't have to translate but can simply read and receive. Here's the crucial question: How does one pass from one to the other? How does one come to *know* Hebrew?

In his wonderful and amazingly concise *Scripture's Knowing*, a popular level introduction to biblical epistemology, Dru Johnson addresses such questions, surveying some key biblical testimony about knowledge in and of God's world.[3] In the preceding paragraphs, I have imitated Johnson in drawing upon both Scout Finch's self-conception and the matter of learning Hebrew to illuminate how we, as God's human creatures, come to know things. Here I will try to distill the heart of Johnson's argument.[4] In a nutshell, we can say that the path for any of us to come to know Hebrew necessarily goes through, and even consists of, a lot of guided and tradition-based ritual practice. This means that we must heed *authorities* (teachers), who tell us what letters and sounds these signs signify, who guide us in how the language "works," and who lead us along a path that has proved again and again to result in fluency. Such authorities do many things when functioning properly, but two particular responsibilities are worth highlighting.

First, such authorities *pass on a tradition*. Just as the apostle Paul, an authority in the early church if ever there was one, was not coming up with his gospel on the spot but passing on a tradition he himself received (see, e.g., 1 Cor. 15:3; cf. 11:2; 2 Thess. 2:15; 3:6), proper authorities in learning a new language (teachers) are not coming up with the language on the spot. Rather, they are a part of and passing on a tradition of knowing, of etiquette, of habits and practices, of speaking and communicating in the language.

These considerations assume, second, that such authorities are committed to *leading us in doing certain things*, embodied and

---

3   Dru Johnson, *Scripture's Knowing: A Companion to Biblical Epistemology* (Eugene, OR: Cascade, 2015). In this slim volume, Johnson popularizes arguments from his monograph *Knowledge by Ritual: A Biblical Prolegomenon to Sacramental Theology*, JTISup 13 (Winona Lake, IN: Eisenbrauns, 2016).

4   James K. A. Smith offers what I take to be a complementary epistemological account in *Imagining the Kingdom: How Worship Works* (Grand Rapids, MI: Baker, 2013). Whereas Johnson directly roots his account in the biblical testimony, Smith makes his anthropological proposal using the resources of Continental philosophy.

repeated practices that will shape truthful knowers of Hebrew. They essentially command us, "Recite paradigms; take the time to memorize vocabulary; rehearse rules of etiquette called grammar and syntax; posture your body to write paradigms out over and over; drill by rote in pronunciation; submit to periodic exams." These are all rituals. I don't have to crack the code of any of them to have my vision shaped by them. In order to become a knower and speaker of Hebrew, I don't ever have to answer questions like "What does the ritual of writing paradigms *mean*?" and "What 'truth' does this ritual symbolize?" (In fact, I would probably never think to raise questions quite like these of this kind of ritual.) But I *do* need to enact the rituals identified by my teacher. And inevitably bound up with my actual enactment of those practices, I need to submit to my teacher, trusting his or her word that these rituals will enable me to "see"

כְּכֶלֶב שָׁב עַל־קֵאוֹ
כְּסִיל שׁוֹנֶה בְאִוַּלְתּוֹ

as more than unintelligible scribbles.

Interestingly, all readers see the exact same black marks against a white background in the preceding sentence. But some of us can, as it were, see *more* in these blotches than others; just as, to switch fields, some people can hear more in Bach's *St. John Passion* than others. Some of us see and hear the same things differently, see and hear more than others, because we are part of certain traditions and have submitted in hope to certain rituals of knowing. Some of us see and hear more than others because we have undergone a process of transformation, which includes engaging in a trusting dialogue with certain guides and teachers. As Kevin Vanhoozer has quipped, "It is difficult to learn or grow or be transformed when one is in dialogue only with oneself."[5] Anyone who has been transformed into a knower of Hebrew has necessarily submitted in trust, to some degree or another, to the word of proper authorities in a well-ordered tradition.

Of course, the tradition of Hebrew-knowing does not "automatically" produce Hebrew speakers. Neither do the rituals of learning Hebrew magically add some substance to our physical eyes or ears or brains to change our visual, auditory, and intellectual ability; they do not mechanically produce our teacher's favor; they do not earn the right to know Hebrew. But they may be rightly identified as part of the ordinary means for shaping human creatures into Hebrew-knowers.

We were designed to know via tradition and ritual, to mature through submitting to proper authorities. These are the kinds of things that are involved in learning and developing skill in speaking Hebrew. In fact, coming to know *anything at all* is a process of tradition and ritual practice, whether it be learning a scientific discipline,[6] learning the culinary arts, learning healthy and fruitful family togetherness, learning the full counsel of God as revealed in Scripture,[7] or learning the language of prayer and the skill of well-ordered life before the face of God.

---

5 Kevin J. Vanhoozer, "From Speech Acts to Scripture Acts: The Covenant of Discourse and the Discourse of the Covenant," in *After Pentecost: Language and Biblical Interpretation*, ed. Craig G. Bartholomew, Colin Greene, and Karl Möller (Cumbria, UK: Paternoster; Grand Rapids, MI: Zondervan, 2001), 40.

6 Johnson, *Scripture's Knowing*, 85–98; Johnson, *Knowledge by Ritual*, 120–32. See also and esp. Michael Polanyi, *Personal Knowledge: Towards a Post-Critical Philosophy* (Chicago: University of Chicago Press, 1962).

7 Contrary to distorted assumptions about the perspicuity of Scripture, wherein we need no instruction to understand the "clear" message contained throughout, the apostle Paul played a necessary, God-appointed role in proclaiming the whole counsel of God—a coun-

Language Learning in the City of God

Having taken that brief (and far too truncated) detour into a biblical epistemology, we can return to the main matter at hand: how does one learn the language of prayer? What is necessary to learn that language? I am persuaded that such learning requires, at a general level, being guided by proper authorities through certain forms of ritual practice. But we can add some more specific activities and focuses by way of analogy to learning foreign languages such as Spanish, French, and German. If we would seek to learn such languages and, indeed, pursue fluency in them, what would we need? Here is a sampling:

1. We need to memorize vocabulary and the rules of grammar and syntax.
2. We need teachers to come alongside us, teachers whom we trust and submit to, and who can explain the vocabulary and rules and dynamics of everyday discourse, but who will *also* lead us in speaking actual sentences, giving us, like a director of a play,[8] cues for saying our lines: "Say with me, 'Où se trouvent les toilettes?'"

---

sel revealed in Scripture, to be sure—to the Ephesian church (see Acts 20:27). Thus, the Westminster Confession fittingly notes that the clear message of Scripture, necessary to be known for salvation, can be sufficiently understood "in a due use of the ordinary means" (1.7). As Augustine wryly noted long ago, those who most forcefully claim no need of human teachers, for being directly taught the things of God by the Spirit, tend ironically to be the ones most eager *to teach others* what they have received (see his preface to *On Christian Doctrine*, §8).

8 See Kevin J. Vanhoozer, *The Drama of Doctrine: A Canonical-Linguistic Approach to Christian Theology* (Louisville: Westminster John Knox, 2005), 447–49; cf. Vanhoozer, *Faith Speaking Understanding: Performing the Drama of Doctrine* (Louisville: Westminster John Knox, 2014), 146–47.

3. The preceding point implies that we need to actually *use* the language, to speak it (to be *led* in speaking it) and not just to think about it.

We can view such practical use, or on-the-ground practice, from several angles:

a. It is advantageous to use the language with several different kinds of conversation partners—teachers, yes, but also other native speakers who provide an everyday apprenticeship in the language; and other fellow learners with whom we can relate (and commiserate); and acquaintances serendipitously encountered; and persons with whom we enjoy great intimacy.

b. Growth unto fluency is especially the fruit of language use in a variety of contexts—some anticipated, but also and especially many unanticipated; some formally set up for learning and cultivating proficiency, but also other "in the wild" opportunities to speak the language.

c. Best of all is when we can relocate to places where the language is spoken as the mother tongue, and where the culture, history, landscape, and lived patterns make sense of and sustain the language. For example, if I want to become fluent in German, it is best to dwell in Deutschland for a while.

If learning to pray wisely, knowledgeably, fervently, and perseveringly may, indeed, be likened to learning and becoming fluent in a foreign language, then consider how these aspects of foreign-language learning help us to think about learning and becoming fluent in the language that is prayer.

1. Think of *Scripture* as a kind of language book. Scripture provides vocabulary. That is, it gives us the words and meanings needed to wield words in prayer well—to name God as Father, Son, and Spirit in our invocation; to name Jesus as God's only Son and our Savior and King, the one through whom and in whose name we pray; to name ourselves as God's creatures, who benefit from his everyday sustaining provision of bread, as servants who exist for his name's sake and his kingdom, as sinners in need of his redeeming and renewing work in Christ. Such vocabulary informs our supplications.

Scripture also teaches us the grammar and syntax, as it were, of godly speech, rules for fitting discourse. Grammatically, the language of prayer is the language of address and the language of relational intimacy, uttered not in the manner of "Matthew 6:11 teaches us that our daily bread comes from the Father" but thus: "Our Father, give us today our daily bread." Syntactically, prayers should include things such as grounding clauses (reasons) stating why God should act on our supplications (e.g., for his name's sake, for the resounding of thanksgiving to him, for the growth of his kingdom, for the rescue of the helpless and oppressed).

Scripture presents certain rhythms or patterns for the practice of prayer (consider, e.g., the significance of the psalmist's commitment to praising God "seven times" throughout the day in Ps. 119:164; see, further, part 4 below). Scripture even provides practice exercises, model prayers for us to take upon our lips as a needful part of learning the language (as we considered esp. in chap. 5 above).

2. Think of *pastors* as language teachers whose job it is to deepen understanding of the text and the language. Indeed, arguably the "primary educational task" of a pastor is "to teach people to pray."[9]

---

9 Eugene H. Peterson, *The Contemplative Pastor: Returning to the Art of Spiritual Direction* (Dallas: Word, 1989), 96.

It is no accident that most historic catechisms, typically divided into three or four major parts, devote one of those parts to instruction through the Lord's Prayer. At the heart of pastoral responsibility is the duty to shepherd God's people in the language that is answering speech. God provides pastors to help clarify vocabulary, teach and answer specific questions about grammar and syntax (i.e., doctrine), and offer input concerning the challenges of speaking the language of prayer "in the wild" (i.e., in everyday need and responsibility).

But pastors also do another puzzling, and for some a troublingly tyrannical, thing as language teachers. They *tell us to pray with them*—for example, when we are gathered in the liturgical assembly: "Let us pray as our Lord has taught us, saying together . . ." Answering speech is not self-initiated, and in more than one way. It is responsively attentive to the God who first addresses us. But it is also surprisingly responsive, for the sake of discipleship, to prompts from our teachers in prayer and the tradition of praying of which we are a part. Eugene Peterson explains:

> We learn to pray by being led in prayer. We commonly think of prayer as what we do out of our own needs and on our own initiative. . . . But in a liturgy we do not take the initiative; it is not our experience that precipitates prayer. Someone stands in front of us and says, "Let us pray." We don't start it; someone else starts it, and we fall into step behind or alongside. Our egos are no longer front and center. . . . We pray not when we feel like it but when someone, the pastor, the priest, the "choirmaster"! says, "Let us pray." We lose nothing of our emotions except their tyranny.[10]

10 Eugene H. Peterson, *Answering God: The Psalms as Tools for Prayer* (San Francisco: Harper & Row, 1989), 86–87.

This, too, is the pastor fulfilling the responsibility of a language teacher. For learning a language requires not just knowledge *about* the language but also guided language *usage*. And this implies that learning a language requires a larger context for learning, a language school or society of speaking where such guidance can be found and takes place, where one can engage in certain linguistic practices, where one is immersed in a larger tradition of language speaking.

3. Therefore, think finally of *the church* as a tradition of linguistic sensibilities and a society of cultural rituals that provides the necessary context and exercise for learning the language of prayer and using the language well.

a. The church includes pastor-teachers, but it also includes all the saints, a many-colored kingdom of diverse experiences. We are blessed in the church to find battle-tested "prayer warriors"—some living in our midst, many dead but whose voices can still be heard—who are eager to apprentice us in the language. We find many others who are chunking it along with us, with whom we can relate and sympathize and experience mutual encouragement. And many other varieties of relationships and serendipitous encounters in the life of the church offer so many opportunities for growth in language fluency: the church is not just good teachers and I, nor just my handpicked cronies and I, nor just people I know and agree with, but also a whole lot of other people I didn't expect (and perhaps would have preferred *not*) to find here. (Serendipitous encounters are among the key things conspicuously absent in most of what goes by the name of "online church" and "Zoom community.") Learning to pray with them is also part of the life of the church. Learning to pray with them is also part of learning to pray.

b. The life of the church implicates us in a variety of prayerful engagements. In the church's gathering for Lord's Day liturgy, we the people of God can get practice in prayer, can experience the repetition and rote (in the best senses of the terms) necessary to learn anything foreign to us. Such practice includes taking the Psalms and other set prayers (whether in prose form or in lyrical form set to music)[11] upon our lips corporately. And it involves building "muscle memory" about the dialogical rhythm of life with our covenantal Lord (*call to worship* leads to *psalms of praise*; *reading of the law* leads to *confession of sin*; *proclamation of the word* leads to *confession of faith*, etc.). At its best, corporate worship is a guiding and directing of our speech in the proper forms and patterns of answering the God who addresses us. It is the best of language schools,[12] which teaches us the language of prayer chiefly by actually having us address God rather than simply "teaching about" prayer and helping us "think rightly about" God. For example, "Come, Thou fount of every blessing" is not only or fundamentally a truth to think upon but a word of personal address. It is a vocative word, a speech act that does not chiefly teach or remind us about truth but addresses God.

11 If the notion of "set prayers" is anathema to you, take a moment to consider what's going on when the lowest of low-church assemblies joins together *with one voice* to sound forth the latest praise chorus that tells God how much we love him or trust him or yearn for his glory. These are often beautiful enactments, in no small part because the congregation is being led to pray as one. The words of such a song form a prayer, one we did not spontaneously come up with as individuals, one that we are—from the "top down," as it were—compelled to join everyone else in praying. It may be couched in rhyme, with contemporary musical accompaniment, but it's as much a set prayer as anything found in a service book, though perhaps less Scripture-saturated and Scripture-responsive. Unfortunately, beyond these set prayers in disguise, low-church assemblies generally "give congregants almost no help" in praying wisely ordered, time-tested, biblically responsive prayers (Timothy Keller, *Prayer: Experiencing Awe and Intimacy with God* [New York: Dutton, 2014], 246). For a recent thoughtful proposal on how modern worship songs might contribute to a rich tapestry of liturgical prayer, see Andy Crouch, "Antiphons. We've Been Singing Antiphons," *Andy Crouch* (blog), September 21, 2022, https://andy-crouch.com/articles/antiphons.

12 See also Peter J. Leithart, *Against Christianity* (Moscow, ID: Canon, 2003), 73; Thomas G. Long, *Testimony: Talking Ourselves into Being Christian* (San Francisco: Jossey-Bass, 2004), passim, e.g., at 32, 54–57.

But the church is not only the church in its gathering. It is equally the church in its *sending* into the world for vocational labor from Monday to Saturday. Here, too, the church has ample opportunity for the practice of prayer, understood now not as pedagogical exercise but as practical enactment in contrast to mere theory. "In the wild," we find many on-the-ground reasons for thanksgiving, confession, supplication, lamentation, and praise. For all of our life "in the wild" is lived out before the God who grants us gifts warranting our thanksgiving, and whose way we frequently offend, and whose help we constantly need, and whose purposes seem oh-so long in coming to fruition, and whose glory fills the whole earth. We find that what we've practiced during our liturgical gathering expands into the rest of our lives. For the God with whom we engage in our liturgical gathering is present and active outside it, and the same drama we enact liturgically in miniature in the sanctuary is performed in all the places to which we are called. While engaged in the missional labors to which we are sent, we may find that we need further help, further formation and discipleship, further instruction in the language, and so gain newfound appreciation for the language school that is corporate worship. At the same time, we may find that as God answers prayers—both corporate and individual—by empowering our vocational labors in the world for Christ's glory and the good of our neighbors, we have increased reason and excitement and practical preparation for festive celebration, for a banquet at the table of the King. That is, we may discover that the life of prayer from Monday to Saturday is not separate from but of a piece with and flows into our prayerful praise in each celebratory Lord's Day gathering.

c. In the preceding points, we have some seeds for growing a much more robust and responsible ecclesiology than may be common today. The church is, indeed, best understood to be a kind of foreign land where a foreign tongue is voiced in the world. Or, as I suggested in the last chapter, the church is an outpost of the City of God among the cities of the earth. In this outpost, this peculiar political body, we hear the Christian mother tongue regularly spoken. We get practice and have regular responsibility in speaking it. We are immersed and discipled in the history and the culture, the rituals and the rhythms, the contexts and the engagements that sustain the language and help make sense of it. If we would pray, if we would learn to pray, if we would become fluent in our mother tongue, then let us devote ourselves to the life of the church, the living temple of the living God, which is called to be nothing less than a house of prayer for all nations. Discovering our lives caught up in the rhythms of the church, we may find that what at first struck us as gibberish becomes surprisingly the truest language of the heart.

———

O Thou Guide unto wisdom, Bestower of prudence, Instructor of the foolish, and Defender of the poor: establish and grant understanding unto my heart, O Master. Grant me speech, O Word of the Father; for behold, I shall not keep my lips from crying unto Thee: Have mercy, O Merciful One, on me who have fallen.

PRAYER FOR THE SUNDAY OF FORGIVENESS
COMMEMORATING ADAM'S EXILE FROM PARADISE[13]

---

13 From the Triodion in *A Prayerbook for Orthodox Christians*, 2nd ed. (Boston, MA: Holy Transfiguration Monastery, 2014), 161–62.

PART 4

RHYTHMS

With one accord, they lifted a voice to God and said,
"O Lord, you are the one who made the heaven and
the earth and the sea and all things in them."

ACTS 4:24 (MY TRANS.)

The paradigmatic prayer is not solitary but in community.
The fundamental biblical context is worship. . . . If
somebody comes to me and says, "Teach me how to pray," I
say, "Be at this church at nine o'clock on Sunday morning."
That's where you learn how to pray. Of course, prayer is
continued and has alternate forms when you're by yourself.
But the American experience has the order reversed. In
the long history of Christian spirituality, community
prayer is most important, then individual prayer.

EUGENE H. PETERSON
The Contemplative Pastor

Much of our ability to put faith into words outside of
church depends . . . on seeing connections between "Sunday
morning" and "Saturday night," between the words we use
in worship and the words we speak the rest of the week.

THOMAS G. LONG
Testimony

10

The Weekly Rhythm of Prayer

YOUR PRAYER LIFE IS BETTER THAN YOU THINK. That's what
I sometimes say to Christians who express to me guilt or discouragement about the state of their prayers. Your prayer life is better
than you think . . . *if you are faithfully present with the gathered body
for Lord's Day worship.* The condition is crucial, reflecting certain
convictions about Christian identity and ecclesiology. To explain,
let's travel to Germany.

A Day in the Life Together

As Adolf Hitler's dark star was rising over Europe, Dietrich Bonhoeffer was developing a vision for "a new kind of monasticism" as
a communal, liturgical training ground for pastors.[1] In late spring
of 1935, he got to translate vision into action: Bonhoeffer was
invited by the Confessing Church to open an "illegal" seminary at
Finkenwalde, where for two years, he taught, counseled, engaged
in manual labor, and shared all things with some twenty ordinands
at a time. The seminary was a demanding program in which, as

---

1   See, further, Eric Metaxas, *Bonhoeffer: Pastor, Martyr, Prophet, Spy* (Nashville: Thomas Nelson,
    2010), 246–60.

Bonhoeffer boasted, "academic and practical work are combined splendidly."[2] Life was highly regimented, echoing monastic traditions: forty-five minute prayer services bookended each day, with personal Scripture meditation, theological/exegetical/dogmatic study, confession of sin, various chores (e.g., kitchen work, building projects), and shared meals scheduled in between. There was also no shortage of games, laughter, and musical joy.[3] Some of the daily patterns at the renegade seminary have been recorded in Bonhoeffer's brief but much celebrated book *Life Together*, first published in 1939.

My edition of *Life Together* comes with publisher's copy on the cover touting it as "the classic exploration of faith in community." That word "community" is important but slippery. Sometimes it amounts to little more than a shorthand for "group in which camaraderie is enjoyed" or "group that I agree with" (as in, "I'm looking for good community"). Frequently community is presented as something an individual *stands apart from* until personal volition intervenes (hence, "Are you a part of a community?"). Here the lone, autonomous "I" may decide to associate with others to form a "we." I dare say that this parallels more or less exactly the dominant functional ecclesiology of many churchgoers today: First, there is "I, the individual believer." Then, should this "I" choose to find one, there are churches to join, perhaps because "I" desire "good community," or "good teaching," or music that "resonates with me," or "like-minded" and "serious" Christians to

2 Letter to Karl Barth, September 19, 1936, in *A Testament to Freedom: The Essential Writings of Dietrich Bonhoeffer*, ed. Geffrey B. Kelly and F. Burton Nelson, rev. ed. (New York: HarperOne, 1995), 431, quoted in Metaxas, *Bonhoeffer*, 270.
3 See Metaxas, *Bonhoeffer*, 267; and William Samson, "The Finkenwalde Project," in *Monasticism Old and New*, ed. Robert B. Kruschwitz, Christian Reflection 37 (Waco, TX: Center for Christian Ethics at Baylor University, 2010), 21–22.

help my personal growth; or because "I" want to "use my spiritual gifts," or simply to obey biblical commands about church participation. In other words, church is part of Christian *responsibility* only and not, first, part of Christian *identity*. Common though this sensibility may be, it is decidedly not what Bonhoeffer is about in *Life Together*.

> You are called into the community of faith; the call was not meant for you alone. You carry your cross, you struggle, and you pray *in the community of faith, the community of those who are called*. You are not alone even when you die, and on the day of judgment you will be only one member of the great community of faith of Jesus Christ. If you neglect the community of other Christians, you reject the call of Jesus Christ.[4]

For the Christian, community is not an optional add-on to self-standing individual existence. Rather, it is already, before our personal decision to join it, bound up with our identity in Christ. It is not only that I in Christ can "find good community" in church but also that I in Christ am perforce a community member. Whether I choose to "go to church" or not, whether I feel "plugged in" or not, if I am united to Christ the head, then I am part of his body. The church is, then, not an elective aid to the Christian's *well-being* but intrinsic to the Christian's *being*.

The notion that we are thrown into community prior to our individual choosing is deeply counterintuitive to reigning sensibilities, both outside *and* inside the church. The assertion that "community prayer is most important, then individual prayer,"

---

4   Dietrich Bonhoeffer, *Life Together*, Dietrich Bonhoeffer Works, Reader's Edition (Minneapolis, MN: Fortress, 2015), 56, emphasis added.

and that the best place to learn the latter is in the former, may leave many scratching their heads. But that our individuality flows not only into but also from corporate life is not, in itself, hard to explain as a fitting description of human nature. For example, at an obvious level, no individual can possibly *exist* except as the fruit of a union of persons (a biological mother and father) to whom we are necessarily related and with whom we are ever identified. Our individuality only is and makes sense as part of that small community, at least. It's no less true for those in Christ. As Saint Paul declares, we are "individually members one of another" (Rom. 12:5). Our individuality in Christ is understandable and realized *as* members of his body.[5] Bonhoeffer wrote *Life Together* out of this same conviction—the life of the community, the life of the church, is intrinsic to Christian identity.

More than that, I suggest that *Life Together* represents a wise pedagogy in harmony with this conviction. To demonstrate this, we can point out a feature of the structure of *Life Together* that is as easy to spot as it is to ignore. After an important introductory chapter setting forth the theme of Christian community, Bonhoeffer goes on to survey a typical day at Finkenwalde, beginning with a chapter entitled "The Day with Others," then moving to a chapter entitled "The Day Alone." The chapter ordering might go largely unnoticed; and when it is pointed out, we might think it materially insignificant. But, arguably, Bonhoeffer means for the structure of the day to be instructive. By beginning with practical communion in the body (the day together), our individuality (the day alone) is contextualized so that it makes most sense and can be most fruitful. At Finkenwalde, common worship preceded and

5   For Paul's point in agricultural terms, see Wendell Berry, "Men and Women in Search of Common Ground," *Sunstone*, July 1987, 9.

provided coordinates for reverent life alone before God. Common prayer was part of the single cloth of the individual Christian's life of prayer, and it also was necessarily, given the structure of the day, the framework and leading guide for private prayer.

A Week in the Life of Prayer

To be sure, Bonhoeffer and friends had a distinct advantage: they lived communally. From their first waking moment, they were together. They had to make deliberate moves to pursue God in "the day alone." The practical shape of life at Finkenwalde embodied, and therefore reinforced, the theological truth that life individually flows from, is part of the fabric of, and is formed by life together. This is nearly opposite to our lived experience today: most of us wake up in our bedrooms alone; we eat breakfast and do "morning devotions" in isolation; only much later, should we so decide, do we join others for fellowship and worship. As a result, it is hard for many Christians to imagine that community isn't an optional aid to personal (or nuclear family) betterment but the abiding context of our being. But this does not mean the pedagogical logic of *Life Together* cannot be reproduced in our lives. It can and it must.

In fact, the formative potential of common-prayer-flowing-into-individual-prayer may already be lurking in the patterns of our lives. We often envision "the Christian life" in such a manner that larger lived *patterns* go unnoticed. That is, we imagine the stuff of the Christian life to be mainly or mostly thoughts, feelings, belief systems, and individual moments in which we deliberate, make decisions, and generally are mindful of God or not. But the Christian *life* is not summed up in any one of these but enfolds them all in a lived history. No life, Christian or otherwise, is just moment-by-moment decision and crisis, each moment disconnected from the others, each meaningful or evaluated separately. It is not the case that Monday, Thursday, Sunday, and all days are the same, so that we need only focus on the general call for decision: "Choose ye this day life!" Choosing life and receiving God's grace practically take different specific forms from day to day. Being created as temporal and "storied" creatures, we inhabit and enact days differently, according to different opportunities, locations, seasons, and responsibilities. Thus, the Christian life is not best considered in small, momentary chunks. It is better assessed in terms of temporal progressions, trajectories, and lived patterns and rhythms. The Christian life is *the whole rhythm of being gathered and being sent*, of corporate worship together in the sanctuary and personal vocational neighbor-love in our towns, of common prayer and private prayer.[6]

To specify further, this rhythm of gathering and sending is played out weekly, at least.[7] It is a rhythm, if we "tell time" according to Scripture, that *begins* on Sunday, the first day of the week. The first day of the week is theologically significant. Mary Magdalene visited the empty tomb on "the first day of the week," John 20:1 tells us. A few paragraphs later, John repeats himself word for word: the disciples gathered "on the evening of that day, *the first day of the week*" (John 20:19). The narrator doesn't strictly need to restate those italicized words, since he already identified the day in verse 1. The comment is an unnecessary interruption in the telling.

---

6 Cf. R. Paul Stevens, *The Other Six Days: Vocation, Work, and Ministry in Biblical Perspective* (Grand Rapids, MI: Eerdmans, 1999), 8; Nicholas Wolterstorff, *Until Justice and Peace Embrace* (Grand Rapids, MI: Eerdmans, 1983), 146–61; D. A. Carson, "Worship under the Word," in *Worship by the Book*, ed. D. A. Carson (Grand Rapids, MI: Zondervan, 2002), 43–44.

7 Elsewhere, I have argued for the value of theologically attuned annual patterns as well; see Daniel J. Brendsel, "A Tale of Two Calendars: Calendars, Compassion, Liturgical Formation, and the Presence of the Spirit," *BET* 3, no. 1 (2016): 15–43.

Or rather, John is flagging something. What's so significant about it being the first day? In the beginning, the first day, day one, was the day of creation, the day when light first dawned on a newborn world (Gen. 1:3–5). John underlines "the first day of the week" to help us recognize the resurrection account for what it is—the beginning of a new creation bathed in the light of the world, with a new and true gardener raised from the dust (see John 20:15; cf. Gen. 2:15) and a new Spirit-inbreathed humanity (John 20:22; cf. Gen. 2:7) given a new commission (John 20:21; cf. Gen. 1:28).[8] The first day of the week is a new day one.

Every week the church reenacts this drama, even enters it as characters. Each new week begins (we might say, is *created*) on Sunday, the day of resurrection, as Christ's people meet with their risen Lord to be covenantally renewed through the word of God and covenantal signs. And every Lord's Day service ends properly with a *sending* into the world on mission till Christ returns—which is to say, the necessary sequel to the Lord's Day is Monday through Saturday. Sunday is to Monday through Saturday as chapter 1 is to chapters 2–7 in the story of new creational life and mission. Monday through Saturday are not rightly understood as detached from their theological beginning in the Lord's Day; rather, they are more clearly seen for what they are meant to be in the new creational light of the Lord's Day.[9]

The twofold point we have been building up to is this: the Christian life is a matter of weekly rhythms, and those weekly rhythms properly *begin* on the Lord's Day in corporate worship.

8   See also Edward W. Klink III, *John*, ZECNT 4 (Grand Rapids, MI: Zondervan, 2016), 828–29; and esp. Jeannine K. Brown, "Creation's Renewal in the Gospel of John," *CBQ* 72, no. 2 (2010): 283–84.

9   Cf. Long, *Testimony*, 40–43.

With some modulation, we can see that Bonhoeffer's daily practice and pedagogy of the day together flowing into the day alone has an analogue in the shape of our lives at a weekly level: the beginning of the week together flows into, and has formative potential for, the rest of the week "alone." Stated specifically with respect to prayer: the life of prayer (the *life* of prayer, not merely this or that individual prayer) is a patterned and rhythmic life, and that rhythm properly *begins* in common prayer. When I tell people, "Your prayer life is better than you think if you are faithfully present at and attentively participating in Lord's Day services of the church," I mean that (1) the common prayer of the gathered church is not icing on the cake of the individual's prayer life but part of the cake, and (2) more than one equal part among many, the common prayer of the church is the theological launching pad and a ready-made training ground for growing personally in the life of prayer.[10]

Corporate Worship as Dialogue with God

I have spent some time trying to reshape our imaginations so that we conceive of our lives not only on the daily level but also and especially on the weekly level. This has been with a view to helping us appreciate that our corporate engagements in prayer every Sunday are not to be segregated from our individual prayer lives; rather, common prayer is, to put it somewhat provocatively, something of the doorway to our prayer closets. In this final section, I want to point out that the Lord's Day covenant assembly *is all about prayer*, and not just because what we typically think of as prayers get said at discrete points in the worship service.

10 Cf. Robert Taft, *The Liturgy of the Hours in East and West: The Origins of the Divine Office and Its Meaning for Today*, 2nd rev. ed. (Collegeville, MN: Liturgical Press, 1993), 68.

The Lord Present at the Assembly

Here are some common assumptions about what Lord's Day worship is, all of which largely miss the mark: Lord's Day worship is an opportunity to fellowship with other believers and to be encouraged; or it is a meeting where spiritual gifts are exercised; or it is an outlet to express our emotions to God; or it is a "refueling station" for the week ahead; or it is a bunch of decorations, with varying degrees of artfulness, piled on top of what really matters, a lecture (in more polite discourse: it's an opportunity to get good teaching in the sermon). I don't doubt that all those things happen, or have the potential for happening. And I don't dispute that, in many respects, these are wonderful benefits enjoyed in and through corporate worship. I say that these assumptions about corporate worship miss the mark of what worship *is*, not because they are bad in themselves but because the focus of them all is on the benefit to us of worship. That is to focus on everything but the main thing.

Imagine the festive celebration of an ancient king's victory over enemies. How odd would it be for the king's attendants in that celebration to focus on what they might get out of it, on the ways in which they might be able to use it and capitalize on it, and not *first* on whether the king is duly honored by and pleased in assembly with his people! After the assembly, such people would well ask as "the decisive question," to use Nicholas Wolterstorff's language, not "What did I get out of it?" but "How did we do?"[11] We may be inclined to think that ancient royal attendants had much more practically on the line (i.e., their necks) than we do when we "go

11 Wolterstorff, *Until Justice and Peace Embrace*, 148.

to church." But we would be wrong in such an assumption (see 1 Cor. 11:27–32).

"How did we do?" when applied to a worship service is, of course, not immune to a slew of wretched diseases and disorders. But the question put to corporate worship does put in stark relief what worship *is*, which is otherwise easy to miss. We call it a worship *service* not because it is a service *to us* but because by it we render the service proper and due to the King. Liturgy is, etymologically, the *service of the people* (not *for* the people). Corporate worship is worshipful service and tribute, like that performed by the priests in the temple,[12] rendered to the divine King, who dwells among us and whose presence we enjoy.

The Lord is, indeed, present to meet us when we gather in covenant assembly on the Lord's Day. Better stated, it is Almighty God, present and active by his Spirit, who gathers us for a meeting and a meal with our risen King. There is gravity to this assembly because profound glory, that of the Creator and King of the cosmos, is present at it, and this is, ideally, something that even unbelieving visitors should sense: "God is really among you!" (1 Cor. 14:25). In this light, everything we say and sing, every thought we think, and all our "body language" in Lord's Day assembly is before our God, as our proper service and tribute to him. To put it in language that shows that worship is squarely in the orbit of prayer, corporate worship is a *dialogue* between the covenant Lord, who is present and speaks in the assembly, and his covenant people.

---

12 Though English translations almost always refer to a "grain offering" in Lev. 2:1, "tribute offering" is arguably a much better rendering of מִנְחָה. It is a word often used with reference to a present given to a leader/king by a subordinate or one who feels in a position of dependence and weakness (see, e.g., Gen. 32:13–15; 43:11; 1 Kings 10:25; also 2 Sam. 8:2, where the term is translated "tribute").

The Lord Answered with One Voice in the Assembly

It is important to clarify that we are especially concerned here with our corporate enactments and answers before God. The stuff of corporate worship involves us in a doing and saying *together*. It is a matter of collective speech or common praying. The Lord's Prayer is something that Jesus expects us to recite ("When you pray, *say* . . ."—Luke 11:2), and to do so together, not just individually ("*Our* Father in heaven . . ."—Matt. 6:9).[13] Our blessedness in Christ is "to live in such harmony with one another, . . . that together you may *with one voice* glorify the God and Father of our Lord Jesus Christ" (Rom. 15:5–6). In keeping with every scene of worship in the heavenly throne room from the book of Revelation, our corporate gatherings on earth are opportunities for us as one body, with one voice, to answer our covenant Lord.[14]

This is not to deny that we can and should pray individually "in" church, which Scot McKnight explains as happening "whenever an individual prays exactly and only what is on his or her heart."[15] But that by itself falls short of corporate worship, which is not just something we could do well enough alone but, for excitement's sake or other reasons, like to do with others around. *Corporate* worship is the covenant people's response with one voice to the God present among them. Participation in the gathered assembly on the Lord's Day invariably constrains us to pray not only "in" but especially "with" the church—praying *at the same time* (a fixed hour), praying

---

13 See esp. Cyprian, *De dominica oratione* 8.

14 For the preceding biblical observations, see Scot McKnight, *Praying with the Church: Following Jesus Daily, Hourly, Today* (Brewster, MA: Paraclete, 2006), 5, 62–63.

15 McKnight, *Praying with the Church*, 1.

in the same place (the sanctuary), praying *the same words* (set prayers). It all amounts to corporate responsiveness to the Lord who addresses us. It's dialogue. Through Scripture publicly read (1 Tim. 4:13) and through authorized heralds (i.e., ordained ministers), God speaks his initiating word; and through psalms and hymns and songs, through set prayers and representative spontaneous prayers, through communicative bodily acts (e.g., kneeling, raising hands, eating bread and drinking wine), the assembly as one body renders to God their answering speech. At its best, worship is the drama of the life of prayer enacted in and as a covenant assembly.

Liturgy as Common Answering Speech

Consider the "order" of a typical service of worship in the Reformed tradition (and roughly discernible in other creedal traditions). When we get to church on the Lord's Day, in almost all churches in all times and places, the first words voiced are a summons, such as,

> Oh come, let us worship and bow down;
> let us kneel before the LORD, our Maker! (Ps. 95:6)

The worship service opens with a public invitation to use our voices and bodies to worship God. We call this a call to worship. It is *God's* word of address to his gathered people, his invitation verbalized (not a private thought or a text read silently) by an appointed minister set apart to serve as God's mouthpiece. This call of God is what gets worship going, properly speaking. Every Sunday, at the outset, we are "created" by God's sovereign, initiating word.

God's word is not data to compute and/or store away in our minds. As a personal address, it anticipates a personal word of response. The gathered people fittingly respond to the call to worship with answering (and very frequently sung or chanted) speech—psalms, hymns, and spiritual songs of praise to our God and King. One of the oldest (from the fourth century or earlier) and continuously used opening responses of praise is the Gloria Patri:

Glory be to the Father, and to the Son, and to the Holy Spirit;
as it was in the beginning, is now, and ever shall be,
world without end. Amen.

What often follows the people's initial response of praise is a prayer of invocation, calling upon the name of the Lord to come and help the congregation in this gathering. Then the minister will call the flock to confession of sin: "Let us confess our sins before God and one another," perhaps adding a scriptural sentence explaining the gospel confidence with which we can boldly approach God's throne of mercy: "If we confess our sins, he is faithful and just to forgive us our sins and to cleanse us from all unrighteousness" (1 John 1:9). To this call the congregation responds with a public confession, whether representatively in the person of the pastor, or corporately, reciting, for example, a traditional confession or a penitential psalm:

Have mercy on me, O God
    according to your steadfast love;
according to your abundant mercy
    blot out my transgressions.

Wash me thoroughly from my iniquity,
  and cleanse me from my sin!

For I know my transgressions,
  and my sin is ever before me. . . .

Create in me a clean heart, O God,
  and renew a right spirit within me. (Ps. 51:1–3, 10)

What is the Lord's just response to those who confess their sins? As 1 John 1:9 assures us, it is nothing less than a glad, glorious, and unhesitatingly swift word of forgiveness in the crucified and risen Christ—the preceding "within me" is barely off our lips! God's ordained minister pronounces an assurance of pardon (or absolution), such as this wonderful word based on 1 Timothy 1:15 from Martin Bucer's 1539 *Church Practices*:

> This is certainly true and a very precious word: Christ Jesus came into the world to save sinners. Let everyone truly confess with Saint Paul in his heart and believe in Christ. Thus, I promise you in his name the forgiveness of all your sins and I declare you to be loosed of your sins on earth, and that you are loosed of them also in heaven, forever. Amen.[16]

This is good news, indeed. It is such good news that it cannot help but elicit an exuberant reply from the assembly, fittingly and almost irresistibly *sung*:[17]

---

16 In *Reformation Worship: Liturgies from the Past for the Present*, ed. Jonathan Gibson and Mark Earngey (Greensboro, NC: New Growth, 2018), 284.

17 See, further, Eugene H. Peterson, *Answering God: The Psalms as Tools for Prayer* (San Francisco: Harper & Row, 1989), 88; Peter J. Leithart, *Revelation 1–11*, ITC (London: Bloomsbury T&T Clark, 2018), 246–47, 262–63.

Long my imprisoned spirit lay
Fast bound in sin and nature's night;
Thine eye diffused a quickening ray,
I woke, the dungeon flamed with light;
My chains fell off, my heart was free;
I rose, went forth, and followed Thee.

Amazing love! how can it be
That Thou, my God, shouldst die for me?[18]

Various Scripture lessons from "the Word of the Lord" may follow, to which the assembly responds, "Thanks be to God!" and utters their dedication to the way of the Lord:

What shall I render to the LORD
    for all his benefits to me?
I will lift up the cup of salvation
    and call on the name of the LORD,
I will pay my vows to the LORD
    in the presence of all his people. (Ps. 116:12–14)

In table 2, I have provided a visual presentation that, while simplified, fills things out a bit further. What should be unmistakable is that corporate worship is nothing if not purposefully developing dialogue between God and the gathered church.

Worship gets going and is sustained by the initiating word of the covenant Lord (the left-hand column), and our involvement throughout as his assembly is a matter of rendering fitting answering speech (the right-hand column). If prayer is answering speech, then Lord's Day

---

18 Charles Wesley, "And Can It Be, That I Should Gain?" (1738), https://www.hymnal.net/.

covenant renewal is the body of Christ at prayer. Corporate worship is—or at its best it can be—training in answering the God who speaks to us, training in answering *attentively, responsively, and fittingly* to the many different kinds of things the Lord says, training in the words and patterns and logic and vibrancy of communion with God.

Table 2. An order of worship in the Reformed tradition

God Calls Us		
Call to Worship	⇨	Psalms, Hymns, Prayers of Adoration
Welcome	⇨	Invocation and the Lord's Prayer
God Cleanses Us		
Call to Confession of Sin (sometimes preceded by a Reading of the Law)	⇨	Confession of Sin
Word of Pardon	⇨	Songs of Praise and Thanksgiving (sometimes accompanied by the Passing of the Peace)
God Consecrates Us		
Scripture Lessons	⇨	"The Word of the Lord." / "Thanks be to God." Prayers of the People, Psalm of Response
Proclamation of the Word	⇨	Profession of Faith (Creeds and Confessions)
God Communes with Us		
Words of Institution of the Lord's Supper	⇨	"Lift up your hearts." / "We lift our hearts up to the Lord." Thanksgiving
Distribution of Elements	⇨	Partaking of Elements Acclamation
God Commissions Us		
Call to Service	⇨	Doxology Closing Prayers
Benediction Sending	⇨	"Amen!"
God's Word of Address		Our Answering Speech

The weekly rhythm of the life of prayer properly begins with Lord's Day worship of the gathered people of God. That engagement both *is* prayer and is one of the most important forms of discipleship in prayer. To the degree that we individually are members of the body of Christ, and to the degree that we are attentive participants in these weekly dramatic engagements, our prayer life may be better than we might at first think.

———

O God, who hast made us glad in the service of Thy house; may the blessing we have received pass not away from us, but abide in the sanctuary of our hearts; that we, being helped by Thee, may be able in all things to please Thy loving eyes; through Jesus Christ our Lord. Amen.

PRAYER TO CONCLUDE MORNING PRAYER SERVICES
FROM THE SERVICE BOOK AND ORDINAL (1918)[19]

19 The Presbyterian Church of South Africa, *Service Book and Ordinal* (Glasgow: Maclehose, Jackson, 1921), 161–62.

For the Christian everything, including the morning and the evening, can be a means of communication with God.

ROBERT TAFT
The Liturgy of the Hours in East and West

How we spend our days is, of course, how we spend our lives. What we do with this hour, and that one, is what we are doing. A schedule defends from chaos and whim. It is a net for catching days. It is a scaffolding on which a worker can stand and labor with both hands at sections of time. A schedule is a mock-up of reason and order— willed, faked, and so brought into being; it is a peace and a haven set into the wreck of time; it is a lifeboat on which you find yourself, decades later, still living.

ANNIE DILLARD
The Writing Life

11

The Daily Rhythm of Prayer

WHAT DO WE HAVE THAT WE DID NOT RECEIVE? Chapter 10 outlined a way in which this apostolic question applies to our know-how and categories for engagement in prayer. Corporate worship has a theological, sociological, and epistemological primacy for the life of prayer. The Lord's Day covenant renewal service, as a well-ordered, covenantally keyed dialogue with God, is our first school of prayer.

Nevertheless, the Lord's Day gathering by itself is not a *life* of prayer but what we could call a *public event* in the whole life. Our theological starting point is the "[Lord's] day with others," but what of the "[week]day alone"? If the weekly rhythm of the life of prayer begins with common prayer in the Sunday gathering, what constitutes wise and fructifying rhythms of prayer in the Monday-through-Saturday dispersion?

Daily Punctuation

Naturally, we should think of good punctuation. "There are so many things to fear in life," comments Lauren Oyler, "but punctuation is not one of them." The benefits of punctuation are incalculable. For example, "when you use [a semicolon], you are doing something purposefully, by choice, at a time when motivations are vague and intentions often denied."[1] Daily set-apart times of prayer, like punctuation marks, form an intentional, communicative framing and directing of my days to God. They clarify how my days are meaningful. They help me to speak, as it were, with proper theological grammar, so that I might name my days as from the Lord, lived out before the face of the Lord, and for the glory of the Lord alone.

Capital Letters: Daily Morning Prayer[2]

> In the morning, Lord, You will hear my voice;
> In the morning I will present my prayer to You and be on the watch. (Ps. 5:3 NASB)

Prayer at one's rising is like a capital *T* crucially signaling the start of a new sentence with "Today" (Heb. 3:13) or "The day of salvation" (2 Cor. 6:2). Through morning prayer, we set apart this day as a day in which to hallow the name of our Father and to submit to his will (Matt. 6:9–10). Morning is the time of supplications for bread from the Father's hand (Matt. 6:11), as well as for the guidance, strength, and insight necessary to engage in wise cultural labor toward the making of bread (which isn't some "natural resource"). The day's first hours are also a fitting time to voice "first of all" prayers (1 Tim. 2:1–4)—to voice, that is, not only petitions for *our* daily bread but also intercessions for the world's needs besides. In the morning, we declare our desire and intention for the day: "O God, you are my God; earnestly I seek you" (Ps. 63:1). We confess anew our common

---

1   Lauren Oyler, "The Case for Semicolons," *New York Times Magazine*, February 9, 2021, https://www.nytimes.com/.

2   I know capital letters aren't punctuation marks. But, as Ralph Waldo Emerson famously quipped, "A foolish consistency is the hobgoblin of little minds."

faith: "I believe in God, the Father almighty, Creator of heaven and earth."[3] And above all, like the sun rising in joyful might for praise (Ps. 19:1–6), our rising is the proper time to praise our great God, singing psalms such as Psalms 148–50, hymns such as "Holy, Holy, Holy," and canticles such as the Magnificat (Luke 1:46–55).

To be sure, mornings are often hectic, and not all of us are "morning people." But intentionality at the outset of the day is crucial. Kathleen Norris explains:

> When I allow busy little doings to fill the precious time of early morning, when contemplation might flourish, I open the doors to the demon of acedia. Noon becomes a blur—no time, no time—the wolfing down of a sandwich as I listen to the morning's phone messages and plan the afternoon's errands. When evening comes, I am so exhausted that vespers has become impossible. It is as if I have taken the world's weight on my shoulders and am too greedy, and too foolish, to surrender it to God.[4]

Aligning the rising of our bodies in the morning with the raising of prayers to the Father of lights, we consecrate through prayer the day ahead to the Lord.[5]

---

3 From early times Christians were in the practice of creedal confession *both* at morning *and* at evening, a practice that corresponds to Yahweh's injunction to Israel to have the Shema on hearts and lips "when you lie down, and when you rise" (Deut. 6:4–7; see Joachim Jeremias, *The Prayers of Jesus*, trans. J. Bowden, C. Burchard, and J. Reumann [Philadelphia: Fortress, 1978], 67–69).

4 Kathleen Norris, *The Quotidian Mysteries: Laundry, Liturgy and "Women's Work"* (Mahwah, NJ: Paulist, 1998), 25.

5 See, further, Robert Taft, *The Liturgy of the Hours in East and West: The Origins of the Divine Office and Its Meaning for Today*, 2nd rev. ed. (Collegeville, MN: Liturgical Press, 1993), 42–47, 84–87, 353–54.

Periods: Daily Evening Prayer

> Let my prayer be counted as incense before you,
>> and the lifting up of my hands as the evening sacrifice!
>> (Ps. 141:2)

Evening is the time for acknowledging all the Lord's faithfulness in the day just completed (Ps. 92:1–2). At the break of day, we prayed for our daily bread; at the close of day, we can give thanks for bread received and, what's more, for the Father's kind answers to our prayers. As we gather around the evening meal, we can with all fittingness punctuate the day's conclusion with prayerful thanksgiving. All meals are *eucharistic*, in that they are opportunities for thanksgiving (*eucharistia*) to God for his loving, merciful, plentiful provision (see, e.g., Matt. 15:36; Luke 22:19; Acts 27:35). The evening meal is the icon and culminating instance of God's daily provision, so it is an eminently fitting opportunity for a household to raise its cup of eschatological wine in celebratory gratitude to God. The day has come to its end, and the Lord has shown himself in giving bread (and much more) to be faithful, wise, mighty, merciful, present, responsive, generous, and good.

Of course, it is safe to assume that since we are still on the near side of *the* end and our glorification, the day just concluded has involved not only God's faithful provision but also our sin and unbelief. So prayerful punctuation of the day's conclusion can also include confession of sin. Psalm 141, quoted above, could be called the quintessential vesper (evening) psalm, being recited transtraditionally and from early ages in Christian evening prayer services, in large part, John Chrysostom observed, because of its penitential nature.[6] Evening is the time for repentance and reconciliation with God and neighbor, as Ephesians 4:26–27 insinuates with the example of sinful anger: "Do not let the sun go down on your anger, and give no opportunity to the devil."

The Lord is gracious and merciful, slow to anger and abounding in steadfast love and mercy through the crucified, risen, and ascended Christ. Therefore, for the Christian, the evening is time once again to profess faith in Christ, to rest in his completed work, and to give thanks now not only for God's creation and providence but also and especially for his redemption. The eventide can be stamped with a period, such as the hymn "Abide with Me," or the ancient prayer appearing at the end of this chapter. As the sun's light fades, with gratitude, repentance, and renewed gospel confidence, Christians rightly set their hope on the never-fading and gladsome light of Christ.

Other Punctuation Marks: Toward a Daily Rhythm

> Seven times a day I praise you
> for your righteous rules. (Ps. 119:164)

Beyond capital letters and periods, other punctuation marks are in our repertoire: commas when we pause for prayer (e.g., before lunch), semicolons signaling a transition in the day (e.g., a midmorning break; the time of laying one's head on a pillow), em dashes separating longer seasons from the typical daily flow (e.g., all-night prayer vigils). Daniel, at great risk to himself, prayed three times a day (Dan. 6:10). Peter apparently viewed the sixth

---

6 Chrysostom, *Commentary on Psalm 140* 1, quoted in Taft, *The Liturgy of the Hours in East and West*, 356.

hour (noon) as a time for prayer (Acts 10:9). Our Lord kept vigil through the night (Luke 6:12). Basil of Caesarea, in his *Longer Rules*, instructed monasteries about morning and evening prayer, and about several other set-apart times of prayer—the sixth hour (see Ps. 55:17; cf. 91:6), the ninth hour (see Acts 3:1), midnight (see Ps. 119:62; Acts 16:25), and so on.[7] Basil reflects a tradition that identifies *seven* set times for prayer throughout the day (variously called the hours of prayer, the daily prayer cycle, or the divine office).

Be that as it may, there is, I believe, an elegant simplicity to the basic practice of morning and evening prayer as a frame for the day. We may view it as a corollary and a typological fulfillment of the morning and evening offerings at the temple (see, e.g., Ex. 29:38–41; 30:7–8; Num. 23:3–8; Lev. 6:20; cf. Ezra 9:5–15; Ps. 141:2; Dan. 9:20–21; Luke 1:10; Acts 3:1).[8] It comes with the precedent of our incarnate Lord's own practice (see Mark 1:35; 6:46–47). And it aligns with the natural rhythms of the created world (of which we are a part) and thus has, as it were, a kind of built-in alarm clock for reminding us.[9]

I recommend daily morning and evening prayer as a starting point for those seeking to develop healthy rhythms in the life of

---

7 Basil of Caesarea, *Longer Rules* 37.2–5, quoted in Taft, *The Liturgy of the Hours in East and West*, 85–86.

8 Frequently, biblical commentaries and literature on the daily offices insinuate a genetic historical relationship between morning and evening sacrifice (and other Jewish prayer practices) and fixed-hour Christian prayer (see, e.g., Jeremias, *The Prayers of Jesus*, 72; Scot McKnight, *Praying with the Church: Following Jesus Daily, Hourly, Today* [Brewster, MA: Paraclete, 2006], 64). While the scenario is plausible, it is a matter of considerable historical complexity and speculation; see, e.g., the discussion in Jeremy Penner, *Patterns of Daily Prayer in Second Temple Judaism*, STDJ 104 (Leiden: Brill, 2012), 35–72. Cf. the prudent comments offered by Taft, *The Liturgy of the Hours in East and West*, 3.

9 Cf. Taft, *The Liturgy of the Hours in East and West*, 11.

prayer. From there we might begin to notice other times when "a natural break in the day" occurs,[10] which we might well set apart regularly for prayer. Personally, I have found great help in the long-standing practice of praying the Nunc Dimittis (Luke 2:29–32) at bedtime. Simeon's comfort at seeing the Lord's salvation freed him to close his eyes in peace; in like manner, we are freed to enter the rest of sleep in peace through the door of resting in Christ. Every nighttime becomes practice for dying well. I suspect most Christians already keep three set times daily for prayer, though we might not think of them as such—namely, moments of thanksgiving at breakfast, lunch, and dinner. It is worth trying to build on that momentum. For a wisely structured rhythm of daily praying is communicative scaffolding for "receiving the day"[11] with two open palms as the gift that it is.

On Spontaneity and Structure

"But wait a minute!" some might object. "All this talk of fixed hours and rigid structure sounds suffocating of spontaneity and heartfelt expression. What's more, it smacks of legalistic fixation on times and seasons, which Jesus came to abolish." A few responses come to mind.

What Jesus Condemns

A first and simple response is this: so far as I am aware, Jesus nowhere condemns praying at fixed hours (in fact, he seems to have happily prayed at set times in his earthly ministry). What he condemns is the lust to be noticed and admired by others as

10 McKnight, *Praying with the Church*, 40.
11 Dorothy C. Bass, *Receiving the Day: Christian Practices for Opening the Gift of Time* (San Francisco: Jossey-Bass, 2000).

pious, and the assumption that long prayers somehow have better chances of getting God's attention (see, e.g., Matt. 6:5–15). The Pharisee and the tax collector in Luke 18:9–14 gather at the temple at the same time to pray—at the same time, apparently, because it was a set, habitual, public time for prayer.[12] Jesus condemns the Pharisee not because he prayed at a set time but because he relied on his own righteousness in a prideful comparison with others. On the flip side, the tax collector went home justified because he cast himself solely on the mercy of God, a casting that was not at odds with praying at a set time but took place *through* it.

Defining What "Counts" in the Life of Prayer

Second, we can question a facile definition of true prayer that may lurk behind the objection. Likely, at least part of what often drives doubts about set, structured times for prayer is an unspoken (and unexamined) assumption that if you're not "feeling it"—not "fully emotionally engaged," not fired by the flames of intimacy—then you're not *really* praying but only "going through the motions" in the worst possible sense. But this is as reductionistic as it is wrongly focused.

Included in the life of prayer, as our Lord well knows, are seasons of weariness, and of what we tend to call "dryness," in which we are tempted to lose heart (see Ps. 69:3; Luke 18:1). So too are dark nights of the soul, in which God feels most distant, but through which he may, in fact, be especially near and growing us. Gideon's lack of *feeling* empowered by the Spirit-presence of God led him

---

12 It is reasonable to suppose that it was at the time of the morning offering; for discussion, see Kenneth Bailey, *Poet and Peasant, and Through Peasant Eyes: A Literary-Cultural Approach to the Parables in Luke*, 2 vols. (1976, 1980; repr., Grand Rapids, MI: Eerdmans, 1983), 2:144–47.

to try to bargain with God (Judg. 6:36–40). Yet the Spirit had already "clothed" Gideon, as the narrator makes plain (Judg. 6:34). Our perceived sense of the Spirit and the actual presence of the Spirit may need to be distinguished.[13] In any case, I suggest that Gideon's answering speech to God was real praying, even if it was weak and in much need of maturation. Reducing "real" prayer to only our spontaneous moments of "feeling it" wrongly excludes numerous other parts of the life of prayer in which God is near to us, continually seeking our response, and in which we are, however haltingly or fumblingly, responding to him.

I say, "I love you," to my wife every morning as I leave for work. Is that legalistic for being routine? Do the words lose their meaning for their formulaic and circadian use?[14] Does the fact that I feel it more on some mornings make the statement *untrue* on other mornings of rush or emotional dryness? Should I refrain from saying it when I "feel dry"? Such questions seem inappropriate and ill-fitted to the marital relationship. Such questions treat marriage in a reductionistic way, as a thin commercial enterprise of so many isolated transactions, each evaluated separately. By the same measure, similar questions applied to the life of prayer can be misleading about our relationship with the God who addresses us. Prayer is not defined by some predetermined amount of emotional engagement, nor ought we to assess our prayers only with a view to whether we deem ourselves to have attained that sum, for prayer is not a commercial transaction but part of a relationship always played out in a larger embodied, temporal, communicative, covenantal context. So there are additional measures by which to evaluate our prayer practice (e.g., our attentiveness to the Father,

13 Barry G. Webb, *The Book of Judges*, NICOT (Grand Rapids, MI: Eerdmans, 2012), 239.
14 Cf. McKnight, *Praying with the Church*, 50.

our attentiveness to his other children, our fidelity to his word, our sincerity and honesty before him, our motivations and aims, the direction of our lives).

Better still is to get our focus off ourselves and onto the God to whom our prayers respond. Strangely, the moments when I most "feel it" are those moments when I am paying *least attention to my feelings* but most attention to the God who is not I, to his splendor and beauty, to his awesome justice and power, to his unthinkable mercy, to the wonder of what he has done, is doing, and promises to do for me and for the world. The trick in the life of prayer, then, is to get our eyes and ears on what God says and does. This is one reason, among others, why something as mundane as punctuating our days with set times of prayer is so valuable: it clears space for setting our eyes and ears on God's word, space for responding to the speaker of that word, space in which the Spirit might blow and cause the embers of our hearts to glow.

Spontaneity within and through Structure

Holy wind *does* blow in such ordinary spaces. True, Spirit-filled spontaneity and feeling can and does spring up within such mundane things as planned structures, daily rhythms, and set times for prayer, and this reality forms a third response to common suspicions. The Spirit who hovered over chaotic waters fructified the earth through the structure of six wisely ordered days (Gen. 1:2–31). The Corinthians were to earnestly desire the Spirit-empowered gifts (1 Cor. 12:31; 14:1, 39), and they were to seek them within the good order, intelligibility, and ordinary peace practiced by all the churches of Christ (1 Cor. 14:33, 40). The Spirit was poured out at Pentecost at a regular third-hour gathering time for prayer (see Acts 2:1, 15). John found himself "in the Spirit *on the*

Lord's day" (Rev. 1:10). The presence of God is promised not only in the spectacular but also in the ordinary gentle breeze (1 Kings 19:11–13). I suppose that structure and set times *might* under certain conditions suffocate life and vibrancy, but they certainly *need* not. Indeed, wise structure and rhythm form the context in which Spirit-wrought spontaneity and feeling in prayer normally spring up.

We can't control when and how that happens. The wind blows as it wills. But we can plan our days so that we regularly stand in the fields where it normally happens. It's possible to pursue well-ordered daily rhythms and fixed hours of prayer precisely because we yearn for spontaneity and heartfelt prayer and want to give it space to grow. We may even find that, like mint in a garden that takes root in one place a first year and in coming years begins to sprout all over, vibrant and spontaneous communicative communion with our ever-present Lord begins to sprout far beyond the borders of our planned times of prayer.

In *The End of the Christian Life*, Todd Billings tells the story of Claude, hospitalized and at the end of his long and intense suffering under a degenerative illness, his body now reduced to reliance on a ventilator.[15] Friends, pastor, and family gather at his bedside to express their love and to prayerfully commend Claude's soul to the Lord. But Claude beats them to the punch: he pulls off his ventilator and, gasping through his final breaths, says: "What is your only hope in life and death? That I am not my own, but belong—body and soul, in life and in death—to my faithful Savior Jesus Christ." Claude was shaped by years of prayer practices and rhythms, practices and rhythms that long preceded him, practices

15 J. Todd Billings, *The End of the Christian Life: How Embracing Our Mortality Frees Us to Truly Live* (Grand Rapids, MI: Brazos, 2020), 145–46.

and rhythms that had everything to do with the hour of his greatest need, practices and rhythms in which words from the Heidelberg Catechism also became his words spontaneously voiced with his final breaths. Structure may prove to be not only a *context for* healthy spontaneity but also part of its *cultivation*.

A Few Suggested Patterns and Practices

Cultivation in the Life of Prayer

I have frequently used agrarian terms like "growing," "fructifying," "fruitfulness," "cultivation." This is no accident but is intentionally keyed to Scripture, which often portrays mature Christian practice and piety with botanical and agricultural images: a tree firmly planted (Ps. 1:1–3; Jer. 17:7–8), a vine carefully kept (John 15:1–11). The language of cultivation also highlights that praying implicates us in a *culture* (which, it must be remembered, is an agricultural metaphor),[16] and that maturing in the life of prayer is a matter of *being cultivated*. Culture is never solely about individual intention and action, but always involves a people, a history, a tradition of reception and formation. The cultivation of a mature life of prayer involves formation within a tradition and a people. Hence, in the preceding chapter, I spotlighted corporate worship. The common prayerful dialogue which is corporate worship is formation in the tradition of God's praying people, an instance of the church's material culture that cultivates us for fruitfulness in the life of prayer.[17]

16 See D. Stephen Long, *Theology and Culture: A Guide to the Discussion* (Cambridge: James Clarke, 2010), 8–14.

17 I have pursued this line of thought with a view to cultivating wisdom in our technological age in Daniel J. Brendsel, "The Path More Traveled: The Place of the (Missing) Church in Christian Engagement of Technology," in *Technē: Christian Visions of Technology*, ed. G. Hiestand and T. A. Wilson (Eugene, OR: Cascade, 2022), 16–35.

But this does not mean that being sent from the sanctuary we are left to fend for ourselves in figuring out daily rhythms of prayer. Even in this we can learn from and follow the lead of others. Something of this is presented pictorially by the nineteenth-century French painter Jean-François Millet (see fig. 1).

Figure 1. *The Angelus*, by Jean-François Millet*

* Jean-François Millet, *The Angelus*, 1857–1859, oil on canvas, 21.65 × 25.98" (55 × 66 cm), Musée d'Orsay, Paris, https://commons.wikimedia.org/, public domain.

Millet depicts two humble farmers with heads bowed. As the title suggests, they are praying the *Angelus*, a prayer of wonder and supplication in the light of the incarnation. These two pray the *Angelus* at this time because the church in the distance is ringing its bells to signal the day's end and the time for prayer. Their daily prayer is intertwined with the rhythms and practices of the church of Christ. For these two, that clearly doesn't mean every waking or spare moment is spent gathered at the building. But their identity and habits as praying bodies are inseparable from the praying body. While few of us live within hearing distance of church bells (or have working bells in our churches), we still can seek to better harmonize the private and the common—that is, to better perceive, prize, and promote their proper interplay.[18]

Help from Prayer Book Traditions

In light of the preceding, there is much to be gained by following the lead of traditional daily prayer services, such as those found in the traditions of the Book of Common Prayer, the Lutheran Service Book, and the Book of Common Worship. The general framework for regular prayer advised by the Westminster Divines in the 1647 Directory for Family Worship is also a helpful guide. With the exception of the last, each of these is properly at home in corporate liturgical use. They are meant, first, to be the stuff of common prayer, not resources for "personal devotions."[19] But traditional prayer books and services can have an overflow benefit of helping us order our individual lives of prayer, especially as we remain aware of and grateful for their origins, and as we appreciate

18 Note, e.g., how Daniel's private prayer was directed *toward the temple in Jerusalem* (Dan. 6:10; cf. 1 Kings 8:41–43; Jonah 2:4) and offered *at the same time as the regular corporate worship practices in the temple*, even though the temple in his day lay in ruins (Dan. 9:21; cf. Ezra 9:4–5). See, further, Timothy Keller, *Prayer: Experiencing Awe and Intimacy with God* (New York: Dutton, 2014), 246–47.

19 On the historical circumstances that led to the *liturgy* of the hours, a corporate enactment, being reduced to the *divine hours* observed by clerics and individual monastics, see esp. Taft, *The Liturgy of the Hours in East and West*, 297–306; cf. Milton Walsh, *Witness of the Saints: Patristic Readings in the Liturgy of the Hours* (San Francisco: Ignatius, 2010), 21–30, esp. 28–30; McKnight, *Praying with the Church*, x–xi.

how individual and corporate prayer are inextricably intertwined historically and theologically.

Each prayer book and daily prayer tradition has its own distinctives and logic. We can leave introductions to such things for others[20] while here simply highlighting two advantages of using traditional structures and prayers.

First, it gives us an objective starting point. It can be immensely freeing to realize that *getting started doesn't depend on our own strength and creativity*. Far too often "I don't know where/how to begin" gets in the way of making a beginning. Perhaps we imagine that if we don't come up with something original and "our own" on the spot, then we haven't earned the right to pray. Maybe we're like the pietistic pastor Fridfeldt in *The Hammer of God*, who was "bothered . . . to be bound by a fixed ritual. It had therefore always been his practice to make little changes, additions, and to put as much feeling and personal touch into it as possible." But at story's end, Fridfeldt found himself exhausted by his self-reliance, despairing of himself, broken by the word (the hammer) of God. In this weary and humbled state, he knelt at the altar needing to lead the congregation in prayer. Normally, he would have sought to pray with all the personal flair and fervor he could muster, but "today he did not feel able to do this." To his great surprise, he discovered a mercy heretofore hidden to his eyes: "Strangely enough, it was a relief to be allowed to read them [i.e., the prayers of the liturgical service] as they were, ancient and hallowed words that

---

20 Helpful primers on the Book of Common Prayer and its history can be found at https://anglican compass.com. For an introduction to principles at work in the Westminster Directory for Family Worship, see Joel R. Beeke, *Family Worship*, 2nd ed. (Grand Rapids, MI: Reformation Heritage, 2021). Taft, *The Liturgy of the Hours in East and West*, 320–22, briefly discusses the background and makeup of Lutheran daily prayer. McKnight, *Praying with the Church*, 69–150, provides accessible introductions to daily prayer traditions outside the Protestant world.

fell as heavy, life-giving drops in his heart."[21] Content and structure
that has stood the test of time is sturdy enough to withstand the
tremors of our insecurity, ignorance, and exhaustion. We need an
objective launching pad. We might not, by the Spirit's guiding,
end where we begin. But we will not end up anywhere if we never
begin somewhere.

Second, following an established order and pattern of prayer
can help pull our attention, so prone to drifting, back into place.
Perhaps, like me, you can easily identify with Marie Howe:

> Every day I want to speak with you. And every day something
> > more important
> calls for my attention—the drugstore, the beauty products,
> > the luggage
>
> I need to buy for the trip.
> Even now I can hardly sit here
>
> among the falling piles of paper and clothing, the garbage
> > trucks outside
> already screeching and banging.
>
> The mystics say you are as close as my own breath.
> Why do I flee from you?
>
> My days and nights pour through me like complaints
> and become a story I forgot to tell.

21 Bo Giertz, *The Hammer of God*, rev. ed., trans. Clifford Ansgar Nelson and Hans Andrae
(Minneapolis: Augsburg Fortress, 2005), 171.

Help me. Even as I write these words I am planning
to rise from the chair as soon as I finish this sentence.[22]

While no silver bullet against distraction, a regular and established pattern of prayer is worth having in our armory. Such a
pattern to follow is like a well-worn path through a confusing
thicket, surely directing us toward our best destination. The rich
substance of time-tested prayer services is like ballast at the bottom
of a buoy, which helps keep it pointed heavenward when waves of
distraction abound.

Other Methods, Varieties of Engagement, and Adaptability

Of course, many other patterns and structures for theologically
focused and fruitful times of prayer have appeared across times
and traditions. One well-known method for structuring prayer is
the ACTS model: Adoration, Confession, Thanksgiving, Supplication.[23] Regardless of the model we might follow, it is of great benefit
to find one, to learn something of its heritage and the logic of its
makeup, and to allow it to shape our times of answering speech.
The point is finding opportunities to be apprenticed in the life of
prayer at the feet of wise pray-ers and within a praying tradition,
not discovering the "perfect" and "required" method and forms
for praying. Indeed, it seems to me that Hans Urs von Balthasar
is on target when he asserts: "There is no such thing as a necessary
structure or even an 'appropriate' one. At the most, a few suggestions can be offered, useful only to the extent that they do not
interfere with the law of contemplation, which is the free Spirit of

---

22 Marie Howe, "Prayer," in *The Kingdom of Ordinary Time* (New York: Norton, 2008), 27.
23 Matthew Henry's early eighteenth-century *A Method for Prayer* offers a more involved, but
    generally similar, movement through such speech acts in praying.

God, who leads the contemplative along the path of freedom."[24] We should feel freedom from season to season to learn from some new (to us) tradition of praying in response to Scripture. But perhaps I might suggest that we commit to a method for a minimum of two or three months, to give us a chance to actually learn from it and be shaped by it.

Additionally, it is wrongheaded to treat a set order for prayer as a straitjacket from which we can never veer and the whole of which we must complete in one sitting or it doesn't "count." If the Spirit causes a Scripture verse to leap from the page, if a supplication comes spontaneously to mind, if some aspect of God's glory captures your heart, if the beauteous joy of a hymn or canticle warms your soul and fires your imagination, by all means stop. Linger. Don't delay in responding to God. Taste and see that the Lord is good. Well-ordered methods for prayer clear space for the surprise of such encounters, even as they help us continue faithfully pursuing the life of prayer in seasons when such encounters seem less in abundance.

Frameworks for Reading God's Word

Since prayer is fundamentally *responsive* to God's initiating word to us, it is of utmost importance to link a pattern of praying with a pattern of reading Scripture. Here's where prayer books especially excel beyond other thematically oriented methods of prayer. Prayer books are saturated with Scripture.[25] More particularly, their ser-

---

24 Hans Urs von Balthasar, *Prayer*, trans. G. Harrison (San Francisco: Ignatius, 1986), 132.
25 Nearly all the Scriptures I cite in the initial section of this chapter ("Daily Punctuation," p. 181) either appear in various prayer services across traditions or are appealed to repeatedly in pastoral reflection on and encouragement to daily prayer throughout the ages (see, e.g., Origen, *On Prayer* 32; Basil, *Longer Rules* 37, both cited by Taft, *The Liturgy of the Hours in East and West*).

vices are ordered so as to make it clear that our praying is always answering speech—for example, by providing scriptural sentences that invite us to praise (the words of an "Invitatory" are always Scripture texts), offering explicit scriptural calls to confession, and giving voice to our thanks that fittingly follows the reading of Scripture (e.g., "The Word of the Lord" / "Thanks be to God").

Additionally, prayer books can be seen from a bird's-eye view to be frameworks for the regular recitation of the Psalter and the comprehensive reading of Scripture. They are, in other words, prayer-saturated Bible-reading plans.[26] The morning and evening prayer services found in the 2019 Book of Common Prayer are a clear case in point, for they include the recitation of all the Psalms on a thirty- (or sixty-) day cycle, as well as a system of daily Old Testament and New Testament lessons in which nearly the whole of Scripture is read over the course of a calendar year. Many of us are already committed to daily Bible-reading plans. Why not situate this planned and set-apart time of Godwardness within a theologically thoughtful framework of prayer?

Baby Steps

Let me close with some encouragement. All this may sound daunting and unrealistic to many: having set times for extended prayer every day just doesn't seem doable in our frenetic and jam-packed schedules. While it may be worthwhile for us to ask *why* our schedules are like this (and why our existing schedules so *dominate* our lives), my aims here move in a couple of different directions.

---

26 One of the great achievements of Thomas Cranmer's 1549 Book of Common Prayer was to tie daily prayer services to a calendar of lections so that nearly the whole of Scripture was read through the year. See Alan Jacobs, *The Book of Common Prayer: A Biography* (Princeton, NJ: Princeton University Press, 2013), 26–27.

On the one hand, I have used several differing prayer services to structure my times of morning prayer and (haltingly) evening prayer. They do not take as long to work through as might at first be expected. For example, the morning prayer service provided in *Psalms for All Seasons* takes maybe ten to fifteen minutes to pray through at a slow pace, allowing for moments of lingering and reflectiveness and spontaneous response, perhaps with an additional several minutes if one incorporates extended Scripture readings. There are available abbreviated services for "Family Worship," which take even less time. The goal, of course, is not to "get through the material" in as little time as possible. But we might just discover that spending time daily in intentionally patterned prayer is not as daunting as we at first assumed.

On the other hand, it seems sensible to encourage those who have never really established a habit and daily rhythm of praying to start small. Many a good practice has drowned in a flood of grandiose intentions and thoughtlessly unrealistic or narrowly conceived commitments. I have never learned how to play piano, though several years ago I made a "commitment" to teach myself with YouTube videos. Grandiose intention + foolish and unrealistic strategy = abandoned endeavor. Don't let pride or foolishness get in the way of forming a daily rhythm of praying.

I might suggest the following as a realistic, highly flexible starting point: commit to framing your days with morning and evening prayer, using the orders for "Family Worship" from the 2019 Book of Common Prayer as a guide,[27] incorporating whatever regular

---

27 Anglican Church in North America, *The Book of Common Prayer* (Huntington Beach, CA: Anglican Liturgy Press, 2019), 67–75. A PDF download of the BCP is available at https://bcp2019.anglicanchurch.net/. The Daily Office for family prayer is also provided in convenient form at https://www.dailyoffice2019.com/family/, or via mobile app.

Scripture reading you are engaged in at the appropriate place. (Another convenient help is your local church's weekly service bulletin. Your church's order of worship can provide structure for your daily times in prayer. This method has the added advantage of linking your individual daily prayer directly to the weekly Lord's Day gathering as its launching point.) For brevity and focus, each day of the week can be planned in such a way as to zero in on a different object of supplication and intercession (e.g., the Lutheran Service Book helpfully suggests as a practice of "daily prayer for individuals and families" a different intercessory prayer focus for every day of the week). All of this should take you maybe five to fifteen minutes, morning and evening, which seems a workable starting point for cultivating healthy daily rhythms of prayer.[28]

———

O God . . . who has made the day for the works of light and the night for the refreshment of our infirmity . . . mercifully accept now this, our evening thanksgiving. You who have brought us through the length of the day and to the beginning of the night, preserve us by your Christ. Grant us a peaceful evening and a night free from sin, and give us everlasting life by your Christ.

EVENING PRAYER FROM
THE APOSTOLIC CONSTITUTIONS
(LATE FOURTH CENTURY)[29]

28 Other concrete suggested plans are provided by Keller, *Prayer*, 252–55, 263–64.
29 Quoted in Taft, *The Liturgy of the Hours in East and West*, 355.

Almighty and everlasting God,
you are always more ready to hear than we to pray
and to give more than either we desire or deserve:
pour down upon us the abundance of your mercy,
forgiving us those things of which our conscience is afraid
and giving us those good things which we are not worthy to ask
but through the merits and mediation
of Jesus Christ your Son our Lord,
who is alive and reigns with you,
in the unity of the Holy Spirit,
one God, now and for ever. Amen.

CA. FIFTH-CENTURY COLLECT

The Rhythm and Shape
of a Typical Prayer

GOOD ORDER IS ULTIMATELY about good theology. The apostle Paul called for things to be "done decently and in order" at the Corinthian assembly (1 Cor. 14:40) because "God is not a God of confusion but of peace" (1 Cor. 14:33). God through the Word and by his Spirit creates order out of chaos (Gen. 1–2), and does so in an ordered manner (i.e., through seven intentionally, artfully structured days). God cares about order, and order plays a key role in our relationship with God. Order is not merely about sociological efficiency, equity, and productivity. It is also part of what goes into the shaping of mind, heart, and body, as Ellen Charry has commented, "so that knowledge of the love of God fits into a life prepared to interpret it properly."[1] Good order is ultimately about good theology.

Our concern in part 4, therefore, has been to explore how well-ordered rhythms, patterns, and practices in our praying life, at

---

1   Ellen T. Charry, *By the Renewing of Your Minds: The Pastoral Function of Christian Doctrine* (Oxford: Oxford University Press, 1997), 28.

weekly and daily levels, might contribute to the pursuit and knowledge of God. That is to look at the order of the life of prayer through a broad-angle lens, as it were. It's also possible, with a zoom lens, to probe the order of small-scale practices, even as small as specific speech acts. That's what this final chapter seeks to do. Specifically, we will explore the order—the rhythm, progression, and shape—of a long-used type of prayer.

There is an old maxim, as old as the fifth century: *lex orandi, lex credendi*, the law of praying is the law of believing. The meaning of the maxim is hotly debated, and I do not intend to enter the debate.[2] But we can at least say this: prayer and belief are intertwined. How we pray is a window on what we believe and may in certain ways shape belief, even as what we believe typically informs and directs what we pray. When right belief has informed well-ordered forms of praying, those forms are of tremendous benefit for believers. Good order in prayer is good theology enacted. So, good order in prayer can massage the muscles of our believing hearts in proper directions.

One of the oldest and most enduring forms of prayer in the Western church is the "collect" ('käl-ekt), though many today may have never heard the term applied to prayer. A collect prayer is a brief, tightly structured supplication, progressing in a simple but meaningful way. It is, I believe, a form of praying that is well worth knowing and practicing.

Collective Order

We have a wealth of collect prayers from the fifth century and earlier, many of which are still prayed today by churches and individual Christians across the globe. This is entirely fitting, since etymologi-

---

2 See Geoffrey Wainwright, *Doxology: The Praise of God in Worship, Doctrine and Life* (New York: Oxford University Press, 1980), 218–84.

cally the term "collect" comes from the Latin *collecta*, "gathering." A collect prayer *gathers together* the prayers of the saints—the prayers, spoken and silent, of a body gathered together for Lord's Day assembly or a liturgical prayer office; and also the prayers of the saints across the centuries.[3] Collects have been used at the beginning of services as forms of supplicating the Lord's help (e.g., in the 1537 Danish Church Order), or following the Eucharist to conclude the service of the table (e.g., in Luther's 1523 and 1526 Lord's Supper services),[4] or at the end of morning and evening prayer services as a way of gathering together the supplications made therein (e.g., in the tradition of the Book of Common Prayer).

Collects are generally brief, with a readily identifiable form and flow.[5] Consider, for example, this medieval collect for purity, which is still regularly prayed across many traditions:

[a] Almighty God,

[b] to you all hearts are open, all desires known,
    and from you no secrets are hid:

[c] Cleanse the thoughts of our hearts by the inspiration of your
    Holy Spirit,

[d] that we may perfectly love you,
    and worthily magnify your holy Name;

[e] through Christ our Lord. Amen.[6]

---

3 Cf. C. Frederick Barbee and Paul F. M. Zahl, *The Collects of Thomas Cranmer* (Grand Rapids, MI: Eerdmans, 1999), ix–x.

4 On the Danish Church Order and Luther's services of the table, see Jonathan Gibson and Mark Earngey, eds., *Reformation Worship: Liturgies from the Past for the Present* (Greensboro, NC: New Growth, 2018), 247–75, and 75–135.

5 In the examples that follow, I have added superscript letters to highlight their structure and for later reference.

6 According to Potts, a form of this prayer appears in the Gregorian Sacramentary (J. Manning Potts, ed., *Prayers of the Middle Ages* [Nashville: Upper Room, 1954], 9). The translation

The same structure is seen in this collect for prisoners used, in particular, by Lutheran congregations:

> [a] Almighty God,
> [b] who didst bring the Apostle Peter forth out of prison,
> [c] have mercy upon all who are suffering imprisonment
> and set them free from their bonds
> [d] that we may rejoice in their deliverance
> and continually give praise to Thee;
> [e] through Jesus Christ, Thy Son, our Lord. Amen.[7]

As is clear, these collects have a shared form and flow. Collects are patterned prayers with a meaningful movement, consisting of most or all of these five elements:

a. an *invocation*, or direct address, of God (the Father)
b. an *identification* of some attribute or work of God
c. an *imploration*, or an appeal/supplication, for God to act now
d. our *intention*, or purpose/grounds, stated
e. the *intermediary* named (the Son) through whom our prayer is raised, frequently woven into a Trinitarian doxological formula[8]

It should be apparent that collects are tightly bound to Scripture. The *content* of traditional collects is regularly rooted in the word

---

used here comes from the 2019 Book of Common Prayer. Many from low church traditions also pray at least part of the prayer, likely unwittingly, in a modified and abbreviated musical form, as they sing Sandra McCracken's "Almighty God" from her 2015 album *Psalms*.

7 *The Lutheran Hymnal* (St. Louis, MO: Concordia, 1941), 105.
8 For alternative descriptive schemes, see Barbee and Zahl, *The Collects of Thomas Cranmer*, x–xi; John D. Witvliet, "Collective Wisdom: A Pattern for Prayer," *Christian Century*, July 29, 2008, 24.

of God (see "Scripture-Saturated, Scripture-Keyed, and Scripture-Cast," below, p. 209). In terms of the *progression* of collects through the year, some traditions link specific collects to specific days in the church's liturgical calendar. This, too, reflects the linking of collects to Scripture, inasmuch as the liturgical year is a calendrical enactment of the story of Christ, the key to the story of Scripture.[9] In any case, the collect *form* parallels paradigmatic prayers from Scripture. Consider, for example, the Lord's Prayer: "Our Father [invocation], who art in heaven [identification], hallowed be thy name . . . [implorations], for thine is the kingdom and the power and the glory forever [intention (grounds) flowing into a doxological formula]" (see also the early church's prayer in Acts 4:24–30).[10]

Collective Wisdom[11]

Since there is good biblical sense in the content and form of collect prayers passed down through the ages, consideration of collects is a means whereby we may cultivate wisdom for praying. Indeed, praying a collect embodies much of what we have explored in these chapters regarding answering speech. Among other things, a collect is all of the following.

A Word of Address

Calling upon God by name with its opening words, a collect is unmistakably vocative speech. It is a personal word of address.

---

9 For explanation and discussion, see Daniel J. Brendsel, "A Tale of Two Calendars: Calendars, Compassion, Liturgical Formation, and the Presence of the Spirit," *Bulletin of Ecclesial Theology* 3, no. 1 (2016): 16–19; also 40.

10 Observed by Witvliet, "Collective Wisdom," 24.

11 I have stolen the title for this section from John Witvliet's wonderful essay of the same name, on which I lean heavily in what follows.

Conforming prayers to the vocative model of collects gives us built-in accountability and prompting, which we need, since prayer can easily get off the rails and be used for something other than answering God. "Prayer" can be mistakenly thought of—or perhaps more often, unthinkingly treated—as detached contemplation of an object (God), as a way of teaching good theology, as so much talking *about* God in the third person, while speaking *with* God in the second person is eclipsed. While good theology and good praying go hand in hand, praying is not, at bottom, theologizing. It is communicative communion with the Father of our Lord Jesus Christ. Through words of invocation, a collect turns to God not as an object for detached contemplation or as a powerful tool to try to manipulate but as a Father whom we would answer and who hears and responds to us.

God-Centered

One remarkable thing about collects, often in contrast to extemporaneous praying, is how consistently focused they are on the God whom we address, on his names and character and ways and works. In traditional collects, at least as much time is devoted to reverencing who God is and what he does as there is to stating specific petitions, and often much more (notice the relative brevity of petitions [letter *c*] in the collects for purity and prisoners, above, p. 205). John Witvliet observes, "People who replace a typical five minute extemporaneous prayer with a set of five or so collects often remark on the experience of spending that much time in prayer thinking about God rather than about their own needs."[12] This is as it should be, because prayer is possible only because God has

12 Witvliet, "Collective Wisdom," 25.

preceded our praying, and all our praying is "pulled forth" from who he is, what he has done, what he has said. Prayer is answering speech.

Scripture-Saturated, Scripture-Keyed, and Scripture-Cast

Collects are saturated with Scripture, God's initiating word of address to us his covenant people. How do we know to name God as a Father who is always "more ready to hear than we to pray" and who gives "more than either we desire or deserve"? By being taught, for example, from Isaiah 65:24 and Luke 15:20–24. Where would we have learned that "all hearts are open" and "all desires known" to God, and "no secrets are hid" from him? From God's word to us in Hebrews 4:12–13. Why would we think to make reference to when God "didst bring the Apostle Peter forth out of prison"? Because we have read or heard Acts 12. The best collects are an engagement with Scripture through and through.

More dramatically, collect praying experientially "plots" us within the scriptural storyline. At its best, a collect is not simply biblical (in the sense of being filled with content derived from the Bible). The theo-logic behind pleading with the God who once delivered Peter from prison to so act now is that Acts 12, ostensibly about what happened in the past, is in truth for us and our salvation (cf. Rom. 15:4; 1 Cor. 10:6). We are dealing with the same God, who is up to the same things today. The biblical drama is not merely to be comprehended but also to be participated in through our turning prayerfully to the drama's divine protagonist. By prayer keyed to the biblical text and plotline, we show that our lives are implicated—indeed, we are cast as characters—in the biblical drama. Witvliet well observes that collect praying "fosters a theocentric hermeneutic which resists any supersessionism," inasmuch as "the pattern resists setting up a wall between God's actions with Israel and God's actions in Jesus, between God's actions in the Bible and God's actions today."[13]

Biblical Reasoning

Healthy supplication is inseparable from Holy Scripture in a way that goes far beyond the Bible simply informing the content of our prayers. Scripture also shapes our prayer at the level of *reasoning*, a point that collect prayers put into helpful relief.

Some methods of prayer, *like* collects, intentionally move through differing areas of focus—for example, adoration, confession, thanksgiving, supplication. But they are perhaps not as transparent with respect to how various focuses of prayer may be interconnected, how they might develop in a meaningful and logical flow.[14] In contrast, a collect moves purposefully from one element to the next: we invoke God and identify him as having some glorious attribute or having done some mighty deed, and *therefore* we are so bold as to supplicate that he act similarly today. (In the collects above [see p. 205], note how the implorations in letter *c* naturally arise from what is acknowledged about God in *a* and *b*.) We always pray through Christ, our mediator, and only on the basis of his name; so collects wisely state this as the ground of our praying (see *e*). This is biblical reasoning in action, arguing with God in the best sense of the word. Collects are part of how Christians' minds are not simply *filled* with the right data but also and especially *transformed* to think along with and through the word (cf. Rom. 12:2).

13 Witvliet, "Collective Wisdom," 25–26.
14 Witvliet, "Collective Wisdom," 25. But R. C. Sproul points out that the order of ACTS matters—when we front-load supplication and pay little attention to the what or how of the other elements, we more often than not wind up with SCAT (Sproul, *The Prayer of the Lord* [Sanford, FL: Reformation Trust, 2009], 63–64).

Attentive to Motivations and Aims

Also a matter of biblical reasoning, but worthy of its own subpoint: collects bring to the level of express articulation the motivations and aims with which we turn to God in prayer (see letter *d* in the sample collects above). Thus, Witvliet observes, "We are forced to say precisely why we want so-and-so to be cured from disease, or what the ultimate purpose of our church building campaign really is."[15] When it comes to purposeless prayer (every prayer, of course, is motivated by some purpose, but often we fail to *articulate and expose to the light* what we're ultimately after), I find that all too often it is selfish and insular prayer, prayer that has only the loosest and most accidental of relations to who God is and what he is up to in the world. But traditional collects plead with God ultimately in order "that we may perfectly love you, and worthily magnify your holy Name," and so that we might "continually give praise to Thee." The end of our prayer proves to be just as important as the middle, inasmuch as it manifests (and, if we are following a faithful model, it can prod and shape for our good and growth) the affections and commitments of our hearts.

For the most part we have been considering the advantage of finding and following traditional collects. But there is also great benefit to shaping our personal prayers today in accord with the collect form. I encourage you to sit down with Scripture open and respond to some passage in the following ways:

- Invoke God by name, a name that relates to something of God's nature and work as revealed in the passage of Scripture under consideration.

15 Witvliet, "Collective Wisdom," 26.

- Identify more expansively the greatness of God's attributes and mighty deeds in the aforementioned passage.
- Implore God to work in accord with what he has shown of himself—perhaps in a matter related to your own life and need, perhaps in the life of your neighbors and neighborhood, or your church and the global mission of Christ.
- State your intention, the purpose of your request, in a way that fits with what God is after in the world (often other scriptures can be drawn on).
- And be explicit about the intermediary in whose name you turn to God, and in whom you are confident that he hears and will act for your good.

So, as one example, you might read Numbers 32, which I read this morning as part of my daily Bible-reading plan, and pray in response:

O great covenant God, who gave to your people Israel a gracious foretaste of the Promised Land by giving to the tribes of Reuben and Gad the regions on the other side of the Jordan, but who warned them through your servant Moses not to forget or forsake their brothers and sisters: protect us your people from divisions rooted in selfishness, self-preoccupation, laziness, or fear. Help us to labor courageously for the good of one another in sure confidence of your promises, that all the world may through our unity know that you are the one God; through Christ Jesus our Lord, who lives and reigns with you in the unity of the Holy Spirit, forever and ever. Amen.

Collected into the Trinitarian Life

Collects are, like all prayers, Trinitarian. There is no prayer if the name of God is not Father, Son, and Spirit. There is no prayer that is not to the Father through the Son in the power of the Holy Spirit. Every prayer is, theologically speaking, Trinitarian in shape.

Of course, as Fred Sanders wryly notes in *The Deep Things of God*, "Many Christians are getting along just fine saying prayers to God without a single Trinitarian thought in their heads." In fact, it is not uncommon for them to utter prayers in extremely convoluted ways, compared with Trinitarian theology. As Sanders observes, "They thank the Father for dying on the cross, they thank Jesus for sending his only Son, and they suddenly realize that they have no clear ideas whatsoever about the Holy Spirit. Befuddled, they retreat to just praying to God-in-general."[16] One common habitual refrain at the end of our prayers is "in your name," to which we might ask: In *whose* name? Who mediates our prayer to God? Is it just "God-in-general" mediating our prayer addressed to "God-in-general"? Left to our own devices, we often wind up functionally praying to a unitarian God.

But traditional collects, shaped as they are by Scripture, are "particularly significant as a source of trinitarian piety and formation," Witvliet reminds us.[17] For the majority of collects are addressed to *God the Father* either explicitly or implicitly (as the naming of "Jesus Christ *your Son*" as mediator indicates). This is in accord with the pattern of biblical prayers: the vast majority of them are addressed to God the Father, a few are

---

16 Fred Sanders, *The Deep Things of God: How the Trinity Changes Everything* (Wheaton, IL: Crossway, 2010), 224.
17 Witvliet, "Collective Wisdom," 25.

addressed explicitly to the Son (Acts 7:59; 1 Cor. 16:22; Rev. 22:20; cf. 2 Cor. 12:8), and, so far as I am aware, none are explicitly addressed to the Spirit.[18] This is not to say that praying to Jesus is undesirable or praying to the Spirit is contraband (more on this below). It is to show a clear New Testament tendency and pattern that our prayers would do well to reproduce. The tradition of collect praying has wisely reproduced it. For example, the majority of the collects gathered by Thomas Cranmer in the Book of Common Prayer are addressed to the Father, with some few exceptions addressed to the Son, and the collect for Trinity Sunday more inclusive of all three persons of the Godhead in its address.[19] Prayer is normally addressed to "the Father, from whom every family in heaven and on earth is named" (Eph. 3:14–15), the "God and Father of our Lord Jesus Christ" (Eph. 1:3).

Additionally, prayer is always raised in the power of the Holy Spirit. The inseparable connection between the Spirit and prayer is testified to all over Scripture. *Before* prayer, so to speak, the Spirit addresses us and calls us to prayerful response (Acts 13:2–3; cf. Heb. 3:7; Rev. 2:7), even as he inclines us to pray (cf. Rom. 15:30). *After* prayer, the Spirit is, arguably, the central-most and fundamental answer in down payment to all our supplications (Luke 11:13; cf. Acts 4:23–31; 8:14–17; Phil. 1:19[20]). And the Spirit is present and active *during* our praying, praying himself *for* us (Rom. 8:26–27) and *alongside* us (Rev. 22:17), and empowering our appeal to God as "Abba, Father!" (Rom. 8:15; Gal. 4:6; cf. Eph. 6:18; Jude 20).

18 Sanders confirms this NT pattern (*The Deep Things of God*, 224).

19 Barbee and Zahl, *The Collects of Thomas Cranmer*, x.

20 I believe Phil. 1:19 links prayer and the Spirit in the closest possible way, much closer than English translations are capable of indicating. See, rightly, Gordon D. Fee, *God's Empowering Presence: The Holy Spirit in the Letters of Paul* (Peabody, MA: Hendrickson, 1994), 740.

In chapter 6 above, I suggested that proper prayerfulness attuned to Scripture is something of a seven-*i*'d being. I had an eye on Scripture, which links the seven eyes of the Lamb with "the seven Spirits of God" (Rev. 5:6)—that is, the Holy Spirit (cf. Zech. 3:9; 4:1–10; Rev. 1:4; 3:1; 4:5; and the sevenfold Spirit of LXX Isa. 11:2).[21] Praying with seven *i*'s on Scripture hints at the necessary work of the Spirit to enable and enliven our prayer in Christ.

Traditional collects clarify the proper and necessary role of the Spirit in prayer. Rarely are collects addressed to the Holy Spirit. Yet the Spirit's role of empowering and inspiring is frequently highlighted in them (e.g., "Cleanse the thoughts of our hearts by the inspiration of your Holy Spirit" in the collect for purity cited above), and the Spirit's unifying presence is named in the Trinitarian formulas with which they typically conclude (e.g., "through our Lord Jesus Christ, your Son, who lives and reigns with you in the unity of the Holy Spirit, one God, world without end").

Again, the point here is not to condemn all praying *to* the Spirit, or similarly to suggest that praying *to* the Son should be exceedingly rare. The point is to illuminate, with the help of collective wisdom keyed to God's self-revelation in the Son and in Scripture, the true shape and reality of any prayer, which can be obscured by our disordered *understandings* of what's going on and our disordered *speech* taken up in prayer. As C. S. Lewis proposed: "The whole purpose for which we exist is to be thus taken into the life of God. Wrong ideas about what that life is, will make it harder."[22] Wrong ideas about who God is as we turn to him in prayer will make it

---

21 G. K. Beale, *The Use of Daniel in Jewish Apocalyptic Literature and in the Revelation of St. John* (Lanham, MD: University Press of America, 1984), 210–11.

22 C. S. Lewis, *Mere Christianity*, rev. ed. (New York: Collier, 1952), 141, quoted in Sanders, *The Deep Things of God*, 227.

harder to enjoy the communion he so wondrously offers. Prayer shaped in a properly Trinitarian manner, and the theological vistas it unfolds, is finally about making it easier to be "taken into the life of God"—that is, to enter more deeply into communion with the Father, through the Son, in the power of the Spirit. Always and in everything, including in prayer, "through him [Christ] we both [Jews and Gentiles] have access in one Spirit to the Father" (Eph. 2:18).

Sanders's discussion is both sensible and characteristically reliable: Jesus and the Spirit are divine persons, so we can rightly address them in prayer, but we can do so only *because of Jesus's merit* (in his name), not because of our own, and *by the Spirit's power*, not in our own strength and human craft. As a result, even when we pray to Jesus or pray to the Spirit, the prayer is, in fact—if not in our specific articulation—thoroughly Trinitarian.[23] You don't *need* to realize the Trinitarian shape of prayer or verbalize it every time you bow your head, close your eyes, fold your hands, and open your mouth, any more than children need to understand the full scope of the self-sacrificial labors of love that have taken place in order to gratefully enjoy dinners set before them. But when a child grows in understanding and becomes able to articulate knowledgeable thanksgiving to mother and father at table, that helps to deepen the communion in love between them. So, similarly in the life of prayer, it is helpful to realize and give voice to what must be happening if any of us enjoys communion with God, who is Father, Son, and Spirit. Verbally shaping our prayers in a Trinitarian manner as a general rule of thumb, as our primary practice, and in keeping with collective

23 Sanders, *The Deep Things of God*, 224–26.

wisdom goes with the grain of prayer and thus frees us for more fruitful prayer.[24]

When we pray, whether we realize it or not, we are in fact coming to the Father in the name of the Son empowered by the Holy Spirit. "The only thing you have to add," Sanders remarks, "is your attention, to begin taking notice of what's Trinitarian about prayer."[25] We can say it still more stunningly: when we pray, whether we realize it or not, our communication with the Father is *a participation in the Son's everlasting communion of love with the Father*, being lifted up by the power of the Holy Spirit. But to properly appreciate this final and remarkable point, we must turn in conclusion to consider the middle that has, to this point, mostly been left unaddressed.

———

Almighty and everlasting God, you have given to us your servants grace, by the confession of a true faith, to acknowledge the glory of the eternal Trinity, and in the power of your divine Majesty to worship the Unity: Keep us steadfast in this faith and worship, and bring us at last to see you in your one and eternal glory, O Father; who with the Son and the Holy Spirit live and reign, one God, for ever and ever. Amen.

COLLECT FOR TRINITY SUNDAY
FROM THE BOOK OF COMMON PRAYER (2019)[26]

---

24 Sanders, *The Deep Things of God*, 211–14.
25 Sanders, *The Deep Things of God*, 212.
26 Book of Common Prayer (2019), 615.

Q. What is prayer?

A. Prayer is an offering up of our desires unto God, for things agreeable to his will, in the name of Christ, with confession of our sins, and thankful acknowledgment of his mercies.

WESTMINSTER SHORTER CATECHISM

When a man is indeed sensible of his sin and God's curse, then it is a hard thing to persuade him to pray; for, saith his heart, "There is no hope," it is vain to seek God. (Jer. xviii. 12.) I am so vile, so wretched, and so cursed a creature, that I shall never be regarded. . . . Oh, how great a task it is, for a poor soul that becomes sensible of sin and the wrath of God, to say in faith, but this one word, "Father!"

JOHN BUNYAN
"Discourse on Prayer"

More important than our experience of Christ is the Christ of our experience.

JAMES B. TORRANCE
Worship, Community and the Triune God of Grace

Conclusion

In Jesus's Name

PRAYER IS ANSWERING SPEECH. It is response to the God who first addresses us. But to leave the matter at that risks our stepping out on the wrong foot. Therefore, I conclude with what could well have come at the outset.[1] For when we, fallen and self-reliant creatures as we are, hear only that we are called to respond to God, our natural instincts kick in, resulting in two grave missteps: we muster up the best response we can offer, and we offer it to an unspecified "God-in-general."

We've already begun to address the latter misstep at the end of the last chapter. There is never any dealing with some "God-in-general," but the one particular God with whom we always have to do is Father, Son, and Spirit. Even if in our muddled thought and speech what we frequently say in prayer functionally implies a unitarian god, that doesn't change who *God actually is*. Still, in the long run, functionally unitarian

---

1   For a terrific example of starting with the crucial matter that I have left for the end, see Bryan Chapell, *Praying Backwards: Transform Your Prayer Life by Beginning in Jesus' Name* (Grand Rapids, MI: Baker, 2005). Though I have mostly deferred the discussion till the conclusion, I did focalize the confidence we can have when praying "in Jesus's name" in chap. 3.

prayer likely stirs up major obstacles for *our motivation* to pray earnestly and perseveringly.

Let us imagine, for the sake of argument, that unitarianism is the truth of the matter, that God is some supreme, all-powerful *monadic* divine being. Why would we ever imagine that our prayer would influence the Deity and redirect, as it were, or otherwise affect the Deity's sovereignly determined course of action? Fred Sanders alerts us to precisely this line of questioning raised by Andrew Murray, the nineteenth-century Dutch Reformed missionary to South Africa: If God is the unmoved and sovereign determiner of all that is, then can speaking of the power of prayer be "anything more than an accommodation to our mode of thought, because the Deity can never be dependent on any action from without for its doings? And is not the blessing of prayer simply the influence it exercises upon ourselves?"[2] That is to say, is the assertion that prayer changes things merely self-referential (it "changes me," as a film once put it), or simply pious code for self-coaching toward the development of a healthy mindset? The resolution, for Murray, is Trinitarian.

> In seeking to answer such questions, we find the key in the very being of God, in the mystery of the Holy Trinity. If God was only one Person, shut up within Himself, there could be no thought of nearness to Him or influence on Him. But in God there are three Persons. In God we have Father and Son, who have in the Holy Spirit their living bond of unity and fellowship.[3]

2 Andrew Murray, *With Christ in the School of Prayer: Thoughts on Our Training for the Ministry of Intercession* (New York: Revell, 1895), 130–31, quoted in Fred Sanders, *The Deep Things of God: How the Trinity Changes Everything* (Wheaton, IL: Crossway, 2010), 222.

3 Murray, *With Christ in the School of Prayer*, 131, quoted in Sanders, *The Deep Things of God*, 222.

Murray exults in the fact that this eternal fellowship is *communicative*. We get a truthful revelation of the life of God in Jesus's earthly ministry. When Christ prays to his Father as in the upper room (John 17), and when the Father responds to the Son with the power and form of the Holy Spirit, as at Jesus's baptism (Mark 1:9–11), what is revealed is exuberant, joyful communicative communion and responsiveness in the life of the one and only God. So Murray concludes: "Prayer has its rise and its deepest source in the very Being of God. In the bosom of Deity nothing is ever done without prayer—the asking of the Son and the giving of the Father."[4]

When we imagine or try to engage with God in a unitarian way, as if he were merely the solitary Unmoved Mover, we bump up against all the problems of prayer and the sovereignty of God that were stirred up in our opening chapter. They were stirred up, and they felt especially troubling, in part because we had held in abeyance any responsible reflection on the name of God as Father, Son, and Spirit. We can have confidence in the "power of prayer," and that prayer really does move "God" not, finally, because we can come up with an airtight philosophical argument for the necessity of such convictions but because Scripture reveals the sure truth that the Father listens and responds in love to the Son. With this in view, Sanders puts his finger on the marvelous good news: "There is always already a conversation going on among Father, Son, and Holy Spirit. When we pray, we are joining that conversation. We have been invited to call on God as Father, invited by a Spirit of sonship

---

4   Murray, *With Christ in the School of Prayer*, 132, quoted in Sanders, *The Deep Things of God*, 222–23.

that cries out 'Abba, Father' as the eternal Son does."[5] That is to say, "Christians are people who talk to God like they are Jesus Christ,"[6] and who have all the confidence that *Christ* has in the praying.

This leads to a consideration of the second great misstep—namely, trying to respond to the God who addresses us as best *we* can. A theologically faithful description of prayer must state not merely that it is our answering speech to the Father but also and especially that it is our participation by the power of the Spirit in the answering speech offered by the Son.

We pray "in Jesus's name." This means, to be sure, that our prayer is raised on the basis of Christ's merits, not ours. We can come to the Father, we can be so bold and seemingly reckless as to *call him Father*, because Christ has shed his blood, the just for the unjust, to bring us to the holy God as adopted children (1 Pet. 3:18). It is from that Christ-won status and new relationship that we, empowered by the Spirit, can pray to our "Abba, Father" (Rom. 8:15; Gal. 4:6). But make no mistake, the prayer to "Abba, Father" is first and properly *Christ's*. The God of grace has so worked through Christ's life and death and the outpouring of the Spirit to unite us to Christ so that his prayer becomes ours.

So praying "in Christ" and "in Jesus's name" means not only coming to God on the basis of Christ's shed blood and justifying work but also participating in Christ's proper and pleasing prayer to God, which preceded us (John 17), continues now at the Father's right hand (Rom. 8:34), and is formed in us by the power of Christ's

---

5 Sanders, *The Deep Things of God*, 215. He goes on to clarify that he is engaging in analogy, so that we should understand that our participation in the "eternal conversation" is "in an appropriately lower, creaturely way."

6 Sanders, *The Deep Things of God*, 216.

own Spirit poured out in our hearts (cf. Rom. 8:14–17; Gal. 4:4–6). Prayer "in Jesus's name" is participation in Jesus's faithful praying, and it moves God as surely as Jesus's own prayers move the Father.

James Torrance has well advised that the pastoral task "is not to throw people back on themselves with exhortations and instructions as to what to do and how to do it." Prayer is answering speech, but ours is not to try to generate the best answer we can come up with, to study up on the most biblically correct forms of prayer, to conjure our most fervent emotional engagement. If that is the kind of response this project has stirred up, then it is a failure. For the true pastoral task is "to direct people to the gospel of grace—to Jesus Christ, that they might look to him to lead them, open their hearts in faith and in prayer, and draw them by the Spirit into his eternal life of communion with the Father."[7] The good news is that "God in grace gives us what he seeks from us—a life of prayer—in giving us Jesus Christ and the Spirit."[8] Or in simpler terms, as has been said elsewhere, God himself, in the fullness of joy and love among Father, Son, and Spirit, *is* the gospel.[9] By inviting us to pray in Jesus's name, God would welcome us to himself that we may participate in his intra-Trinitarian life of love and joy.

The life of prayer is wondrously expansive. My hope and prayer in Jesus's name for you is that these reflections might stir up eagerness, earnestness, and practical wisdom for entering more fully into it.

---

7   Torrance, *Worship, Community and the Triune God of Grace*, 45.

8   Torrance, *Worship, Community and the Triune God of Grace*, 64.

9   John Piper, *God Is the Gospel: Meditations on God's Love as the Gift of Himself* (Wheaton, IL: Crossway, 2005).

We ask not of Thee, O Father, silver and gold, honour and glory, nor the pleasures of the world, but do Thou grant us grace to seek Thy Kingdom and Thy righteousness, and do Thou add unto us things necessary for the body and for this life. Behold, O Lord, our desire; may it be pleasing in Thy sight. We present our petition unto Thee through our Lord Jesus Christ, Who is at Thy right hand, our mediator and Advocate, through Whom Thou soughtest us that we might seek Thee; Thy Word, through Whom Thou madest us and all things; Thy only begotten Son, through Whom Thou callest us to adoption, Who intercedeth with Thee for us, and in Whom are hid all the treasures of wisdom and knowledge; to Him, with Thyself and the Holy Spirit, be all honour, praise, and glory, now and forever. Amen.

PRAYER OF AUGUSTINE (397–400)[10]

---

10 In *Prayers of the Early Church*, ed. J. Manning Potts (Nashville: Upper Room, 1953), 62. The prayer, variously appearing, seems based on Augustine's *Confessions* 11.4.

Discussion Questions

THE FOLLOWING QUESTIONS are meant to further individual reflection after each chapter but also, and especially, group discussion. The questions address key themes or challenges from the chapter, invite prayerful engagement on a specific passage of Scripture related to the chapter, and encourage avenues of direct prayerful response. In this last respect, I encourage you to start a prayer journal in which your times of meditation and prayerful response can be written out. I believe this can aid in clarifying your words of prayer to the Lord; additionally, it provides a helpful way to retrace your steps at the conclusion of the book to better see and notice—and give thanks for—how God has been present and active and responding throughout. The Lord be with you.

Chapter 1. Answering the Sovereign God

1. Has the doctrine of God's sovereignty over creation and history ever caused you to think that prayer is pointless? Spend some time sharing together (or in personal reflection) questions you wrestle with, or have wrestled with, about God's sovereignty. How might this chapter have helped address and clarify some of your confusion? What questions and unresolved confusion remain?

2. In *Evangelism and the Sovereignty of God*, J. I. Packer observes that "the Christian is at his sanest and wisest when he prays." Specifically, Packer suggests that when you pray to God for the conversion of unbelievers whose salvation you long for, "by your practice of intercession, no less than by giving thanks for your conversion, you acknowledge and confess the sovereignty of God's grace."[1] What do you think he means by this? How does intercession for the conversion of unbelievers bear witness to our implicit conviction in God's sovereignty over our lives? Why might we think that prayer makes no sense *unless* we are praying to the sovereign God?

3. The logic of biblical lamentation helps us to understand the crucial interconnection between prayer and the sovereignty of God. The Psalms are filled with prayers of lamentation to God. One of the longer and most striking ones is Psalm 89. Read it in its entirety (preferably out loud). In what verse does the psalmist begin to voice his lamentation in earnest? What is the psalmist so upset about? What is the point of the many, many verses that precede his overt lamentation? On what basis (or bases) does the psalmist expect God to act?

4. Consider starting a prayer journal in which you write out, or at least keep track of, your prayers and God's various responses to them over the course of the coming days and weeks. For your first entry, return to Ephesians 1:3–23. Following the lead of the apostle Paul, let what has already been revealed of God's good character and work in Christ from verses 3–14 inform your prayers for yourself, for one

1   J. I. Packer, *Evangelism and the Sovereignty of God*, rev. ed. (Downers Grove, IL: InterVarsity Press, 2012), 19.

another (if you are reading this in a group), and for the members of your congregation.

Chapter 2. When the Dialogue Seems One-Sided

1. What is, so to speak, the "easy answer" to the problem of unanswered prayer? Why is this answer necessary and important to be aware of? Why might it be important also to note that this answer is, as suggested at the beginning of the chapter, "insufficient"? In what way is it insufficient?

2. With a concordance or an online search engine (e.g., at biblegateway.com), survey the number of times in Scripture when biblical pray-ers cry out to God, "How long?" (or simply scan through the Psalms and observe how often the psalmists make this plea). What might we learn from the frequency of this plea in the inspired Scriptures? Why do the biblical pray-ers keep turning to God after suffering such long "silence"?

3. Think about and share an experience you have had of some seemingly long-unanswered Christ-honoring prayer. How have you responded to this experience? What biblical testimony have you turned to for help?

4. Of the four biblical insights offered in this chapter, which one proved most fortifying of your prayer life, and why? In light of the encouragement you may have received from this chapter, perhaps also still battling discouragement and weariness of heart, offer up a renewed prayer for some matter for which you have long lifted up supplications to God. Pray with and for others in the group in

their battle with weariness in prayer and for God's sustaining grace in their waiting. If you are keeping a prayer journal, write out your prayers there.

Chapter 3. The End and the Beginning of Prayer

1. The Heidelberg Catechism (A. 116) says that "prayer is the most important part of the thankfulness God requires of us." Why is prayer so tightly bound to and "part of" thankfulness? (There is more than one fitting way to answer.) What does this chapter mean when it claims that gratitude is "the test of all truly happy (in the sense of 'blessed' and 'felicitous') prayers"?

2. This chapter has emphasized that explicitly identifying the purposes (the ends or goals) tied to our supplications is crucial for a healthy life of prayer. We will return to the matter in the final chapter. For now, how do we know what are good ends and goals for our supplications to God?

3. Take stock of your habits in prayer. What do you regularly ask God for *first*—that is, how do you typically begin your prayers, and what sorts of things do you regularly request from God first of all? Why do you think that is?

4. Read Numbers 14:1–19. In verses 13–19, Moses intercedes on behalf of the rebellious wilderness generation of Israel. What reasons or purposes does Moses offer to God for *sparing* this rebellious people?

5. Having completed part 1 of the book, spend some extended time together and/or in your prayer journal responding to God

and what he has revealed of himself through the Scriptures you have been engaging. Pay special attention both to giving thanks for what God has been teaching you, and to offering supplications for still more growth in the weeks to come while expressly mentioning some of the purposes for which God might act on your requests.

Chapter 4. Praying in Response to Scripture

1. How would you describe the difference between "Here I am" and "I see/understand" as responses (postures) to our reading and hearing of Holy Scripture?

2. As we will consider in greater detail in the next chapter, the Psalms are the "prayer book of the Bible." The Psalter is a book of God-inspired prayers collected in one place to help us grow in our own life of prayer. But how this prayer book opens is telling. Read Psalm 1. It is not a prayer addressed to God but a declaration of the blessedness of the one who "meditates day and night" (v. 2) on God's law (his word). Why is it significant that this book of *prayers* begins with a psalm about meditating on the word?

3. This chapter addresses two "problematic postures toward the word": on the one hand, praying that isn't tethered to Scripture because we presume that Scripture is largely "irrelevant" to our problems and needs today; on the other hand, praying that isn't tethered to Scripture because all our attention to Scripture is in the mode of study rather than of hearing God's word of address. Do you find you are prone to fall off the horse on one side or the other, and if so, why? What are some reasons why you might

fail or forget to respond to God's word with prayer? In your prayer journal, write out a prayer acknowledging to God if you have discerned an unhealthy disconnect between God's word and your prayer life, and asking for help and guidance to grow into a more healthy union of these two realities that properly "go together."

Chapter 5. Praying Scripture

1. Based on what you read in this chapter, and on your own reflections now, why is it important that *Scripture itself*, its very words and its inscripturated prayers, be our first form of prayer—that is, prayers we ourselves take up on our lips?

2. Praying the words of Scripture as our first form of prayer can be awkward and uncomfortable (leaving a bad "taste" at first). Why might this be? If you have tried to pray biblical prayers and found it difficult, what difficulties did you encounter? Or, if you and your church are not in this habit, what struggles and awkwardness can you envision? What might be some good and wise responses to such challenges?

3. Meditate on the biblical prayers shown as examples under the heading "The Prayer Book of the Bible" (p. 82). What questions are stirred up about these prayers as you contemplate taking them on your own lips? How might they be easy and uncomplicated to pray? How might they be difficult and complicated?

4. Might there be any prayers in Scripture that we ought not to pray? Why or why not?

5. Select three psalms, preferably different *kinds* of psalms (e.g., a psalm of praise or thanksgiving, a psalm of confession of sin, a psalm of lamentation, a historical narrative psalm). With one another or in your prayer journal on different days in the week ahead, write out a psalm as the beginning of your prayer to God, and then with the remainder of your prayer add your own words of praise or confession or lamentation or inquiry or whatever is stirred up in response to your "first form of prayer."

Chapter 6. Praying (in the Story of) Scripture

1. Which of the seven *i*'s of praying with Scripture open did you find most helpful and illuminating? Why? Which of the seven *i*'s was most confusing or otherwise challenging, and why?

2. Explain in your own words why it is important to sometimes pray psalms (and other scripturally rooted prayers) that we might not *feel* at the time.

3. Discuss where we are in the biblical storyline, and think of some specific ways in which that might direct what and how we pray with and as the church of Christ.

4. Having completed part 2, spend the next week (seven days) putting into practice the suggestions of these chapters regarding "praying with Bible open," focusing each day on a different *i*. For example, on Sunday, *imitate* a biblical prayer: record in your prayer journal a prayer beginning with a psalm (or perhaps pay careful attention to a psalm prayed or recited during Lord's Day worship with the gathered church, and afterward write a prayer in your journal that

builds on it). On Monday, *invoke* God by a revealed name: focus on a particular name or title by which to call upon God, and prayerfully respond to what that particular name says about God's identity and character. Progress through the week in this way.

Chapter 7. Naming and Receiving Reality Aright

1. This chapter seeks to answer the question of why God calls us to pray for things that seem "natural" and automatic. How would you answer that question?

2. Matthew Myer Boulton comments, "We ask for bread, then, not only so that we might receive it, but also and principally so that when we receive it, we might actually experience it as it is." What is the significance of the modifier "also and principally"? Why might the more important matter for our lives not be to receive daily bread per se but to "experience it as it is"?

3. Psalm 104 is a hymn of praise to God for his works of creation and providence. Pray this psalm, taking note of, and pausing to express adoration and gratitude for, the indications in the psalm that God is always near to you in everyday life with his fatherly protection and provision and care.

4. This chapter lays the foundation for what we will return to commend in chapter 11, below—namely, the habit of beginning each day with prayer and ending each day with prayer and thanksgiving. We can begin the practice before getting to chapter 11. In the week ahead in your prayer journal, record morning prayers and supplications to God, and in the evenings write out your thanksgivings

for the ways in which God may be at work, near and attentive and responsive, to answer your morning supplications.

Chapter 8. The Language of the City of God

1. In your own words, explain why a book on prayer would address the civic identity of the church. What does Paul's exhortation to "behave as citizens worthy of the gospel" have to do with the life of prayer? Why is the life of prayer in the church of Christ of utmost importance for the good of the nations of the world?

2. What does Eugene Peterson mean when he speaks of "the language of information," "the language of motivation," and "the language of intimacy and friendship"? Do you share his opinion that the first two dominate in contemporary society, while the last is increasingly rare? In your own life, does one or the other dominate? If so, why?

3. Explain in your own words the responsibility to "voice creation's praise." Read and meditate on Romans 8:18–30. Notice, in particular, Paul's reference to creation's "groaning." Why is the non-human creation groaning? For what is it eagerly longing? What might be the reason it so longs for this? There are some obvious and perhaps not obvious reasons. Prayerfully respond to Romans 8— perhaps with a groaning lament at the present sufferings of this age, perhaps with hope at God's promises and invincible love made known in Christ.

4. Using as a model the list from the Book of Common Prayer's litany in this chapter (p. 138), or the prayer in the coda to the chapter from the Palatinate Church Order (p. 144), spend a season journaling

in intercessory prayer for your church, your neighborhood, your community, and the needs of your state, nation, and the globe.

Chapter 9. Learning the Language

1. Have you ever thought of the process of coming to learn and know a language as a matter of *rituals*? How might the crucial role of rituals in learning relate to the life of prayer? How might it relate to and imply the necessary role of the church in the life of prayer?

2. *Tradition* is for some evangelical Christians something of a dirty word. Why do you think that is? How does the present chapter understand the nature and significance of tradition?

3. Review the list of analogies under the heading "Language Learning in the City of God" (p. 153) between things in church life and the process of learning a new language. Which parallel stands out to you as most illuminating? Why?

4. Read and prayerfully respond to Psalm 133. In particular, meditate upon and seek the Lord's wisdom with regard to its important final lines as a testimony to what is to be enjoyed among the people, the fellowship, the family of God.

5. Part 3 has entered into the realm of *ecclesiology*, or the theology of the church. In what ways have these chapters challenged or grown your understanding of what the church is? Or what questions or concerns or disagreements have they stirred up about the nature and importance of the church vis-à-vis the life of prayer? Spend time discussing these matters among your group. In your prayer

journal, give thanks to God for the ways in which the church has served as a "language school" and "culture" to help you grow in your prayer life; pray for wisdom and grace, that we may be able more gracefully to "devote ourselves to the life of the church."

Chapter 10. The Weekly Rhythm of Prayer

1. What is the significance of Dietrich Bonhoeffer's *Life Together* having a chapter titled "The Day with Others" *preceding* a chapter titled "The Day Alone"?

2. Do you tend more often to consider and evaluate your Christian life "in small, momentary chunks" or "in terms of temporal progressions, trajectories, and lived patterns and rhythms"? What are some reason why the latter might be an important way of taking stock of our lives?

3. Read Nehemiah 8–9. Highlight and meditate on points of connection between Nehemiah 8–9 and the explanation of corporate worship as dialogue with God given in this chapter.

4. Have you been in the habit of thinking that the King is actually present at corporate worship to meet his gathered people by the Spirit? Have you been in the habit of thinking of corporate worship as a whole as a *dialogue* with this King, who is present and addresses us? Have you been in the habit of *expecting* to meet and hear him address us in corporate worship? Why might these convictions be transformative for our understanding of corporate worship, and for our experience of it? Spend time prayerfully reflecting on these questions in your prayer journal, variously giving thanks for how the Lord

has worked through corporate worship in your life, or confessing and repenting of your neglect of the covenantal assembly, or seeking still more mercy and grace from the Lord for you and your brothers and sisters in your congregation in the Lord's Day assemblies to come.

Chapter 11. The Daily Rhythm of Prayer

1. Did the section "On Spontaneity and Structure" (p. 187) address some potential concerns or frustrations you may have brought to the chapter? Did it leave others unaddressed? If so, discuss them in your group.

2. Share with the group some of the daily rhythms of prayer with which you have had good traction. Why have these rhythms "fit" for you? Are there other ways, other "natural breaks in the day," in which you might pause for prayer? Together, or individually, meditate and pray through Psalm 113.

3. Review some of the suggested prayer book resources in this chapter, perhaps with others in the group, or maybe even others in your church more broadly. Taking stock of your daily prayer habits, come up with a workable plan for regular prayer over the course of the next month. Make use of whatever you find helpful in your review of prayer book material and/or the weekly service materials from your local congregation. Take into consideration Bible-reading plans you either are already committed to or would like to try, and how that reading might fit in your overall plan. Again, perhaps you and others in your group could commit to roughly the same plan. If your church already holds a regular weekly prayer service, seriously consider attending it as part of your plan. To reiterate, the plan is

not meant to be a straitjacket but can be a helpful scaffolding to stand on in getting started. Be realistic, prayerfully acknowledging what you think your limits are, what you are anxious or concerned about in starting such a plan, and asking for wisdom to come up with something feasible for you.

Chapter 12. The Rhythm and Shape of a Typical Prayer

1. In many ways, this chapter distills the arguments of the whole book by considering a specific model of prayer, the collect. What, if anything, in this chapter helped to crystallize in your mind and heart earlier parts of the book?

2. Why is it so significant for collects (and for any of our prayers) to name and praise the *intermediary* through whom we pray?

3. Using the collect form, pray in response to a passage or passages from Scripture that you have read most recently in your daily Bible reading. Try continuing to do so daily for the coming week, or one morning a week for the coming month.

4. Having completed the four parts of the book, review in prayer where the Lord has led you. Retrace your steps in your prayer journal. What has the Lord taught you? Does the life of prayer now appear more expansive than you had at first thought? How has your gratitude and eagerness and earnestness for the life of prayer grown? Where would you like your pursuit of the life of prayer to grow still more? Give thanks for where the Lord has brought you, and pray for grace to "excel still more" (1 Thess. 4:1) in the name of Jesus.

Sources of
Chapter-Opening Epigraphs

Introduction

Anselm of Canterbury, *Proslogion*, in *Anselm of Canterbury: The Major Works*, ed. Brian Davies and G. R. Evans (Oxford: Oxford University Press, 1998), 86–87.

Chapter 1

John Calvin, *Institutes of the Christian Religion*, ed. John T. McNeill, trans. Ford Lewis Battles (Louisville: Westminster John Knox, 1960), 3.20.3.

Chapter 2

Andrew Peterson, "The Silence of God," copyright ©2003 New Spring Publishing Inc. (ASCAP) (adm. at CapitolCMGPublishing.com). All rights reserved. Used by permission.

Chapter 3

Kevin J. Vanhoozer, "What Is Everyday Theology? How and Why Christians Should Read Culture," in *Everyday Theology: How to Read Cultural Texts and Interpret Trends*, ed. Kevin J. Vanhoozer, Charles A. Anderson, Michael J. Sleasman (Grand Rapids, MI: Baker, 2007), 45.

Chaim Potok, *In the Beginning* (New York: Knopf, 1975), 3.

Dwight L. Moody, "The Eighth Chapter of Romans," in *Moody's Last Sermons: Authorized Edition Printed from Verbatim Reports* (Chicago: Moody, n.d.), 43–44, quoted in Fred Sanders, *The Deep Things of God: How the Trinity Changes Everything* (Wheaton, IL: Crossway, 2010), 121.

Chapter 4

Michael S. Horton, *The Christian Faith: A Systematic Theology for Pilgrims on the Way* (Grand Rapids, MI: Zondervan, 2011), 85, emphasis original.

Helmut Thielicke, *A Little Exercise for Young Theologians*, trans. C. L. Taylor (Grand Rapids, MI: Eerdmans, 1962), 34.

Chapter 5

Tish Harrison Warren, "By the Book," *Comment* 34, no. 4 (2016): 44–49, https://www.cardus.ca/comment/article/by-the-book/.

Mikhail Bakhtin, "Discourse in the Novel," in *The Dialogic Imagination: Four Essays*, ed. Michael Holquist, trans. Caryl Emerson and Michael Holquist (Austin, TX: University of Texas Press, 1981), 282.

Chapter 6

George Herbert, "The Bunch of Grapes," in *The Complete English Poems*, ed. J. J. M. Tobin (New York: Penguin, 2004), 119–20.

Lesslie Newbigin, *The Open Secret: An Introduction to the Theology of Mission*, rev. ed. (Grand Rapids, MI: Eerdmans, 1995), 82–83.

Chapter 7

Iris Murdoch, *Metaphysics as a Guide to Morals* (New York: Penguin, 1992), 315.

John Ames, in Marilynne Robinson, *Gilead* (New York: Farrar, Straus and Giroux, 2004), 27–28.

Piscator, in Izaak Walton with Charles Cotton, *The Compleat Angler, or the Contemplative Man's Recreation* (1653; repr., London: Dent, 1973), 190–91.

Chapter 8

Eugen Rosenstock-Huessy, *Speech and Reality* (Norwich, VT: Argo, 1970), 111.

Robert Louis Wilken, *The Spirit of Early Christian Thought: Seeking the Face of God* (New Haven, CT: Yale University Press, 2003), 210.

Chapter 9

Esther L. Meek, "Learning to See: The Role of Authoritative Guides in Knowing," *Tradition and Discovery* 32, no. 2 (2005–2006): 41, emphasis original.

Pirke Aboth 1.6, from *The Mishnah*, trans. Herbert Danby (Oxford: Oxford University Press, 1933), 446.

Chapter 10

Eugene H. Peterson, *The Contemplative Pastor: Returning to the Art of Spiritual Direction* (Dallas: Word, 1989), 15–16.

Thomas G. Long, *Testimony: Talking Ourselves into Being Christian* (San Francisco: Jossey-Bass, 2004), 47–48.

Chapter 11

Robert Taft, *The Liturgy of the Hours in East and West: The Origins of the Divine Office and Its Meaning for Today*, 2nd rev. ed. (Collegeville, MN: Liturgical Press, 1993), 348.

Annie Dillard, *The Writing Life* (New York: Harper & Row, 1989), 32.

Chapter 12

Ca. fifth-century collect. A Latin form of the prayer appears as early as the Leonine Sacramentary (C. Frederick Barbee and Paul F. M. Zahl, *The Collects of Thomas Cranmer* [Grand Rapids, MI: Eerdmans, 1999], 92). The version quoted above is the collect for the twelfth Sunday after Trinity, in the Church of England's Common Worship (https://www.churchofengland.org/prayer-and-worship/worship-texts-and-resources/common-worship/common-material/collects-and-post-24).

Conclusion

Westminster Shorter Catechism, question and answer 98.

John Bunyan, "Prayer," in *The Complete Works of John Bunyan*, 3 vols. (Marshallton, DE: National Foundation for Christian Education, 1968), 1.1.268. It should be noted that this "discourse" of Bunyan is especially stinging in its contempt for prayer books and established forms of prayer, matters I have treated in these pages as of some benefit for the Christian life. Bunyan gives voice to many nowadays who equate prayer books with dead letters, sterile tradition, and "man-made" religion. I cite Bunyan here to indicate that I am in agreement with the spirit of his pursuit, though I think the way he wields his particular criticisms begs several questions and poses some false alternatives.

James B. Torrance, *Worship, Community and the Triune God of Grace* (Downers Grove, IL: InterVarsity Press, 1996), 34.

Bibliography

Anglican Church in North America. *The Book of Common Prayer*. Huntington Beach, CA: Anglican Liturgy Press, 2019.

Ansberry, Christopher B. *Be Wise, My Son, and Make My Heart Glad: An Exploration of the Courtly Nature of the Book of Proverbs*. Beihefte zur Zeitschrift für die alttestamentliche Wissenschaft 422. Berlin: de Gruyter, 2011.

Anselm. *Anselm of Canterbury: The Major Works*. Edited by Brian Davies and G. R. Evans. Oxford: Oxford University Press, 1998.

Anselm. *The Prayers and Meditations of St. Anselm with the Proslogion*. Translated and edited by Benedicta Ward. New York: Penguin, 1973.

Arnold, Clinton E. *Ephesians*. Zondervan Exegetical Commentary on the New Testament 10. Grand Rapids, MI: Zondervan, 2010.

Athanasius. "The Letter of Athanasius to Marcellinus on the Interpretation of the Psalms." In *On the Incarnation*. 2nd rev. ed, translated and edited anonymously, 97–119. Crestwood, NY: St. Vladimir's Orthodox Theological Seminary Press, 1953.

Bailey, Kenneth. *Poet and Peasant and Through Peasant Eyes: A Literary-Cultural Approach to the Parables in Luke*. 2 vols. Grand Rapids, MI: Eerdmans, 1976, 1980. Reprinted in one volume, Grand Rapids, MI: Eerdmans, 1983.

Bakhtin, Mikhail. "Discourse in the Novel." In *The Dialogic Imagination: Four Essays*, edited by Michael Holquist, translated by Caryl Emerson and Michael Holquist, 259–422. Austin, TX: University of Texas Press, 1981.

Balthasar, Hans Urs von. *Prayer*. Translated by G. Harrison. San Francisco: Ignatius, 1986.

Barbee, C. Frederick, and Paul F. M. Zahl. *The Collects of Thomas Cranmer*. Grand Rapids, MI: Eerdmans, 1999.

Barrett, C. K. *The Gospel according to St. John*. 2nd ed. Philadelphia: Westminster, 1978.

Bass, Dorothy C. *Receiving the Day: Christian Practices for Opening the Gift of Time*. San Francisco: Jossey-Bass, 2000.

Bauckham, Richard. *The Theology of the Book of Revelation*. New Testament Theology. Cambridge: Cambridge University Press, 1993.

Beale, G. K. *The Book of Revelation*. New International Greek Testament Commentary. Grand Rapids, MI: Eerdmans, 1999.

Beale, G. K. *The Use of Daniel in Jewish Apocalyptic Literature and in the Revelation of St. John*. Lanham, MD: University Press of America, 1984.

Beasley-Murray, G. R. *The General Epistles: James, 1 Peter, Jude, 2 Peter*. London: Lutterworth; New York: Abingdon, 1965.

Beeke, Joel R. *Family Worship*. 2nd ed. Grand Rapids, MI: Reformation Heritage, 2021.

Begbie, Jeremy S. *Resounding Truth: Christian Wisdom in the World of Music*. Grand Rapids, MI: Baker, 2007.

Bennett, Arthur, ed. *The Valley of Vision: A Collection of Puritan Prayers and Devotions*. Edinburgh: Banner of Truth, 1975.

Berry, Wendell. "Men and Women in Search of Common Ground." *Sunstone*, July 1987, 8–12.

Billings, J. Todd. *The End of the Christian Life: How Embracing Our Mortality Frees Us to Truly Live*. Grand Rapids, MI: Brazos, 2020.

Billings, J. Todd. *The Word of God for the People of God: An Entryway to the Theological Interpretation of Scripture*. Grand Rapids, MI: Eerdmans, 2010.

Bonhoeffer, Dietrich. *Life Together*. Dietrich Bonhoeffer Works, Reader's Edition. Minneapolis: Fortress, 2015.

Bonhoeffer, Dietrich. *Meditating on the Word*. Translated and edited by David McI. Gracie. 2nd ed. Lanham, MD: Cowley, 2000.

Bonhoeffer, Dietrich. *Psalms: The Prayer Book of the Bible*. Translated by J. H. Burtness. Minneapolis: Augsburg Fortress, 1970.

Borger, Joyce, Martin Tel, and John D. Witvliet, eds. *Psalms for All Seasons: A Complete Psalter for Worship*. Grand Rapids, MI: Brazos, 2012.

Boulton, Matthew Myer. *Life in God: John Calvin, Practical Formation, and the Future of Protestant Theology*. Grand Rapids, MI: Eerdmans, 2011.

Brendsel, Daniel J. *"Isaiah Saw His Glory": The Use of Isaiah 52–53 in John 12*. Beihefte zur Zeitschrift für die neutestamentliche Wissenschaft 208. Berlin: de Gruyter, 2014.

Brendsel, Daniel J. "The Path More Traveled: The Place of the (Missing) Church in Christian Engagement of Technology." In *Technē: Christian Visions of Technology*, edited by G. Hiestand and T. A. Wilson, 16–35. Eugene, OR: Cascade, 2022.

Brendsel, Daniel J. "Scripture in Scripture: Reading the Old Testament with the Apostles." Desiring God, September 8, 2020. https://www.desiringGod.org/.

Brendsel, Daniel J. "The Spirit after Pentecost: Three Facets of His New-Covenant Glory." Desiring God, January 28, 2022. https://www.desiringGod.org/.

Brendsel, Daniel J. "A Tale of Two Calendars: Calendars, Compassion, Liturgical Formation, and the Presence of the Spirit." *Bulletin of Ecclesial Theology* 3, no. 1 (2016): 15–43.

Brown, Jeannine K. "Creation's Renewal in the Gospel of John." *Catholic Biblical Quarterly* 72, no. 2 (2010): 275–90.

Bunyan, John. *The Complete Works of John Bunyan.* 3 vols. Marshallton, DE: National Foundation for Christian Education, 1968.

Calvin, John. *Commentary on the Book of the Psalms.* Vol. 1. Translated by James Anderson. Edinburgh: Calvin Translation Society, 1845.

Calvin, John. *Institutes of the Christian Religion.* Edited by John T. McNeill. Translated by Ford Lewis Battles. Louisville: Westminster John Knox, 1960.

Carson, D. A. "Worship under the Word." In *Worship by the Book,* edited by D. A. Carson, 11–63. Grand Rapids, MI: Zondervan, 2002.

Chapell, Bryan. *Praying Backwards: Transform Your Prayer Life by Beginning in Jesus' Name.* Grand Rapids, MI: Baker, 2005.

Charry, Ellen T. *By the Renewing of Your Minds: The Pastoral Function of Christian Doctrine.* Oxford: Oxford University Press, 1997.

Chesterton, G. K. *Orthodoxy.* 1909. Reprint, Peabody, MA: Hendrickson, 2006.

Dillard, Annie. *The Writing Life.* New York: Harper & Row, 1989.

Edwards, Jonathan. *The Works of Jonathan Edwards.* 2 vols. Edited by Sereno E. Dwight. Revised and corrected by Edward Hickman. Edinburgh: Banner of Truth, 1974.

Episcopal Church in the United States of America. *The Book of Common Prayer.* New York: Church Publishing, 1979.

Evangelical Lutheran Synodical Conference of North America. *The Lutheran Hymnal.* St. Louis, MO: Concordia, 1941.

Fee, Gordon D. *God's Empowering Presence: The Holy Spirit in the Letters of Paul.* Peabody, MA: Hendrickson, 1994.

Fretheim, Terence E. *God and World in the Old Testament: A Relational Theology of Creation.* Nashville: Abingdon, 2005.

Gibson, Jonathan, and Mark Earngey, eds. *Reformation Worship: Liturgies from the Past for the Present*. Greensboro, NC: New Growth, 2018.

Giertz, Bo. *The Hammer of God*. Translated by Clifford Ansgar Nelson and Hans Andrae. Rev. ed. Minneapolis: Augsburg Fortress, 2005.

Goldingay, John. *Genesis*. Baker Commentary on the Old Testament. Grand Rapids, MI: Baker, 2020.

Goldingay, John. *Psalms 1–41*. Baker Commentary on the Old Testament. Grand Rapids, MI: Baker, 2006.

Hafemann, Scott J. *2 Corinthians*. NIV Application Commentary. Grand Rapids, MI: Zondervan, 2000.

Harris, Mark. "'The Trees of the Field Shall Clap Their Hands' (Isaiah 55:12): What Does It Mean to Say That a Tree Praises God?" In *Knowing Creation: Perspectives from Theology, Philosophy, and Science*, edited by Andrew B. Torrance and Thomas H. McCall, 287–304. Grand Rapids, MI: Zondervan, 2018.

Herbert, George. *The Complete English Poems*. Edited by J. J. M. Tobin. New York: Penguin, 2004.

Hodge, A. A. *The Westminster Confession: A Commentary*. 1958. Reprint, Edinburgh: Banner of Truth, 2002.

Holy Transfiguration Monastery, trans. *A Prayerbook for Orthodox Christians*. 2nd ed. Boston, MA: Holy Transfiguration Monastery, 2014.

Horton, Michael S. *The Christian Faith: A Systematic Theology for Pilgrims on the Way*. Grand Rapids, MI: Zondervan, 2011.

Horton, Michael S. *Covenant and Eschatology: The Divine Drama*. Louisville: Westminster John Knox, 2002.

Howe, Marie. *The Kingdom of Ordinary Time*. New York: Norton, 2008.

Hymns Ancient and Modern. Historical ed. London: Clowes, 1909.

Jacobs, Alan. *The Book of Common Prayer: A Biography*. Princeton, NJ: Princeton University Press, 2013.

Jeremias, Joachim. *The Prayers of Jesus*. Translated by J. Bowden, C. Burchard, and J. Reumann. Philadelphia: Fortress, 1978.

Johnson, Dru. *Knowledge by Ritual: A Biblical Prolegomenon to Sacramental Theology*. Journal of Theological Interpretation Supplements 13. Winona Lake, IN: Eisenbrauns, 2016.

Johnson, Dru. *Scripture's Knowing: A Companion to Biblical Epistemology*. Eugene, OR: Cascade, 2015.

Johnson, Keith L. Review of *Between Cross and Resurrection: A Theology of Holy Saturday*, by Alan E. Lewis. *Perspectives in Religious Studies* 35, no. 3 (2008): 338–43.

Keener, Craig S. *The Gospel of John*. 2 vols. Peabody, MA: Hendrickson, 2003.

Keller, Timothy. *Prayer: Experiencing Awe and Intimacy with God*. New York: Dutton, 2014.

Kierkegaard, Søren. *For Self-Examination and Judge for Yourselves!* Translated by Walter Lowrie. Princeton, NJ: Princeton University Press, 1944.

Kierkegaard, Søren. *Provocations: Spiritual Writings of Kierkegaard*. Compiled and edited by Charles E. Moore. New York: Plough, 2011.

Kline, Meredith G. *The Structure of Biblical Authority*. 2nd ed. Eugene, OR: Wipf and Stock, 1997.

Klink, Edward W., III. *John*. Zondervan Exegetical Commentary on the New Testament 4. Grand Rapids, MI: Zondervan, 2016.

Lee, Archie C. C. "Genesis I and the Plagues Tradition in Psalm CV." *Vetus Testamentum* 40, no. 3 (1990): 257–63.

Lee, Harper. *To Kill a Mockingbird*. Philadelphia: Harper & Row, 1960. Reprint, New York: Warner, 1982.

Leithart, Peter J. *Against Christianity*. Moscow, ID: Canon, 2003.

Leithart, Peter J. *Revelation 1–11*. International Theological Commentary. London: Bloomsbury T&T Clark, 2018.

Lewis, Alan E. *Between Cross and Resurrection: A Theology of Holy Saturday*. Grand Rapids, MI: Eerdmans, 2001.

Lewis, C. S. *The Discarded Image: An Introduction to Medieval and Renaissance Literature*. Cambridge: Cambridge University Press, 1964.

Lewis, C. S. *Mere Christianity*. Rev. ed. New York: Collier, 1952.

Long, D. Stephen. *Theology and Culture: A Guide to the Discussion*. Cambridge: James Clarke, 2010.

Long, Thomas G. *Testimony: Talking Ourselves into Being Christian*. San Francisco: Jossey-Bass, 2004.

Longenecker, Richard N. *The Epistle to the Romans*. New International Greek Testament Commentary. Grand Rapids, MI: Eerdmans, 2016.

Luther, Martin. "Preface to the Psalms." In *Martin Luther: Selections from His Writings*, edited by John Dillenberger, 37–41. New York: Anchor, 1962.

MacDonald, George. *Unspoken Sermons*, 2nd ser. London: Longmans, Green, 1885.

Mason, Rex. "The Use of Earlier Biblical Material in Zechariah 9–14: A Study in Inner Biblical Exegesis." In *Bringing Out the Treasure: Inner Biblical Allusion in Zechariah 9–14*, edited by M. J. Boda and M. H. Floyd, 2–208. London: T&T Clark, 2003.

McKnight, Scot. *Praying with the Church: Following Jesus Daily, Hourly, Today*. Brewster, MA: Paraclete, 2006.

Meek, Esther L. "Learning to See: The Role of Authoritative Guides in Knowing." *Tradition and Discovery* 32, no. 2 (2005–2006): 38–50.

Metaxas, Eric. *Bonhoeffer: Pastor, Martyr, Prophet, Spy*. Nashville: Thomas Nelson, 2010.

Midrash on the Psalms. 2 vols. Translated by William G. Braude. Yale Judaica Series 13. New Haven, CT: Yale University Press, 1959.

Mihalios, Stefanos. *The Danielic Eschatological Hour in the Johannine Literature.* Library of New Testament Studies 436. London: T&T Clark, 2011.

The Mishnah. Translated by Herbert Danby. Oxford: Oxford University Press, 1933.

Morgan, George Allen. *Speech and Society: The Christian Linguistic Social Philosophy of Eugen Rosenstock-Huessy.* Gainesville, FL: University of Florida Press, 1987.

Murdoch, Iris. *Metaphysics as a Guide to Morals.* New York: Penguin, 1992.

Naselli, Andy. "12 Reasons You Should Pray Scripture." *Themelios* 38, no. 3 (2013): 417–25.

Newbigin, Lesslie. *The Open Secret: An Introduction to the Theology of Mission.* Rev. ed. Grand Rapids, MI: Eerdmans, 1995.

Norris, Kathleen. *The Quotidian Mysteries: Laundry, Liturgy and "Women's Work."* Mahwah, NJ: Paulist, 1998.

Old, Hughes Oliphant. *Leading in Prayer: A Workbook for Ministers.* Grand Rapids, MI: Eerdmans, 1995.

Ong, Walter J. *The Presence of the Word: Some Prolegomena for Cultural and Religious History.* New Haven, CT: Yale University Press, 1967. Reprint, Minneapolis: University of Minnesota Press, 1981.

Oyler, Lauren. "The Case for Semicolons." *New York Times Magazine,* February 9, 2021. https://www.nytimes.com/.

Packer, J. I. *Evangelism and the Sovereignty of God.* Rev. ed. Downers Grove, IL: InterVarsity Press, 2012.

Patton, Matthew H. "Searching for a Truly Penitent Israel: Ezra-Nehemiah and Restoration Prophecy." Unpublished paper presented at the Wheaton College PhD Colloquium, February 4, 2010.

Penner, Jeremy. *Patterns of Daily Prayer in Second Temple Judaism.* Studies on the Texts of the Desert of Judah 104. Leiden: Brill, 2012.

Peterson, Eugene H. *Answering God: The Psalms as Tools for Prayer.* San Francisco: Harper & Row, 1989.

Peterson, Eugene H. *The Contemplative Pastor: Returning to the Art of Spiritual Direction.* Dallas: Word, 1989.

Peterson, Eugene H. *The Pastor: A Memoir.* New York: HarperOne, 2011.

Piper, John. *Desiring God: Meditations of a Christian Hedonist.* Rev. ed. Colorado Springs: Multnomah, 2011.

Piper, John. *God Is the Gospel: Meditations on God's Love as the Gift of Himself.* Wheaton, IL: Crossway, 2005.

Piper, John. *The Justification of God: An Exegetical and Theological Study of Romans 9:1–23.* 2nd ed. Grand Rapids, MI: Baker, 1993.

Polanyi, Michael. *Personal Knowledge: Towards a Post-Critical Philosophy.* Chicago: University of Chicago Press, 1962.

Potok, Chaim. *In the Beginning.* New York: Knopf, 1975.

Potts, J. Manning, ed. *Prayers of the Early Church.* Nashville: Upper Room, 1953.

Potts, J. Manning, ed. *Prayers of the Middle Ages.* Nashville: Upper Room, 1954.

Presbyterian Church of South Africa. *Service Book and Ordinal.* Glasgow: Maclehose, Jackson, 1921.

Pritchard, James B., ed. *Ancient Near Eastern Texts Relating to the Old Testament.* 3rd ed. Princeton, NJ: Princeton University Press, 1969.

Roberts, Robert. *Emotions: An Essay in Aid of Moral Psychology.* Cambridge: Cambridge University Press, 2003.

Robinson, Marilynne. *Gilead*. New York: Farrar, Straus and Giroux, 2004.

Rosenstock-Huessy, Eugen. *Speech and Reality*. Norwich, VT: Argo, 1970.

Rossetti, Christina. *Selected Prose of Christina Rossetti*. Edited by David A. Kent and P. G. Stanwood. New York: St. Martin's, 1998.

Sacasas, L. M. "The Material Sources of Free Speech Anxieties." The Convivial Society, July 9, 2020. https://theconvivialsociety.substack.com/p/the-material-sources-of-free-speech.

Samson, William. "The Finkenwalde Project." In *Monasticism Old and New*. Christian Reflection 37, edited by Robert B. Kruschwitz, 19–25. Waco, TX: Center for Christian Ethics at Baylor University, 2010.

Sanders, Fred. *The Deep Things of God: How the Trinity Changes Everything*. Wheaton, IL: Crossway, 2010.

Schmemann, Alexander. *For the Life of the World: Sacraments and Orthodoxy*. Rev. and exp. ed. Crestwood, NY: St. Vladimir's Seminary Press, 1997.

Schmitt, John J. "You Adulteresses! The Image in James 4:4." *Novum Testamentum* 28, no. 4 (1986): 327–37.

Seifrid, Mark A. *The Second Letter to the Corinthians*. Pillar New Testament Commentary. Grand Rapids, MI: Eerdmans, 2014.

Smith, James K. A. *Imagining the Kingdom: How Worship Works*. Grand Rapids, MI: Baker, 2013.

Sproul, R. C. *The Prayer of the Lord*. Sanford, FL: Reformation Trust, 2009.

Spurgeon, Charles H. "Robinson Crusoe's Text." Sermon preached at the Metropolitan Tabernacle, Newington, August 30, 1885. https://archive.spurgeon.org/sermons/1876.php.

Stevens, R. Paul. *The Other Six Days: Vocation, Work, and Ministry in Biblical Perspective.* Grand Rapids, MI: Eerdmans, 1999.

Swale, Matthew. "Power for Prayer through the Psalms: Cassiodorus's Interpretation of the Honey of Souls." *Themelios* 44, no. 3 (2019): 487–502.

Taft, Robert. *The Liturgy of the Hours in East and West: The Origins of the Divine Office and Its Meaning for Today.* 2nd rev. ed. Collegeville, MN: Liturgical Press, 1993.

Taylor, Charles. *A Secular Age.* Cambridge, MA: Harvard University Press, 2007.

Tertullian. *Concerning Prayer.* In *Tertullian's Treatises: Concerning Prayer, Concerning Baptism,* translated by Alexander Souter. London: SPCK, 1919.

Thielicke, Helmut. *A Little Exercise for Young Theologians.* Translated by C. L. Taylor. Grand Rapids, MI: Eerdmans, 1962.

Thielman, Frank. *Ephesians.* Baker Exegetical Commentary on the New Testament. Grand Rapids, MI: Baker, 2010.

Tietje, Adam D. *Toward a Pastoral Theology of Holy Saturday: Providing Spiritual Care for War Wounded Souls.* Eugene, OR: Wipf and Stock, 2018.

Torrance, James B. *Worship, Community and the Triune God of Grace.* Downers Grove, IL: InterVarsity Press, 1996.

Vanhoozer, Kevin J. *The Drama of Doctrine: A Canonical-Linguistic Approach to Christian Theology.* Louisville: Westminster John Knox, 2005.

Vanhoozer, Kevin J. *Faith Speaking Understanding: Performing the Drama of Doctrine.* Louisville: Westminster John Knox, 2014.

Vanhoozer, Kevin J. "From Speech Acts to Scripture Acts: The Covenant of Discourse and the Discourse of the Covenant." In *After Pentecost: Language and Biblical Interpretation,* edited by Craig G.

Bartholomew, Colin Greene, and Karl Möller, 1–49. Cumbria: Paternoster; Grand Rapids, MI: Zondervan, 2001.

Vanhoozer, Kevin J. *Remythologizing Theology: Divine Action, Passion, and Authorship*. Cambridge Studies in Christian Doctrine 18. Cambridge: Cambridge University Press, 2010.

Vanhoozer, Kevin J. "What Is Everyday Theology? How and Why Christians Should Read Culture." In *Everyday Theology: How to Read Cultural Texts and Interpret Trends*, edited by Kevin J. Vanhoozer, Charles A. Anderson, and Michael J. Sleasman, 15–60. Grand Rapids, MI: Baker, 2007.

Wainwright, Geoffrey. *Doxology: The Praise of God in Worship, Doctrine and Life*. New York: Oxford University Press, 1980.

Walsh, Milton. *Witness of the Saints: Patristic Readings in the Liturgy of the Hours*. San Francisco: Ignatius, 2010.

Waltke, Bruce K., and M. O'Connor. *An Introduction to Biblical Hebrew Syntax*. Winona Lake, IN: Eisenbrauns, 1990.

Walton, Izaak, with Charles Cotton. *The Compleat Angler, or the Contemplative Man's Recreation*. 1653. Reprint, London: Dent, 1973.

Warren, Tish Harrison. "By the Book." *Comment* 34, no. 4 (2016): 44–49. https://www.cardus.ca/comment/article/by-the-book/.

Webb, Barry G. *The Book of Judges*. New International Commentary on the Old Testament. Grand Rapids, MI: Eerdmans, 2012.

Weinandy, Thomas G. *Does God Suffer?* Notre Dame, IN: University of Notre Dame Press, 2000.

Weinandy, Thomas G. "Easter Saturday and the Suffering of God: The Theology of Alan E. Lewis." *International Journal of Systematic Theology* 5, no. 1 (2003): 62–76.

Wenham, John. *Christ and the Bible*. 3rd ed. Grand Rapids, MI: Baker, 1994.

Wilken, Robert Louis. *The Spirit of Early Christian Thought: Seeking the Face of God*. New Haven, CT: Yale University Press, 2003.

Wilson, Todd A. "Wilderness Apostasy and Paul's Portrayal of the Crisis in Galatians." *New Testament Studies* 50, no. 4 (2004): 550–71.

Witvliet, John D. *The Biblical Psalms in Christian Worship: A Brief Introduction and Guide to Resources*. Grand Rapids, MI: Eerdmans, 2007.

Witvliet, John D. "Collective Wisdom: A Pattern for Prayer." *Christian Century*, July 29, 2008, 24–27.

Wolterstorff, Nicholas. *Until Justice and Peace Embrace*. Grand Rapids, MI: Eerdmans, 1983.

Wright, Christopher J. H. *The Mission of God: Unlocking the Bible's Grand Narrative*. Downers Grove, IL: InterVarsity Press, 2006.

General Index

Scripture Index